ISRAELI VISIONS AND DIVISIONS

ISRAELI VISIONS AND DIVISIONS

Cultural Change and Political Conflict

Myron J. Aronoff

Transaction Publishers
New Brunswick (U.S.A.) and London (U.K.)

Second printing 1991, First paperback edition 1991

Copyright © 1989 by Transaction Publishers
New Brunswick, New Jersey 08903

Library of Congress Catalog Number: 88-22002
ISBN:0-88738-255-X(cloth); 0-88738-897-3 (paper)
Printed in the United States of America

Library of Congress Cataloging-in-Publication Data

Aronoff, Myron Joel.
  Israeli visions and divisions : cultural change and political conflict / Myron J. Aronoff.
    p. cm.
  Bibliography: p.
  Includes index.
  ISBN 0-88738-255-X
  1. Political parties—Israel. 2. Political culture—Israel.
3. Israel—Politics and government. I. Title.
JQ1825.P37A76 1988
306'.2'095694—dc19   88-22002
                                         CIP

For Miriam and Yael

Contents

Acknowledgments

Thanking all of those who have made it possible for me to write this book is a formidable task. Were I able to do so adequately it would require a book-length section of acknowledgments to express my gratitude to the thousands of individuals and scores of institutions that have cooperated with my research on Israel over the past two decades. Many I have thanked in acknowledgments in previous publications and I reaffirm my gratitude to them here. However, were I even to list the hundreds of people whom I interviewed during my fieldwork in 1982–83, and in 1987–88 I fear that I would task the patience of my readers. Therefore I have listed by name only those whom I have directly quoted in my endnotes to the individual chapters.

Since I did not directly quote even half of those whom I interviewed, and since I learned a great deal from all who so generously gave of their time and expertise, I would like to extend first and foremost my profound gratitude to my informants. They include leading scholars from all of Israel's universities, members of the government and the Knesset, religious leaders, representatives of Israel's cultural establishment, and Israelis of every walk of life and ethnic group. Many are old friends and others are new ones. Indeed, one of the most gratifying aspects of anthropological fieldwork is the personal nature of the research. Every one of the people I interviewed and with whom I interacted provided a different insight and I wish to express my heartfelt gratitude to them all.

I gratefully acknowledge the generous support of the Joint Committee on the Near and Middle East of the American Council of Learned Societies and the Social Science Research Council who granted me funds provided by the National Endowment for the Humanities and the Ford Foundation. In addition Rutgers University awarded me a Faculty Academic Study Program leave and grant for the academic year 1982–83, and sent me back to Israel as director of its junior-year-abroad program again in 1987–88. I have also drawn upon previous research in Israel funded by the Social Science Research Council of the United Kingdom, by the Ford Foundation, and by the Bernstein Israel Research Trust.

I am particularly indebted to those individuals who have permitted me to quote from their unpublished work and to those who have taken the time to read various drafts of individual chapters of this manuscript and who gave me excellent criticism and suggestions for improving it. In many cases they have saved me from blunders or awkward phrases, for which they have my gratitude. They are to be completely exonerated from responsibility for any errors of fact or interpretation or clumsiness of style that may remain. I apologize if I inadvertently forgot anyone whose name should be included on this list. I wish collectively to thank for their helpful comments members of faculty seminars at Bar-Ilan University, Haifa University, the Hebrew University of Jerusalem, Tel Aviv University, and the University of Cape Town where I presented various parts of this work.

I am especially grateful to Rita Aronoff, Benjamin Beit-Hallahmi, Yoram Bilu, Dan Caspi, Jerold Green, Emanuel Gutmann, Don Handelman, Steven Heydemann, Irving Louis Horowitz, Aaron Klieman, Kay Lawson, Arnold Lewis, T. J. Pempel, Gerold Pomper, David Somer, Ehud Sprinzak, Alex Weingrod, and Yael Yishai.

Without the constant help, support, and encouragement of my life partner, best friend, and spouse—Rita—I could never have accomplished any of the things of which I am most proud. Since I have already dedicated my first book to her, she must be content with a very special expression of love and gratitude here.

This book is dedicated to the most important products of our collaboration, our beautiful and bright daughters Miriam and Yael. Besides being the most wonderful daughters parents could ever dream of having, they each made a contribution to this book. Miriam assisted in research on Peace Now, and Yael organized my newspaper files and read and commented on the manuscript. As an expression of gratitude, pride, and love I dedicate this book to them.

Acronyms

CRM	Citizen's Rights (and Peace) Movement, also known as Ratz
Gahal	(Gush Herut Liberalim), alignment of Herut and the Liberals
IDF	Israel Defense Forces, also known as Zahal
IZL	(Irgun Zva Leumi), National Military Organization (NMO)
Lehi	(Lochemei Herut Yisrael), Israel Freedom Fighters
Mafdal	(Mifleget Datit Leumi), National Religious Party (NRP)
NRP	National Religious Party, also known as Mafdal
NZO	New Zionist Organization (founded by Jabotinsky in 1930)
PLO	Palestine Liberation Organization
Ratz	(Reshimat Zchuyot ha Ezrach), Citizen's Rights Movement (CRM)
Shin Bet	(Sherut Bitachone Klalit), General Security Services
WZO	World Zionist Organization
Yesha	Council of Jewish Settlements in Judea and Samaria
Zahal	(Zva Haganah l'Yisrael), Israel Defense Forces (IDF)

Introduction

After all, what is reality anyway? Nothin' but a collective hunch [Jane Wagner, The Search for Signs of Intelligent Life in the Universe].

Social imagination is constitutive of social reality [Paul Ricoeur, Lectures on Ideology and Utopia].

Conceptual Framework

This book examines the relationship between the changing political system and the political culture in Israel, with particular (but not exclusive) focus on the past decade. Since I use the concept "political culture" differently from most political scientists, I shall first define a few of the key terms I use throughout the book in order to clarify my conceptual approach.[1]

My approach, which is anthropological, is based on the observation that human beings universally ascribe meaning to their actions and to those of others with whom they interact. The collective meanings that social groups create, share, and symbolically express, I call culture.[2] Culture is based on assumptions that constitute a "collective hunch," or shared perceptions of reality. Every culture at any given specific historical period will be characterized by a limited repertoire of particularly central and salient themes, which are symbolically expressed through myth and ritual and convey the values and goals most valued by or deemed most sacred to the collectivity at the time.

Two contradictory processes take place concurrently in all societies and cultures. On one hand, patterns of collective behavior become habitual and the collective meanings ascribed to them undergo a process of institutionalization or reification during which they tend to become taken for granted as they come to define reality for the members of the society.[3] On the other hand, the process of reification (or conventionalization) is never completed. Due to the impossibility of achieving perfect socialization and the unequal distribution of status and power (among other factors), there are always those individuals and groups who call into question the taken-for-grantedness of the dominant cultural myths and offer competing definitions of reality. Ricoeur (1986) suggests that a credibility gap exists in all systems of legitimation when they exceed their authority.[4] Wagner (1981:59) conceives of culture in terms of a "dialectic through which meaning is and *must be* continually invented."[5]

Many treatments of culture in the literature assume a level of coherence and integration that is extremely rare in reality. Cultures contain ambiguities and frequently contradictory principles, which allow for a variety of interpretations. Depending on the sociopolitical divisions in the society there can be either a relatively hegemonic situation in which a given cultural definition of reality dominates the society at large or a situation in which significantly different cultural perspectives compete. In extreme cases the absence of a minimally shared symbolic framework or political culture can lead to the breakdown of public order and civil war, as is the case in contemporary Lebanon. In the absence of shared culture, or combined with it, economic interdependence and political coercion (including the use of violence) frequently prevent fragmented nations from following Lebanon's fate.

Cultural forms are related to the forms of political systems. For example, from around the mid-1930s until 1977, Israel had the type of system that Maurice Duverger (1967) identified as a dominant party political system. There are two equally important elements to dominance—political and ideological/cultural. In Israel, for example, Labor established its political control by dominating the center of the political spectrum in such a manner that no coalition could be formed without it, and thereby it maintained control of the most important cabinet portfolios as well as the lion's share of the nation's budgets. Yet equally important to the notion of dominance is the ideological dimension. As Duverger observes:

[A] party is dominant when it is identified with an epoch; when its doctrines, ideas, methods, its style, so to speak, coincide with those of the epoch. . . . Domination is a question of influence rather than strength: it is also linked with belief. A dominant party is that which public opinion *believes* to be dominant. . . . Even the enemies of the dominant party, even citizens who refuse to give it their vote, acknowledge its superior status and its influence; they deplore it but admit it.[6]

Even when there are dominant cultural forms in a society, their endurance may vary depending (among other reasons) on their effectiveness in providing models for dealing with various existential and societal problems. As they become less effective in coping with such problems, the immutability that characterizes cultures at the height of their power becomes undermined, and challenging alternative visions are likely to be advanced. There is no simple functional relationship, since a number of factors (including the power of inertia) can cause a lag in time between the undermining of the taken-for-grantedness of a cultural definition of reality and the acceptance of a viable alternative (when such an alternative is available).

Cultures are neither produced, maintained, nor changed in vacuums. They are always embedded in specific social, economic, and political environments that shape them, and which are in turn shaped by the cultures that they produce. The dialectical nature of the relationship between socioeconomic and political processes and changing cultural forms is the main theoretical focus of this book.

I attempt to relate profound changes in the developing socioeconomic and political system to the equally significant changes in the political culture. One should not assume that there need necessarily be anything approaching a perfect "fit" between a society's sociopolitical system and its political culture. In a stable society in which the sociopolitical environment changes slowly and incrementally, it is more likely that such a fit might be more closely approximated, but never fully achieved. However, in a society as dynamic and rapidly changing as is Israel, it is to be expected that there will be disparities, which are likely to develop as the gap widens between the two.

Most individuals in the society are unlikely to be conscious that their political system and their political culture are not well synchronized. The more astute observers are likely to be aware that changes are taking place, that new groups and parties have achieved political prominence, that old sacred myths have been called into question, that new values are being stressed, that political conflict may become intensified, or that the old rules of the political game no longer seem to apply. Many are likely to sense the uncertainty produced when a society is in a state of flux, which for some results in individual search for meaning through religious revival or collective cultural revitalization through movements such as Gush Emunim (Bloc of the Faithful).[7] However, it requires a certain detachment as well as a conceptual frame of analysis to explain the phenomenon. That is the goal of this book.

At this point it would be useful to make some additional refinements of the notion of culture. I have already used the term "political culture." I define political culture as any part or aspect of the general culture that gives legitimacy to the society as a whole or to the system that allocates power and values within the society. At the broadest level the political culture articulates the society's definition of itself and of its destiny. It commonly contains a myth of origin, which relates how a people came to be or how a society or a nation was created. Even the most modern histories can serve mythological functions, as the constant rewriting of history aptly illustrates. Ezer Weizman has observed, "The one thing that changes very radically in Israel is the past."[8]

Within every society there will be groups who compete for the scarce resources, prestige, and power. The more particular interpretations of the general cultural themes that they articulate I call ideology. These tend to be more conscious and rationalized versions of wider cultural themes, and, not surprisingly, tend to give legitimacy to the claims of the particular party or group that articulates them.[9] Ideology plays an important role in the process of legitimation. As in political culture in general, ideology has both a cognitive and a normative dimension. At the cognitive level, it " 'explains' the institutional order by ascribing cognitive validity to its objectivated meanings." At the normative level, it "justifies the institutional order by giving a normative dignity to its practical imperatives."[10] All forms of cultural expression, from symbols (which are the bricks from which all cultural forms are constructed) to the more elaborated cultural expressions such as myth and ritual, have both cognitive and normative dimensions, although they may emphasize one dimension over the other.

It is useful to make a heuristic distinction between nonrational and rational modes of thought, which are related to the cognitive and normative dimensions of culture. In general rational modes of thought tend to relate to the cognitive dimension of culture and nonrational modes of thought relate to the normative. Most contemporary political science has relied on models that overemphasize the rational dimension of human behavior. Anthropology has tended to recognize the duality of human nature, which was very much a part of the classical tradition of political philosophy ignored by the mainstream of contemporary behavioral political science.

When making heuristic analytical distinctions such as between rational and nonrational thought processes there is a very strong tendency to reify such concepts, to treat them as mutually exclusive categories, and then to go out in the real world and look for cultures that can be labeled "rational" or "nonrational" or "traditional" or "modern." Such is not my intent. On the contrary, I begin with the assumption that all humans share certain universal characteristics, which include the capacity to reason and the ability to feel, express, and respond to emotions and sentiments of a nonrational nature, for example, love, hate, loyalty, altruism, and so forth. All cultures utilize forms that appeal to both dimensions of humanity.

Each major category of cultural form can be subdivided on a basis of whether it tends to relate more to the rational or to the nonrational dimension. Most scholars who have studied symbols have recognized this distinction. For example, Susanne Langer in her classic study *Philosophy in a New Key* (1942) distinguished between conscious, rational discursive symbols (such as language) and presentational symbols. The latter are wordless, unconsciously appeal to the senses through nonrational visual forms, and are grasped simultaneously as integral objects of total reference. Sherry Ortner (1973) distinguishes between summarizing symbols that are essentially sacred and the objects of reverence and the catalysts of emotion, and elaborating symbols that are essentially analytic. The two major types of elaborating symbols are root metaphors, which have conceptual elaborating power as sources of conceptualizing the order of the world (e.g., the wheel in Hindu culture), and key scenarios, which are mechanisms for social action (e.g., the Horatio Alger myth in United States culture).

Similarly, students of rhetoric have made analytic distinctions relating types of rhetoric to degrees of rationality. For example, Bailey (1981) suggests that logical reasoning is related to plain speaking, which appeals to cerebration (the intellect) and occurs in contexts of certainty "ideally" exemplified by science. Deliberative rhetoric, which allows discussion, is characterized by tempered speech, appeals to the pseudo-cerebral (a more limited form of rationality than scientific), and occurs in contexts of consensus such as are approximated in "ideal" stable democratic societies. Hortatory rhetoric relies on grandiloquent styles of speech, which appeal to the emotions and are common in contexts of uncertainty. This style is favored by the political demagogue.

I suggest that similar distinctions can be made between different sets of major cultural forms such as legends and myths, ceremonies and rituals, and civil (or political) religion and traditional religion. The basis of such conceptual distinctions rests on the relative degree to which rational or nonrational thought processes dominate. Which cultural form is emphasized and the degree to which it is successful will depend to a large extent on the appropriateness of the mode to the given sociopolitical context. However, I do not mean to suggest that there is always a conscious decision made by an individual or a group as to which type of cultural form to use on any given occasion. In many cases the culture in which actors are embedded may shape perceptions, for example of time, making the events of the ancient past as real as yesterday's events (which I discuss in detail in later chapters)—which can favor one type of form over another in a given context. For example, the immediacy of the Holocaust for Menachem Begin in the context of the war in Lebanon may have elicited the association of Beirut to Berlin and of Arafat to Hitler (in a letter to

President Ronald Reagan) without his having rationally calculated the utility of such an analogy for propaganda purposes.[11]

Whereas all types of cultural expression will be in the repertoire of most if not all cultures, it is entirely possible that in given historical periods or in certain socioeconomic contexts, specific types of a more rational or nonrational nature may tend to dominate. For example, in times of uncertainty characteristic of major social change it is likely that nonrational forms may predominate. It is also possible that in any given society certain groups may appear predisposed to favor one type of cultural form over another. However, as long as human beings are involved it is highly unlikely that over any lengthy period of time any group will operate exclusively in one mode. Even a group dominated by the most nonrational, mystical orientation will be obliged to engage in forms of rational decision making in order to further its goals. Given these caveats and caution against the tendency to reify such analytic distinctions, I suggest that they have utility in helping to explain the current state of Israeli society. Whereas this frame of analysis informs this entire work, it is most explicitly detailed in the analysis of Israeli political culture.

Zionism: The Dominant Paradigm of Israeli Political Culture

As Ben Halpern (1961) has cogently argued, modern Jewish history begins with the emergence of the "Jewish problem" during the Enlightenment of the eighteenth century because it critically examined the traditional status of the Jew. Emancipation of the Jews ended the consensus as to the nature of the position of the Jew, and in the West undermined traditional culture and ended the uniformity of religious practice.

Zionism as a modern ideological and political movement arose as a response to the problem of the Jews (their persecution and insecurity as a consequence of anti-Semitism), and the problem of Judaism (the threat that assimilation would undermine authentic Jewish culture). It rejected both cultural assimilation, characteristic of Jews of the West, and the passivity of waiting for messianic redemption, characteristic of the more traditional Jews of Eastern Europe. Modern Zionism was an ideological reaction against the emancipation, which it denied as a rational solution to the Jewish problem. Zionism defined the Jewish problem as a national problem, and therefore called for national liberation.

Although it arose as a thoroughly modern national liberation movement, Zionism derived its power and legitimacy from its reinterpretation and adaptation of the traditional eschatological myth of exile and redemption. The most radical innovation introduced was the call for human action to realize national redemption rather than waiting for fulfillment of the biblical divine promise of messianic redemption. This innovation was perceived to be blasphemous by many of the traditional Jews, whose modern descendants continue to reject modern political Zionism and its product, the modern state of Israel, to this day.[12]

The contradiction between claims of Zionism and those of the anti-Zionist Orthodox Jews have not been reconciled. Yet an alternative synthetic ideological interpretation of a national (Zionist) religious movement attempted to bridge Orthodox Jewish tradition and modern political Zionism. The basic conflicting, and even contradictory interpretations over what should be the exact Jewish character of Israel as a Jewish state continues to provide the most serious division among Jews within contemporary Israeli society. The absence of minimal consensus on such basic principles has been the primary obstacle to agreement over a written constitution, and has been one of the primary causes for coalition crises over the years.

For a number of reasons this division is likely to increase in political salience in the future. Given the relative balance of power between the two major political blocs, the Labor alignment and the Likud, the power of the religious parties as key coalition partners has increased tremendously over the past decade. As greater concessions are made to them, the resentment of the non-Orthodox majority grows and signs of a backlash are already apparent.[13] Segregation between ultra-Orthodox, Orthodox, and non-Orthodox Jews is almost absolute in terms of residence, education, and service in the military (even among the national religious who serve in the army, most do so in homogeneously religious units), and marriage.

The other significant minority of the Israeli population for whom Zionist symbols, myths, and rituals are unacceptable are the Arabs. Ironically, one of the consequences of the attempt to socialize Israeli Arab children with the symbols of Zionism has been their tendency to identify the notion of a persecuted people without a homeland with the plight of their fellow Palestinians. Zionism has thereby made a contribution to the developing political culture of Palestinian nationalism. Clearly the most important political and cultural problem facing Israel is how to reconcile the contradictory claims of the Palestinian national movement with those of its own. Arab citizens of Israel have increasingly identified with their brethren in the occupied territories, thereby increasing the stakes and making the resolution of this problem even more imperative.

For the overwhelming majority of Jews in Israel the significant political battles that have been waged since the inception of the Zionist movement and the creation of the modern Jewish state have taken place within, and have been shaped by, the dominant Zionist political culture. From the beginning of the Zionist movement there were significant political/ideological divisions. For example, the political Zionists, led by Theodore Herzl, insisted on diplomatic efforts to gain an internationally backed charter for the creation of a Jewish state in Palestine. Jabotinsky's revisionist movement and its contemporary political descendant, the Likud, claim descent from this stream of Zionism. The practical Zionists, led by Chaim Weizmann and David Ben-Gurion, insisted on creating facts by building the socioeconomic and political infrastructure by a pioneering vanguard of Jewish immigrants even prior to gaining such a charter. The contemporary Labor party claims descent from this school of Zionism, as does Gush Emunim.

Ahad Ha'Am proposed a cultural Zionism, which envisaged Israel as the vital core of a new authentic form of Jewish culture that would renew and nourish the Jewish communities of the Diaspora. To a certain extent the Labor movement incorporated aspects of this cultural emphasis in its vision of the Israeli melting pot (or pressure cooker), which was to produce a cultural revival and the renewal of the Jewish people, but in so doing it strongly negated the Diaspora. The nationalists argue that Jewish national aspirations can be fulfilled only through the struggle for territorial and political rights in the greater land of Israel. Lewis (1984:28) suggests that political debate in contemporary Israel is structured by these two differing interpretations of Zionism.

The Zionist idea provides the root cultural paradigm of Israeli political culture. The enduring cultural themes contained within Zionism have shaped the rhetoric and the discourse of Israeli political debate even for those who reject them. The political polarization between Labor and the Likud are manifestations of competing ideological interpretations of a shared political culture. I examine the extent to which debate conforms to, and thereby confirms, the Zionist political culture. In so doing I follow Gluckman (1967) in distinguishing between political strife and conflict between principles of social organization.[14] I critically examine the contemporary crisis in Zionism in order to determine whether the Zionist vision has sufficient force and salience to withstand the strains and challenges facing it.

Major Theme

Israel is presently in an important transition stage. Significant realignments in relationships of power among groups in the society have taken place. However, the changes are more than the parties that constitute the government. Political realignments have profoundly changed the nature of the political system itself. Those who came to power failed to recognize the nature of the changes in the political system and continued to operate under the old rules of the political game, which were no longer appropriate to the new context.

Whereas Israel had been characterized by a dominant party system from the mid-1930s, when Labor achieved ascendancy in the Jewish-controlled community in Palestine prior to independence, until its first electoral defeat in 1977, it became a competitive party system thereafter.[15] Yet the Likud, which dominated the government coalitions from 1977 through 1984, acted as if it were a dominant party and self-consciously attempted to make its myths and rituals—its interpretation of reality (past and present)—universally accepted.

I have suggested that the Israeli political system is undergoing a crisis of political legitimacy.[16] This crisis is more apparent today than when I originally made this assessment and is likely to become even more apparent in the future than it is today. The serious challenges facing the Israeli political system in the present transition period reveal a nation deeply polarized over the most fateful issues facing it and a government so divided that it is incapable of acting decisively on these very issues.[17]

I have suggested (in an earlier publication) that the proliferation of extraparliamentary political movements was indicative of a decline in confidence in the main political parties. I analyze in this book how Gush Emunim and Peace Now have largely been co-opted by existing parties, especially by newer ones on the opposite ends of the ideological spectrum. This is evidence of the resilience of the party system, but not necessarily of public confidence in it. As Peace Now has become more cautious and conservative in its tactics, a proliferation of new movements has arisen to challenge its leadership of the peace camp. A large segment of the Israeli public feels unable to satisfy its desire to participate in and influence the most vital issues of the day exclusively or even primarily through the established political parties.

There is another consequence of this co-optation process that is less encouraging for the state of democracy in Israel. The co-optation of more "extreme" political views into the parliamentary parties tends to give greater legitimacy to these views. Although the two large parties compete with each other for the support of the floating voters who tend to be more moderate at the center of the political system, they must also compete with the more ideologically "pure" splinter parties on their fringes for the support of a sector of the more ideologically motivated electorate. In so doing some of their representatives are tempted to emulate the more extreme views of the latter in order to compete more successfully with them. When parties are thereby forced into more extreme positions a "chain reaction" of extremism can occur.[18]

An example of such a phenomenon is the call for the "transfer" of

Palestinian Arabs. When Rabbi Meir Kahane first issued such a call he was universally condemned as an extremist and a racist. When similar proposals were made by Deputy Defense Minister Michael Dekel (Likud) and Minister without Portfolio Yosef Shapira (Morasha/National Religious party), they were condemned, but less loudly. The fact that representatives of legitimate mainstream parties articulated such extreme views legitimatize their acceptance by those who do not consider themselves to be extremists or to be on the fringes of society.[19]

The pardoning by the president (prior to their trial and conviction) of the director and key officials of the internal General Security Services (Shin Bet) who were charged with perjury, having framed an army officer, and covering up the murder of two captured Palestinian terrorists precluded the determination of political responsibility for these activities. The report of the commission chaired by a Supreme Court judge, Landau, and comprised of former chief of army intelligence, Yitzhak Hofi, and State Comptroller Ya'acov Maltz, found that the Shin Bet, as a matter of policy, had consistently committed perjury in proceedings related to the admissibility of confessions since 1971; and it concealed its methods of interrogation in cases of terrorism.[20] The absence of a viable parliamentary opposition in the eleventh Knesset meant that serious questions relating to the political responsibility for such systematic undermining of the rule of law went unanswered.

Such flaunting of the rule of law by the crucial agencies of the state hardly facilitates the imposition of the rule of law in the society at large. The widespread incidents of increasing violence, from acts of vigilantes in the territories to confrontations between ultra-Orthodox and secular Jews in Jerusalem, are further evidence of the crisis of political legitimacy. The conspicuous inability of political leadership to curtail such expressions of violence challenges their authority and that of the institutions of the state. In fact, the government itself officially adopted a policy of using physical violence to suppress the uprising in the occupied territories during the winter of 1988.[21]

The increasing reliance by the main political parties on non-Zionist religious parties to form coalition governments is another indicator of the current crisis in Zionism, the dominant motif in Israeli political culture that gave legitimacy to the very creation of the state. The "blackening" (manifestation of increasing religious strictness) of the traditionally more moderate national religious camp portends increasing danger of the possibility of a *kulturkampf* (clash of cultures) between the Orthodox minority and the non-orthodox majority.[22]

The widespread civil uprising of Palestinians on the West Bank and in the Gaza strip, which ushered in the new year of 1988, challenged the status quo of immobilism caused by the divided national "unity" government. The demonstration of widespread support by Arabs holding Israeli citizenship indicates but one of the consequences of the erasing of the Green Line (the pre-1967 borders) so ardently pursued by the Likud and its ultranationalist allies. It challenges the patronizing manner in which all Israeli parties have taken for granted the support of Israeli Arabs without fully integrating them within their frameworks, and indicates that Zionism fails to provide a salient symbolic framework for Israel's Arab citizens.

This work explains the major political divisions within Israeli society and relates them to the differing ideological visions. The analysis traces the relationship between the developing political system, the changing relationships of power, and the ideological interpretations of Zionist reality that have competed in attempting to define reality and guide policy. It analyzes the increasing ideological polarization and the crisis of Zionism as the main agency of legitimation in Israel today.[23]

Methodology

I have been engaged in the systematic study of Israeli society, culture, and politics for the past twenty years. I lived in Israel from 1966 through 1977, interrupted only by a year in England (1968–69) and a sabbatical in Holland (1974–75). During this period I conducted anthropological research in a development town for fifteen months (Aronoff, 1974), and engaged in a long-term study of the then dominant Labor party (Aronoff, 1977). I was also affiliated as a faculty member of Tel Aviv University from 1969 through 1977. During this period I was drafted into the Israeli army where I did basic training and served in a noncombat reserve unit.

In the summer of 1977 I returned to the United States to take up a tenured position at Rutgers University. During 1982–83 I spent a sabbatical year in Jerusalem conducting fieldwork on the changes that had taken place during what has been termed "the Begin era." Since much of the original research that forms the heart of this work derives from the fieldwork I conducted in Israel during that year, I shall describe it in some detail. Another year in Israel during a most eventful period, 1987–88, allowed me to follow up on certain aspects of the research and to complete final revisions of the manuscript.

I regularly attended the plenary sessions of the Knesset throughout the year 1983–84 as well as several Knesset committees, which I attended with some frequency. I conducted many interviews and held even more informal conversations in the Knesset members' dining room with Knesset members, lobbyists, and journalists. During this period I interviewed over half of the members of the Knesset, including several members of the government. I also gained access to several important meetings of the Labor party parliamentary faction.

In addition I conducted archival research in the prime minister's office on the Ministerial Committee on Symbols and Ceremonies. I interviewed all key personnel involved in the implementation of the decisions of this committee, ranging from officials of the Knesset, Zahal (Israel Defense Forces, IDF), the president's office, the Government Information Office, and so forth. I also attended a meeting of the committee to get a sense of how decisions were reached in it.

I attended rallies and meetings of the major peace movements and of Gush Emunim, and also conducted formal interviews of their leaders. I attended practically every professional academic conference and symposium, which pertained to public issues, held in the country during the year. I interviewed, formally and informally, approximately 100 academics, religious leaders, editors, journalists, and Israelis of many walks of life. I also closely monitored the Israeli media, movies, and plays, paying special attention to commentaries on and observations of the society by Israelis.

In short, I attempted to engage in participant observation of the state of the nation. Whereas most anthropologists more modestly confine themselves to a village, a small urban community, or a single corporate institution, I attempted to observe a nation from the perspective of its capital (in addition to many trips throughout the nation). I would never have had the chutzpa (nerve or cheek) to attempt such a challenging task had I not become sufficiently acculturated as an Israeli to overcome my middle-class, middle-western American upbringing, which had failed to bring out that particular trait in my character. Whatever insights I have succeeded in gaining into Israeli society can be largely attributed to my being a professionally trained inside outsider (or outside insider).

The fact that I have spent over half of the past twenty years, in which I have been professionally studying Israel, living and working in the country (which included the wars in 1967, 1973, and 1982–83 and the civil "disturbances" or "uprising" in the territories of 1987–88) has enabled me to get inside the culture in a manner in which most anthropologists who are not native to the culture they study (and who generally spend much briefer periods in the field) are not usually able to achieve. The fact that I have spent the better part of the past ten years living outside Israel and viewing it from a distance has somewhat ameliorated the well-known anthropological syndrome of "going native," that is, losing one's professional detachment or perspective.

I neither claim to have achieved complete objectivity nor even to have a completely dispassionate perspective (which is probably an impossibility—

certainly when it comes to as controversial a focus of study as I have chosen). However, I do think that I have a perspective that, given my professional training and interests and my research experience and contacts in Israel, is unique. I have tried to be candid about my liberal, cosmopolitan, intellectual perspective (some would say bias) so that the reader can take this into consideration when evaluating my interpretations and conclusions.

This book has been written, partly, in response to the many people and groups who have asked me to explain the changes that have taken place in Israel in the past decade. Although there have been a disproportionately large number of books written on contemporary Israel, I (somewhat immodestly) think there is a need for this one. In it I attempt to clarify what to many, if not most, outside observers appears to be a confusing array of parties that seem to undergo constant fission and fusion, and issues that explode and periodically threaten to tear the body politic apart.

Since these have profound regional and international implications, they receive considerable attention in the world news media. Yet rarely does such coverage go beyond the surface issues to get at underlying processes and causes.[24] I do not claim to have all the answers, but I do hope that what follows will shed some light on a number of important issues. Any work written by a professional academic (no matter how much it may be written with a more general audience in mind) usually raises more questions than it answers. This work is not an exception.

Notes

1. Having earned doctorates in both political science (U.C.L.A.) and social anthropology (Manchester, England), I define myself professionally as a political anthropologist. Although I have been introduced by political scientists as "half a political scientist" and by anthropologists as "half an anthropologist," I feel that combining two complementary approaches adds to, more than it detracts from, each. More extensive formulations of the conceptual approach I employ in this analysis can be found in Aronoff (1980a) and Aronoff (1983).
2. Among the many scholars whose work has influenced my understanding of culture, that of Clifford Geertz has been particularly important. See the bibliography for references to some of his publications.
3. For an excellent analysis of the process of institutionalization, see Berger and Luckmann (1966).
4. Ricoeur suggests that the primary function of utopia is to undermine the taken-for-granted perception of reality. By offering an alternative vision of society it allows a possibility radically to rethink relationships in society and notions of authority. Ricoeur (1986:16) claims that "imagination itself—through its utopian function—has a *constitutive* role in helping us *rethink* the nature of our social life."
5. Wagner (1981:59) argues that "because we 'use up' our symbols in the course

of using them, we must forge new symbolic articulations if we are to retain the orientation that makes meaning possible." My own interpretation, while compatible with that of Wagner, places greater importance on the "political" causes of the undermining of taken-for-granted symbolic definitions of reality. My approach is much closer to that of Ricoeur, whose major work on this subject, unfortunately, I read only after completing this manuscript.

6. Duverger (1967:308), quoted in Arian (1985:96). I analyze the role of dominance in the Israeli political system in detail in chap. 1, below.

7. Aviad (1983) analyzes the return to Judaism through the religious renewal movement in Israel, and Beit-Hallahmi (forthcoming) discusses the relative attraction of various new religious sects (or cults) after the decline of the dominant Zionist vision. I analyze Gush Emunim with special attention to its character as a revitalization movement that becomes institutionalized (see chap. 4, below).

8. Quoted from my notes of a Weizman lecture on "Israel and the Peace Process with Egypt" delivered at Haifa University on November 17, 1987, at a colloquium on the subject of the "Tenth Anniversary of the Visit to Jerusalem by President Mohammed Anwar El-Sadat." I explore the notion of the rewriting of history or the invention of tradition in depth in chap. 3.

9. My conceptualization of ideology has been influenced by Geertz (1973). While completing the final revisions of this manuscript, I read Ricoeur's major work on ideology and was struck by the similarity in our approaches. Ricoeur suggests there is an inherent discrepancy between the *claim* to authority by rulers and the ruled's *belief* in their legitimacy. The primary function of ideology is to overcome this discrepancy. (See Taylor's introduction to Ricoeur (1986:xvi–xvii). This is similar to the notion of the "frailty in authority," which Gluckman (1956:27) postulated: "as positions of leadership carry high ideals, and as most men are, well, only men, there develops frequently a conflict between the ideals of leadership and the weakness of the leader. This is the frailty in authority."

10. For a more elaborate discussion of the legitimation process, see Berger and Luckmann (1966:93).

11. Obviously the two are not mutually exclusive. A politician can rationally use a historical analogy that comes naturally to him because of psychological and cultural predispositions. I shall suggest that such statements are much more characteristic of Begin than of Shimon Peres. However, Peres, in his capacity as foreign minister, was recently quoted (Morris, 1987) as saying, "There is no way Israel would support Iran (in the war). Iran is Haman. Is it conceivable that Mordechai (Israel) would help Haman?" The allusion comes from the book of Esther and refers to the evil Prime Minister Haman of ancient Persia who sought the extermination of the Jews. I would suggest, that, since such statements are much less common from Peres, given his background and cultural/ideological orientation, it is more likely that his use of the historical analogy is a more consciously rational choice than was the aforementioned example from Begin's letter to President Reagan. Prime Minister Begin's allusion to the Holocaust is reflective of deeper psychological and ideological/cultural orientations, which I discuss in detail in chap. 6, below.

12. Robert Paine (1987:6) has cogently argued that even the ultra-Orthodox are Zionist in their belief in the eschatological concept of redemption. In fact, he quotes informants among the Haredim (as the ultra-Orthodox are called in

Israel) who claim: "We are more 'Zionist' than they are"; and "We are pre-Herzlian Zionists." He argues that in their rejection of the political claim to the redemptive fulfillment of Herzl, "The Ultra-Orthodox are Zionists who are still in waiting, who are still in Exile." However, since they reject (in varying degrees) the major symbols of contemporary Zionism and in many cases even the legitimacy of the state of Israel, I consider these groups non- and anti-Zionist in terms of contemporary Israeli politics. This is discussed in more detail in my analysis of Israeli political culture.

13. For example, clashes between ultra-Orthodox and nonobservant Jews in Jerusalem over the encroachment of the former into previously nonreligious neighborhoods, the closing of roads to traffic on the Sabbath, and the showing of films and other forms of entertainment on the Sabbath have led to increasingly violent demonstrations.

14. Gluckman says: "I thus restrict 'conflict' to refer to oppositions compelled by the very structure of social organization. . . . For surface disturbances of social life, depending on their nature, we can use competition, fight, etc. I like to reserve 'struggle' for events with deeper and more fundamental roots, and 'conflict' for discrepancies at the heart of the system. But I reserve 'conflict' for the relation between discrepancies that sets in train processes which produce alterations in the personnel of social positions, but not in the pattern of positions. I prefer the already established term 'contradiction' for those relations between discrepant principles and processes in the social structure which must inevitably lead to radical change in the pattern. Conversely, I stipulate that 'co-operation, affiliation, association, ties, bonds,' refer to surface links between persons or combined activities; 'solidarity' to a more deeply rooted interlinking; and 'cohesion' to the underlying principles of structure that give unity to the system of a social field" Gluckman (1967:109–10).

15. I discuss this in more detail in my essay "Significant Trends in Israeli Politics," in Reich and Kieval, eds. (1986).

16. Myron J. Aronoff, "Significant Trends in Israeli Politics." In *Israel Faces the Future,* ed. Bernard Reich and Gershon R. Kieval (New York: Praeger, 1986).

17. The *Jerusalem Post* editorial of March 17, 1988 (p. 10) entitled "Moment of Truth" stated: "Unfortunately, Israel today is saddled with a governmental deformation which, though bedecked with the feathers of national unity, is even less of a policy-making body than the Knesset on the most crucial issue facing the country."

18. I discuss this phenomenon in my critique of an essay by Ehud Sprinzak, "Fundamentalism, Terrorism, and Democracy: The Case of Gush Emunim Underground," Woodrow Wilson Occasional Paper (1987). I also discuss this in more detail in the epilogue of this book.

19. For example Reserve General Rehav'am Zeevi (head of the Ha'aretz Museum) invited some 150 guests to participate in a symposium on "Transfer" in which he called for the mass expulsion of Arabs on February 22, 1988. He claimed, "We have lit the torch—and it shall burn." Some participants warned that such expulsions could lead to civil war in Israel. (Joshua Brilliant, "Zeevi Encouraged by Response to 'Transfer,' " *Jerusalem Post,* February 23, 1988, pp. 1, 4. When he spoke at Tel Aviv University protestors shouted, "Fascism, fascism," and gave mock Nazi salutes, and he was practically prevented from speaking. "Protestors Outnumber Audience at T.A.U. Lecture by 'Gandi,' " *Jerusalem Post,* March 15, 1988, p. 2.

20. See, for example, the coverage of the commission's report by Benny Morris and by Menachem Shalev on the front page of the *Jerusalem Post* on November 1, 1987, and the more detailed elaboration of the part of the report that was released to the public in the same edition.

21. Some of the leading experts in the country consider the government's policies in coping with the uprising to have been contrary to international law. See, e.g., Benny Morris's interview with former Attorney-General Yitzhak Zamir, entitled "Rights and the Man," in the *Jerusalem Post Magazine* (February 12, 1988:4–6).

22. See Abraham Rabinovich, "Split in the Golden Way," the *Jerusalem Post Magazine,* December 4, 1987, p. 4, 6, 13.

23. Although I fundamentally disagree with his analysis of its causes (and even more fundamentally disagree with his political prescriptions), Israel Eldad (a leader of the pre-state Lechi underground and ideologue of Techiya) has made a similar point. He suggests that "What is developing is the crumbling of the fundamentals of Zionism" (Israel Eldad, "A Homeland Can't Be Put Up for Sale," the *Jerusalem Post,* February 26, 1988, p. 11).

24. A noteworthy exception to the generalization is Thomas Friedman, whose in-depth coverage for the *New York Times* is exceptionally sensitive and sophisticated.

1

The Role of Dominance: Labor and the Likud

[A] Party is dominant when it is identified with an epoch. [Maurice Duverger]

The Origins of Labor Dominance

Identification with an Epoch

The dominance of the Labor movement in Israel was established during the crisis of the early stages of nation building in the 1920s through the 1930s. Its main leaders, party, and affiliated institutions (e.g., the kibbutzim and the Histadrut, or labor federation), became identified with the heroic epoch of pioneering and the successful struggle for national independence. Each of the two most important scholarly studies of the establishment of Labor dominance during this period focuses primarily on one aspect of dominance and tends to underemphasize the importance of the other aspect. Yoseph Gorni (1973) emphasized the acquisition of ideological dominance by the party through its exceptional leaders who gained legitimacy because they were considered to be the pioneering vanguard of Zionism. They exemplified the dominant values of the time, *chalutziut* (Zionist pioneering), voluntarism, and egalitarianism. They displayed sufficient flexibility to incorporate a multiplicity of viewpoints as the party co-opted more groups while projecting a coherent vision of national goals and aspirations.

Yonathan Shapiro (1976) analyzed the process whereby Labor gained political dominance through the creation of a number of original sociopolitical institutions through which it mobilized power. The most important of these was the establishment of the Histadrut in 1920. The Histadrut, a unique labor federation that became a virtual state within a state in the period prior to independence, played a crucial role in the creation of, and in shaping the character of, the present state of Israel.

1

It is possible to comprehend the success of Labor in establishing its dominance only by explicating the interactive effect of the ideological/cultural and the political/institutional levels of dominance. They were not merely complimentary. Each was essential for the success of the other. For example, the respect that the Labor leaders received from the nonsocialist middle-class leadership of the World Zionist Organization (WZO) derived from their perception of the Labor Zionists as being the most active and creative force in settling immigrants and reclaiming (literally and figuratively) the land of Israel. Therefore the WZO heavily subsidized the Labor movement's colonization efforts and their urban projects through the Histadrut. Through these resources Labor was able to mobilize greater political support by providing a wide range of services to the new settlers, who became clients of the party, and at the same time Labor leaders refurbished their image as the vanguard of pioneering Zionism.

Conversely, the large and amorphous middle-class General Zionists lacked charismatic leadership and a coherent ideology with a unifying myth; also they failed to build their own institutions. The Revisionist movement, which was founded in 1925, had a charismatic leader and an ideology with a central myth, but it failed miserably to develop strong and viable institutions. The organizational failure in the early period can be largely attributed to strategic errors of the leader, Vladimir Zeev Jabotinsky. As the sworn enemies of the Histadrut, the revisionists could not compete for a share of the valuable patronage of this organization. Jabotinsky focused his primary political activity on central and eastern Europe rather than Palestine, so little effort was made to develop strong organizational bases in the *yishuv* (the Jewish community in Palestine). His primary approach was ideological rather than organizational. His disciple and successor, Menachem Begin, made a similar strategic error in focusing almost exclusively on ideology and ignoring the building of strong institutional bases of support (discussed below). Jabotinsky's decision to split away from the World Zionist Organization and to form his own New Zionist Organization in 1935 enabled Labor to gain a dominant position in the executive of the WZO and thereby to gain control of the valuable resources that accrued from this organization.

Capturing the Political Center

One of the more effective means by which Labor established its dominant position was through the strategic formation of coalitions that effectively made it the indispensable partner for any viable ruling coalition. Although ostensibly a socialist party, under David Ben-Gurion's leadership Labor staked its claim as the main national party in the political center. He declared his readiness to form a coalition with any legitimate Zionist party excluding the Communist party and the nationalist Herut (the political offspring of the Revisionist movement). Ben-Gurion made a historic pact with the National Religious party, which brought it into every government formed by Labor. By balancing coalitions with socialist parties to its left and liberal and conservative parties to its right, Labor ensured its dominance and centrality. Medding (1972) analyzes the strong party machine, controlled by bosses completely loyal to Ben-Gurion, which enabled such coalition flexibility.

Another important tactic was the delegitimation of Labor's rivals. These tactics worked with varying success at different periods with different parties. The parties of the radical left were stigmatized as anti-Zionist and /or having loyalties beyond national ones, and the rightist Herut was declared to be irresponsible and beyond the pale of legitimate Zionist politics because of its dissident activities during the war of independence and the irresponsible behavior of some of its main leaders thereafter. (This is discussed in detail in chapter 2, below.)

Loading the Dice

Lipset and Rokkan (1967) have shown that the mobilization of power in the crucial formative period of a political system determines its development for many years thereafter. James S. Coleman (1957), reanalyzing a large number of studies of community power, has concluded that the manner in which conflicts are resolved in the early stages of the formation of a community "loads the dice" and establishes patterns of conflict resolution that last long after the original issues have been forgotten. My study of a new town (Aronoff, 1974), illustrated such a case in an Israeli context. Shapiro (1976), following Lipset and Rokkan, argues that the leading and dominant role played by Labor in the formative stages of the crystallization of the Israeli political system gave it a unique advantage, which it successfully exploited to maintain a dominant position for nearly fifty years.

The Maintenance of Labor Dominance

The consolidation of Labor dominance came in the period following independence in 1948 with the institutionalization of the bureaucratic agencies of the state. During the postindependence period the character of both the ideological and the political dominance of Labor were significantly adapted to the changing social, economic, cultural, and political conditions. Many of the major services that had previously been provided by the voluntary agencies (such as the Histadrut) prior to independence were transferred to the state bureaucracy after independence. The paramilitary organizations of the various political movements were abolished by the provisional government in one of its first acts, and the Israel Defense Forces (IDF or Zahal) was created. In the ensuing years the labor exchange was transferred from the Histadrut to the Ministry of Labor, and the separate school systems controlled by the political movements were abolished and a state educational system was established, which provided for secular and religious options. The relinquishing by the Histadrut of the socialist-Zionist school system reflected a lengthy process whereby Labor, under Ben-Gurion's leadership, had deemphasized its socialist ideological orientation in favor of a stronger emphasis on nationalism.

David Ben-Gurion articulated a new ideology of *mamlachtiut* (statism), which asserted that the state and its agencies, for example, the army, had taken over the role of pioneering vanguard from the prestate voluntary agencies. This ideology gave legitimacy to the transfer of important functions from the Histadrut to the state. It also appealed to a large constituency of masses of new immigrants who were not particularly attracted by Labor's pragmatic socialism. Whereas the new myths and ceremonies that accompanied the advent of *mamlachtiut* appealed to larger numbers, the intensity of support among those attracted tended to be less fervent than the support of those who had been committed to socialist-Zionism. Statism became the ideology through which Labor institutionalized its authority and attempted to socialize the new immigrants with this new interpretation of Zionist civil religion.

Israel underwent a tremendous growth in population through immigration. The dynamic growth and diversification of the economy, including a stronger private sector, led to a commensurate growth and increasing complexity of government. An enormous state bureaucracy grew. Not only did the civil service grow, but also the party's bureaucracy expanded with the growth of urban machines and a vast patronage system aimed at the mobilization of the immigrants.

Labor maintained its dominant position for as long as it did because it was relatively successful in meeting the major challenges that Israel faced in its first three decades: defense against hostile neighbors, the "absorption" of mass immigration, and the need for economic growth.[1] From the outset Israel's physical existence was challenged, and the leading role that Labor's leaders played in the successful defense of the nation has been one of the most important bases of their authority.[2] It was not until the shock of the surprise attack on Yom Kippur 1973 (termed the "earthquake" in the media) and the protest movements that followed from it that the taken-for-granted assumption of Labor's leadership of the nation and its defense establishment was seriously called into question on a significant scale.

Labor also derived considerable authority from its leading role in the integration of the survivors of the Holocaust from Europe and hundreds of thousands of Jews from Islamic countries of North Africa and the Middle East. The young nation faced an unprecedented challenge of crisis proportions in more than doubling its population in the first few years of its existence. During a period of serious economic hardship, the needs for housing, education, and welfare of these immigrants—a large proportion of whom were indigent—severely taxed the resources of the nation. Even with the considerable help of Jews abroad and foreign nations, the "ingathering of the exiles," which constituted a virtual raison d'être for the creation of the state, was a formidable accomplishment. However, largely in response to this challenge the party developed in directions that ultimately undermined its dominant position in the society.

As with the previous examples of the successful meeting of challenges, Labor's success in helping to achieve high rates of economic growth eventually contributed to the undermining of its dominance. As the economy developed into a healthier and more sophisticated one with high rates of employment, the dependence of citizens on the patronage provided by the government and through the party was drastically reduced. Skills and education rather than party identification became far more important in gaining satisfactory employment. The second and third generations at both ends of the economic ladder became disenchanted with Labor for different reasons.

The Loss of Labor Dominance

> Domination takes the zest from life. . . . The dominant party wears itself out in office, it loses its vigour . . . every domination bears within itself the seeds of its own destruction. [Duverger, 1967:312]

Sometimes the successes of a dominant party can contribute to the eventual undermining of its dominance. Just as the legitimacy derived from an ideology that was central to the political culture paved the way for the political dominance of Labor, the erosion of the authority provided by ideological legitimacy undermined its political dominance. Liebman and Don-Yehiya (1983:123) have speculated that one of the important factors that is likely to have contributed to the decline of statism (*mamlachtiut*) was the successful building of the nation: "As time passed the existence of the state no longer evoked such wonder." Similarly, in *A More Perfect Peace*, Amos Oz (1985:177) observed: "Once, long ago, there was a time when all things done here were done with devotion, even with a kind of ecstasy, sometimes with enormous self-sacrifice. But then the bold dreams came true.''

A woman of the pioneering generation who had been one of the founders of her kibbutz once confided to me: ''I sometimes have to pinch myself to make sure that I am not dreaming that we actually have our own Jewish state!'' For her, the creation of the state of Israel is the fulfillment of a dream, the realization of a vision, which her children take very much for granted.[3] Both the realization of the dream and the sense that the reality fell short of the ideal further contributed to the end of the pioneering epoch with which Labor had been identified and from which it derived its legitimacy. I shall explore the implications of this for the polarization of Israeli society, particularly during the 1981 election campaign and during the war in Lebanon, in chapter 2, below.

One area in which Labor conspicuously failed was in the socialization of succeeding generations. Studies of voting behavior indicate that Labor lost the political support of the younger generations. In most cases they failed to instill the values and ideals for which the party stood. The establishment of a Jewish Consciousness Program in the secular public schools in 1957 to counter the attraction of Canaanism (a nativist ideology that stressed the need to build a Hebrew culture without links to the Diaspora) for the youth is identified by Liebman and Don-Yehiya with the beginning of the decline of statism.

In other cases, having succeeded in instilling the ideals of the party, the leaders lost the support of the youth because their actions and policies failed to live up to these ideals. Such was the case with the National Religious party (NRP), which, through its network of religious schools, succeeded in socializing younger generations who are far more nationalistic, religiously observant, and self-confident than the preceding generation. Consequently they deserted the National Religious party in large numbers for the more militant Gush Emunim (Bloc of the Faithful) movement, the political parties closest to it, Morasha, Techiya, and the Likud.[4] We shall analyze the phenomenon of Gush Emunim in chapter 4, below. The leaders of the younger generation who remained in the NRP and rose to positions of power in it were instrumental in shifting the party's coalition alliance from Labor to the Likud. The failure of Labor to retain the traditional alliance with the NRP, or to replace it with an equally reliable alternative, was another challenge unsuccessfully met, which contributed to its downfall.

Oligarchic tendencies, which were latent from the early formative years, became increasingly manifest with the development of a dominant machine within the dominant party. The machine expanded as a response to the development of elaborate patronage networks designed to mobilize new immigrants. A system of indirect elections to party and Histadrut institutions through the use of appointments committees guaranteed elite domination of these institutions.

Those groups most supportive of the elite were over-represented and other more marginal groups were under-represented on these institutions. As they became mere rubber stamps for decisions made informally by the elite, democratic procedures and the party constitution were increasingly put aside for political expediency. Criticism of the elite and their policies was suppressed, and recruitment and mobility to higher levels became dependent upon loyalty to the elite rather than the display of independence and initiative.

The erosion of responsiveness of the party to the demands of the public coincided with a growing arrogance of the top national leaders, who became preoccupied with the perpetuation of their rule. This resulted in progressively widespread feelings of political inefficacy among the secondary national leaders, the local leadership, and the rank-and-file membership. This contributed directly to the erosion of Labor legitimacy and dominance.[5]

Among the alienated groups that failed to gain sufficient access to the centers of power under Labor, the most politically important were the Jews who emigrated from the Middle East, and particularly emigrants from North Africa, and their offspring. As Labor increasingly came to be perceived to be the party of the European-born veteran elite and their descendants, the Eastern Jews increasingly identified with the antiestablishment leader of the opposition Likud, Menachem Begin.[6] The greater militancy and religiosity of Begin also attracted the religious voters, as they attracted the NRP (under the influence of their young leaders) as a coalition partner.

Whereas in the early years of independence Labor succeeded in denying legitimacy to its main opposition, Herut, over the years it became increasingly difficult, if not impossible, to do so.[7] Although Herut began altering its policies by the mid-1950s, it was not until the resignation of David Ben-Gurion in 1963 that major changes began to take place. In chapter 2, I shall analyze the process that led to the inclusion of Herut (as part of the Gahal electoral alliance with the Liberals) in the government of national unity established during the crisis preceding the war in June 1967. The participation of Menachem Begin and his colleagues in the government until their resignations in August 1970 firmly established their legitimacy and paved the way for their ascension to power in 1977.

Probably the greatest challenge that Labor failed to meet was the crisis of identity experienced by many Israelis. The sense of Jewish isolation, which reemerged as symbols of the Holocaust gained ascendancy in the late 1950s, was heightened during the period immediately preceding the war of June 1967, and reached a peak during the war of October 1973. The invisible seeds of a process that eventually led to a crisis of legitimacy for Labor and the political system in general was precipitated by the consequences of Israel's military victory in 1967, but only became manifest in the widespread political disillusionment and protests that resulted from the shock of the surprise attack and the conduct of the war in the initial stages of October 1973.

Israel's lightning victory in the Six-Day War of 1967 unleashed a number of different processes, which had significant political repercussions. First of all it ended the serious economic recession and unemployment. Although the pioneering values of voluntarism and egalitarianism had ceased to have salience for most of the population long before, after 1967 the vast majority of even loyal Labor supporters ceased to pay lip-service to them. Conspicuous consumption and rampant materialism typified what some came to term the "Americanization" of Israel.

The speed of Israel's victory, the unification of Jerusalem (including the Western Wall of the ancient Temple), and the "liberation" of the areas on the West Bank of the Jordan, which had been the heartland of Jewish settlement in biblical times (including the holiest shrines in Jewish tradition) were felt by some to have been evidence of divine intervention and inspired new forms of nationalism and of religious messianism. These movements claimed to offer an alternative to what they termed the moral bankruptcy of the Labor ideology of statism and the rampant materialism that they blamed on Labor's leadership.

The conquest of the new territories posed especially significant problems for Labor as it created opportunities for the opposition (which at the time participated in the government). The government headed by Prime Minister Levi Eshkol decided on June 19, 1967, that in exchange for peace it was willing to withdraw to the former international borders with Egypt and Syria, and would negotiate the future of the West Bank, Gaza, and the problem of the Palestinians. By August it had already modified its position.[8] In their September meeting in Khartoum the Arab heads of state explicitly articulated their policy of refusal to negotiate with Israel, to recognize the Jewish state, and to make peace with it.

The combination of pressures created by the refusal of the Arab states to negotiate, and the pressures from nationalist and religious groups to annex the territories occupied during the war, pushed the Labor-led government to increasingly tougher stands, which conflicted with many of the liberal, humanistic values held by Eshkol and other Labor leaders who felt uncomfortable in their new roles as occupiers. With the succession of

Golda Meir after the death of Eshkol, Labor moved toward more militant policies thereby blurring the differences between it and the opposition. Rather than being apologetic about their policies, the opposition had a long-standing strong stand on the territories, a stand that had been anachronistic until Israel's victory in 1967.

Labor failed adequately to socialize a new generation of supporters and leaders, to maintain responsive party institutions, truly to integrate the Eastern Jews, to maintain its historic coalition partnership with the NRP, to prevent the main nationalist opposition from gaining legitimacy, and to prevent or to resolve the crisis of identity that emerged between the late 1960s and the mid-1970s. Yet when Labor lost the 1977 election and the Likud formed the coalition government, most of the public, politicians, and pundits were shocked. Perhaps one of the most telling illustrations of Labor's dominance is the fact that so few people had realized that the era of Labor suzerainty was over until their electoral defeat. Even then, many predicted it would be back in power in 1981, and indeed the polls showed a substantial lead for Labor until shortly before the election.

After the Likud formed its second government in 1981, it was clear to all that Labor would not accomplish what the Swedish socialists succeeded in doing, namely, reestablishing their dominant position after a parliamentary defeat. The fact that other dominant parties have been able to revitalize and maintain their dominance (most conspicuously the Japanese Liberal Democratic party), suggests that there was nothing inevitable about the decline of Labor. Rather, most of the party's failures can be attributed to a failure of the leadership to adapt the party and its ideology to changing conditions, or as Schweitzer (1986) put it, failure to set a new national agenda appropriate to the times.

The Likud's Attempt to Attain Dominance

Initially, upon assuming the mantle of leadership of the nation, the leaders of the Likud were cautious and attempted to emphasize continuity rather than a radical break with the past Labor rule. Partly in response to public anxiety created by the transition, and partly because of a lack of qualified and experienced personnel to staff many positions, the Likud government left many key Labor-appointed officials and civil servants in place. Menachem Begin even chose the former Labor defense minister, Moshe Dayan, to serve as his first foreign minister. The most significant accomplishment of the first Likud government, the peace treaty between Israel and Egypt, gained greater parliamentary support from Labor than it did from the Likud members of the Knesset.

The resignations of the most moderate members of the government,

Dayan in October 1979 and Defense Minister Ezer Weizman in May 1980 (both key figures in the successful negotiation of the peace treaty with Egypt), changed the character of the government. Among other things the government began actively to use its patronage to solidify and to broaden its base of support, thereby initiating a new politicization of civil service similar to the earlier days of statehood. However, given its late start, the relatively limited number of qualified personnel loyal to the party, and the short duration of their rule, the Likud never succeeded in building institutional bases of support that were at all comparable to those of Labor at the height of its power.

In chapter 2, we shall see why the 1981 election was the most violent and polarized in recent history. Its unpredictability contributed to tensions and anxiety. Begin was particularly anxious for an additional term so that he could implement his plans for the massive Jewish settlement of "Judea and Samaria," the biblical terms that the Likud government succeeded in substituting for what had previously been called by many the West Bank, the occupied territories, or simply the territories. The successful gaining of the popular acceptance of these terms was a prelude to gaining popular acceptance of the government's settlement policies. If the territories were perceived to be the biblical heartland of the Jewish people, rather than "occupied territories," the legitimacy of the government and its settlement policies would be enhanced.

The Likud's electoral tactics, especially Begin's rhetoric, played an important role in the renewal of political polarization and the escalation of violence. The pursuit of controversial policies such as the extended war in Lebanon with its political as well as military goals provoked widespread opposition. The second Likud government, dominated by Begin, Foreign Minister Yitzhak Shamir, and Defense Minister Ariel "Arik" Sharon, attacked their critics as traitors, fifth columnists, and supporters of the Palestine Liberation Organization (PLO). These attempts to delegitimize the opposition were part of a concerted Likud effort to establish political and ideological dominance.

Having overcome the pariah image that had characterized them in the earlier period, Begin and others in his movement attempted to eliminate the last vestiges of Labor's ideological legitimacy and to establish the Likud's ideological hegemony. The government fully utilized the state agencies to reinterpret Israeli history and to place in a more favorable light the Likud's heroes. They sought to incorporate their own myths as the authoritative means for the interpretation of present realities.

The Likud's attempt to manipulate political culture is illustrated in chapter 3, below, through the analysis of two case studies. The nearly year-long events memorializing Vladimir Zeev Jabotinsky attempted to elevate the ideological guru of the Revisionist movement (and of Herut) to the status of one of the nation's great heroes. Jabotinsky placed great importance on ritual, and his disciple, Menachem Begin, used the occasion of the 100th anniversary of his mentor's birth to launch an unprecedented array of activities to celebrate him as a national hero, and to give legitimacy to their political movement.

Similar events and ceremonies were designed to enshrine the heroes and martyrs of the dissident underground movements—the Irgun Zvai Leumi (IZL, National Military Organization) and Lechi (Fighters for Israeli Freedom; also known as the Stern gang). They aimed at correcting what the government perceived to be the injustice of their having been ignored or maligned by the former Labor establishment. The acceptance of a movement's heroes is a prelude to accepting its values. One of the means by which the Likud government attempted to accomplish this was through the use of ceremonies commemorating historical figures whose heroic acts could be utilized to provide meaningful guides to understanding current problems and dilemmas. The most elaborate of such ceremonies was a state funeral held on May 11, 1982, in the Judean desert for the remains of what were reputedly the fighters and followers of Shimon Bar Kochba, who led the second Jewish revolt against Rome in A.D. 132–35.

Although the bones had been discovered with artifacts in 1960, it was not until Chief Ashkenazi Rabbi Shlomo Goren won the enthusiastic support of Prime Minister Begin that these remains were reinterred. I shall contrast the solemnity of the state rites held before the leading figures of the state and representatives of foreign governments, with the ludic parody of the ceremonies by a group of protestors wearing Roman attire. The parody of the state ceremony undermined the taken-for-granted seriousness of the event. It symbolized the widespread disagreement with the interpretation that the government, articulated in Begin's eulogy at the funeral, attempted to make of this important period and of the controversial figure of Shimon Bar Kochba.

Whereas the Talmud refers to Bar Kochba as a cruel, imperious leader and a false messiah, Begin portrayed him as a heroic freedom fighter. Critics of the interpretation of Begin and his government argued that Bar Kochba waged an unrealistic policy, which led directly to the decimation and exile of the Jewish people, and to make of him a hero is tantamount to rejoicing in policies that led to national suicide.[9]

There was a passionate national debate over the meaning of the Bar Kochba revolt, which involved prominent secular scholars, the prime minister, and the chief Ashkenazi rabbi (among others). On one hand, this public debate highlighted the polarized interpretations of the Zionist vision that characterized the period. Yet the fact that such a diverse group of

Israeli leaders seriously debated the significance and implications of events that took place 2,000 years ago also indicates that they share an underlying Zionist/Israeli worldview, which makes the debate over the meaning of such a root cultural paradigm both possible and significant. The fact that respected national figures challenged the meanings and interpretations made by the government to explain the ceremonies is strong evidence that the Likud had failed to establish ideological dominance or cultural hegemony. I discuss the implications of this in much greater detail in chapter 6, below.

The Likud, even more than preceding Labor governments, utilized history and mythology to interpret contemporary political events, to gain ideological legitimacy, and to attempt to establish dominance. Jabotinsky's notion of Jewish statehood based on the biblical term *malkhut Yisrael* (kingdom of Israel), stressing the sacred right of the Jewish people to the entire land of Israel, combined with a sense of Jewish isolation expressed in the biblical reference to Israel as "a nation that dwells alone," an emphasis on heroism and self-sacrifice, activism and adventurism, were symbolically expressed in the burial of the Bar Kochba bones (analyzed in chapter 3, below).

Although the Likud came to power as the representative of the formerly marginal elements in society, the nationalist right, the Eastern Jews, and the religious, it did so through co-optation rather than incorporation of the latter two groups. For example, the government gave legitimacy, power, and resources to Gush Emunim (Bloc of the Faithful), the militant messianic settlement movement, and derived legitimacy and political support from it without actually gaining the affiliation of the Gush to the Likud. (This is discussed more extensively in chapter 4.) It gained the coalition support of the religious parties, not just through their ideological affinity, but by also paying a high price in portfolios, policy, and financial support for the independent religious institutions. None of these substantially broadened the base of party support. Given the intense rivalry in Herut for succession to the top leadership position, factionalism has reached such a peak that the first party convention after Begin's resignation as prime minister and party leader had to be disbanded because it deteriorated into anarchy. The proposed merger of the constituent units of the Likud have yet to take place. Menachem Begin, the political heir and disciple of Jabotinsky, made the same mistake as his mentor in relying too heavily on symbols and neglecting the vital organizational aspects of politics.

In addition, the Likud was in a much weaker coalition bargaining position than was Labor during the earlier period of its dominance. Whereas Labor had generally twice the parliamentary representation of its nearest rival (except in 1965 and 1973), the Likud led Labor by a narrow margin of eleven Knesset seats in 1977, by a single seat in 1981, and, after postelection splits and mergers, they ended up with equal representation in 1984. This parliamentary balance severely handicapped the Likud's attempt to establish its dominance, since its claims were forcefully resisted by approximately half of the members of parliament.

Evaluation of the Claim for a New Dominance

A strong element of mystical, messianic, nonrational eschatological politics, which was a legacy of revisionism in the Likud, was reinforced with the co-optation of groups like Gush Emunim into the new National Camp (as the Likud labeled itself in the 1984 election). This led a number of prominent scholars to claim that a new dominance had been established. In chapter 6, I shall evaluate the claims of several scholars that Israeli politics has become dominated respectively by "totemic time," "Religious New Zionism," the "new civil religion," and "religion." We shall argue that the differences between the ideologies of Gush Emunim, revisionism, folk or civil religion, and traditional Judaism are not only very significant, but in some cases antithetical. If there were a single new ideological form of Zionist civil religion it could not possibly combine at one and the same time revisionism, national religious messianism, folk religion, and Orthodox tradition.

During the period of early Labor dominance, most scholars identified with Labor's version of the Zionist vision. In fact, their scholarly work tended to contribute to Labor's hegemony. This is in sharp contrast with the scholars who write of the reputed dominance of new nationalistic religious political paradigms. These scholars, as well as the majority of the educational elite and media leaders, tend to be very critical of the various forms of New Zionism or civil religion. This contradicts the assertion that there is a new dominant ideology. The leaders of the nationalist right decry the liberal bias in academe and the media. For example, a body named the Media Consumers Protection League crusades against what they call the "leftist mafia" in the media.

Objective indicators, including the "hard" evidence of voting results and survey data on key issues, and the analysis of the results of elections, tend to refute the conclusion that either political dominance or ideological dominance of any party or worldview has been established. Rather, the picture that emerges is of a society divided fairly evenly, and tending toward polarization, electoral stalemate, and possible political paralysis.

It is considerably more difficult to create an identification with an epoch than it is to fall heir to one as did Labor through its leadership of the movement for national independence and the creation of a new state. Menachem Begin's attempt to identify the Likud with what he projected as the new era of Jewish settlement and effective (if not legal) annexation of Judea and Samaria, the "war of choice" in Lebanon, and the manipulation of symbols and ceremonies failed to establish the hegemony of the Likud for two main reasons. First, the nation was politically and ideologically divided fairly evenly into two major camps. Second, rather than subtly attempting to build unity through symbols that united the camps, Begin's conspicuous attempts to manipulate political culture called into question and undermined his efforts and even further aggravated the already existing divisions.

The Consequences of Dominance

Advantages

The stability and continuity of leadership and policy, which is a characteristic of a dominant party system, is particularly beneficial in the early stages of the development of a new society and political system. Israeli independence was won and has had to be maintained through a brutal, prolonged, and costly series of wars, both conventional and unconventional, which poses a constant challenge to the nation's survival. The mass immigration immediately following independence and subsequent waves of culturally heterogeneous immigration have compounded the "normal" challenges of nation building. In conditions characterized by pervasive change and uncertainty, the predictability of political regime that results when one party dominates a polity can make a significant difference in successfully meeting such challenges.

The fact that most relevant groups could be organized through the agency of the dominant party and its affiliated institutions simplified the task of national mobilization and made it more efficient. The incorporation of such diverse social forces as agricultural settlements, industrial workers, artisans, professionals, and various ethnic groups made an important contribution to national integration in a society where the centrifugal forces have always been strong. The centralization and coordination of leadership selection, decision making, and succession in both the government and the Histadrut was a major contribution of the party, which helped Israel build a strong society within such a relatively short period.

Disadvantages

However, when drawing up a balance sheet one must also account for the negative effects of prolonged dominant party rule. First of all prolonged dominance eventually had a debilitating effect on the party itself. It directly contributed to the strengthening of oligarchic tendencies, the degeneration of decision making in party institutions, and the breakdown of responsiveness of the leadership to the membership and to the public in general. Prolonged rule without serious challenge contributed to the arrogance of leadership, which in exceptional cases resulted in corruption. Whereas cases of personal corruption were relatively isolated, the phenomena of disregarding practices that violated the party constitution and principles were widespread. Recruitment and advancement through patron-client relationships deprived the party and the nation of potential leaders who displayed initiative, independence, and originality.

Prolonged dominance by one party has a serious negative influence on the opposition parties. Perpetual opposition without likelihood of gaining a share in ruling tends to encourage irresponsible behavior. This is particularly the case when the party and its leadership have been defined as pariahs without legitimacy by the dominant party and it is believed by significant sectors of the general public. Lack of access to public office deprives the party leadership of valuable experience in governing, and the party of a potential pool of high-caliber public servants with administrative experience.

This can lead to problems of transition when eventually the dominant party loses its dominant position. It can lead to high levels of anxiety among the public, and potentially to significant problems of implementation of new policy if the civil service is too closely identified with the previously dominant party. Fortunately Israel did not suffer from severe problems of transition. In fact, most observers were surprised and relieved at the smooth transfer of power following Labor's defeat.

One serious problem from which Israel suffered was the polarization that partly resulted from the Likud's unsuccessful bid to delegitimize Labor and to establish its own dominance. The Likud went beyond building its own legitimacy; it vainly attempted to destroy any vestiges of Labor's legitimacy. This arose from the need to overcome their former pariah status and possibly from the desire of certain leaders who had suffered in the past to gain revenge on their political rivals. Also this was the model of politics that had been identified with the political system from the beginning. Consequently the renewal of political polarization reached such a dangerous level of verbal and even physical violence that the president warned of the potential danger of civil war. This was also a legacy of the aftermath of one-party dominant rule.

Whereas the benefits of single-party dominant rule outweighed the costs in the initial stages of nation building, the longer it was perpetuated the more the disadvantages outweighed the advantages. By the 1970s the old dominant party system had long outlived its utility as the dominant party failed to meet critical challenges and was discredited. The unsuccessful attempt by the Likud to replace Labor as the new dominant party indicates that the system of one-party dominance is no longer viable in the conditions that characterize Israel in the 1980s.

Conclusions

Party alignment in Israel is entering a new phase in its development. It has evolved from a dominant party system to a competitive party system in which the two major blocs (but not their associated satellite parties and client religious parties) have moved closer to each other on a range of policy issues. This new constellation is creating a new political center, which has continued to drift to the right of where it was during the height of Labor dominance.[12] This emergent system is still in flux, and there have yet to emerge clear rules of the game appropriate to the new political context. The resultant confusion and uncertainty can be seen in the responses of the unity government formed in 1984 to the various crises that erupted during its tenure.

It would appear that the political system and the balance of forces between the major political groups in the country have developed to a point where the return to one-party dominant rule is neither likely nor desirable. It is particularly important at this juncture in the development of the Israeli political system that the legitimacy of all parties be mutually recognized. The authority of the government and the legitimacy of the nation's institutions require the political actors to abide by the rules of the democratic game. The rule of law must be applied to all individuals and organizations, including the highest levels of government and intelligence agencies. Finally, although certainly not least important, the political culture must evolve to adapt to the changed party system. New interpretations of old Zionist themes and creative ideological innovations must emerge that meet the needs of the rapidly changing conditions. The dialectical relations between political institutions and political culture pertain as much to competitive party systems as they do to dominant party systems.

Notes

1. The main Labor parties underwent several splits and mergers over the years, which resulted in name changes. Mapai was the dominant Labor party from 1930 until 1968 when the Israel Labor party was formed by the merger of Mapai with Achdut Ha'avoda and Rafi. The best study of Mapai is Medding (1972).

For a detailed analysis of the Israel Labor party from its formation in 1968 to the eve of its defeat in 1977, see Aronoff (1977). Analyses of the reasons for Labor's defeat can be found in Aronoff (1979), and of Labor in the opposition in Aronoff (1982).

2. See Peri (1983) for a perceptive analysis of the relation between the military and politics in Israel.

3. Berger and Luckmann (1966:107) have called attention to the intrinsic problem involved in the transmission of culture from one generation to another. Amos Oz (1982 [1985 English edition]) gives an excellent literary illustration of this point as it applies to Israel.

4. See the essays in Newman (1985) for more detailed discussions. The Knesset representation of the NRP declined from 12 in 1977 to 6 in 1981 to 4 in 1984. Chapter 4 contains a more detailed analysis.

5. Medding (1972) and Aronoff (1977) analyze this process in different periods and come to opposite conclusions regarding the degree of internal party democracy in Labor and the responsiveness of the party to societal demands.

6. For an excellent analysis of the appeal of the Likud to the Eastern Jews, see Lewis (1984).

7. Levite and Tarrow (1983) analyze the rehabilitation of Herut and, in chapter 2, below, I shall discuss the consequences of this for the more recent polarization of Israeli politics.

8. See Rabin (1979:135).

9. The leading proponent of this position is Yehoshafat Harkabi (1982).

10. See Hobsbawm and Ranger (1983) for interesting discussions of the notion of "the invention of tradition" and comparative examples.

11. See Arian (1985:217–18) for survey evidence that contradicts Schiff's notion of a new religious hegemony.

12. For an explanation of the difficulty of collapsing the multiple dimensions of issues in Israeli politics into a highly simplified single dimensional continuum implied in the use of "left" and "right," see Dominguez (1984).

2

Political Polarization

*The world grew bitter because the world fell
somehow short of half-remembered Eden [Walter
Miller, A Canticle for Leibowitz].*

One of the most striking developments in Israel in recent years is the
reemergence of political polarization after nearly two decades of relative
political quietude. This polarization, which differs in several important
respects from the divisiveness of the earlier period (to be discussed below),
has been expressed largely through verbal violence, but there have also
been dangerous signs of increasing physical violence as well. It is the
result of the political coming of age and rise to power of formerly marginal
groups that successfully challenged Labor's ideological and political dominance, and of the failure of Labor to adjust to its new status and to play a
more constructive role when it was in the opposition.

During the period in which it constituted the dominant political alignment in the coalition government (from 1977 to 1984), the Likud attempted
to establish its own dominance through the co-optation of new forms of
religious nationalism and the exploitation of ethnic tensions. Labor, and a
significant proportion of the members of kibbutzim, intellectuals, and
others, never fully accepted the legitimacy of the new government. Although they accepted the legality of the election results, they failed to
accept the right of the Likud to impose its ideology and to implement
policies that, they argued, lacked a national consensus. As a result of the
1984 election the two major political blocs, Labor and the Likud, with
their conflicting perceptions and interpretations of reality, have equal
political parity. Although the policies of the two major blocs have converged in several areas when compared with the earlier era, the leaders of
each imply in their public positions that only their policies, particularly
those pertaining to the future status of the territories occupied by Israel in
1967 and with more than a million Palestinians residing within them, will

19

ensure Israel's security and that the rival's are a threat to the nation's survival. These conditions (aggravated by the Palestinian uprising) have resulted in the polarization of politics in Israel today.

In this chapter I analyze the key incidents that led to (1) the intensification of the conflict between the two camps in the periods prior to and after the establishment of the state; (2) the "normalization" of relations in the later period; (3) the renewal of serious political strife in the period of Likud rule; and (4) the relative normalization following the formation of the unity government in 1984. (In the epilogue I shall discuss the renewal of polarization during the 1988 election campaign.)

Early Polarization

The early years of the developing Israeli society and polity were characterized by relatively intense ideological division and political competition, particularly between the main political camps. This rivalry was especially bitter between the Labor camp led by David Ben-Gurion and the Revisionist movement led by Vladimir Zeev Jabotinsky. After Jabotinksky's death he was eventually succeeded by his devoted disciple Menachem Begin, who carried on the struggle against Labor.

The intensity of this ideological debate can be attributed to a number of factors. Among the more important are the influence of Jewish tradition and culture, the intellectual and political climate of Eastern Europe at the turn of the century when Zionism emerged as an ideology and a political movement, and the voluntary and nonsovereign nature of both the World Zionist Organization and the Jewish institutions in Palestine. The visions of the main Zionist movements constituted all-encompassing worldviews, which conflicted with one another. Labor had a universalistic social-democratic ideology, which emphasized pioneering, settlement of the land, and egalitarianism. Labor's leaders perceived the militaristic militant nationalism of the revisionists as fascist. Revisionism was strongly influenced by Pilsudski's Polish nationalism and stressed "blood and iron," the values of martial heroism (Mendelsohn, 1981). The revisionists were convinced that what they perceived to be Labor's universalism was assimilationist and they feared its links with communism. The policies of the two regarding the partition of Palestine, attitude toward the Arabs, and relations with the British Mandatory regime were contradictory (Isaac, 1981:41).

During bitter rhetorical exchanges, Ben-Gurion called the revisionists fascists, referred to his rival Jabotinsky as "Il Duce" (Mussolini's title), and compared him to Hitler (prior to the Holocaust). The revisionists responded in kind by referring to Ben-Gurion as a "British agent" and calling the Laborites "Bolsheviks."[1] Emotions reached a peak on June 16, 1933, when the prominent Labor leader Chaim Arlosoroff was murdered and three members of an extremist faction of the revisionists were charged with the crime. Although there was insufficient evidence to convict them, the incident cast a cloud of suspicion, which was sufficiently salient that fifty years later, after Menachem Begin became prime minister (in 1977), he appointed a government commission of inquiry to investigate the murder (Teveth, 1982).

During the tense atmosphere created by the bitter rivalry between the two largest political movements in the *yishuv* (the Jewish community in Palestine), their leaders, Ben-Gurion and Jabotinsky, met secretly in a series of meetings in London during October 1934. The two great rivals managed to reach agreement to eliminate violence and to regulate the relations between the trade unions of the two movements. However, the agreement on cooperation between the two trade unions met with strong opposition from both movements. It was defeated in a referendum held by the Histadrut (General Federation of Labor) on March 24, 1935. Menachem Begin was among the followers of Jabotinsky who most strongly opposed the cooperative agreement with Labor. At a Revisionist World Conference in Cracow in January 1935, Begin told Jabotinsky: "You may forget, sir, that Ben-Gurion called you Vladimir Hitler. But our memories are better" (Bar-Zohar, 1978:73).

One important factor, which significantly influenced the nature and the outcome of the competition between the two major movements, was the decision of Jabotinsky to lead his revisionists out of the World Zionist Organization (WZO), and to establish the New Zionist Organization (NZO) in 1935 (Schechtman and Benari, 1970). In so doing, the revisionists removed themselves from the most important international forum in Zionist politics at a critical formative period. Labor not only benefited by gaining an increasingly dominant position in the WZO and through it greater access to its vital resources, but Ben-Gurion successfully insinuated that the revisionists' actions had placed them beyond the bounds of mainstream, if not legitimate, Zionist politics.

The military auxilliaries of the two camps came precariously close to clashing during the last phase of the British mandatory rule. Whereas the Haganah, the main Jewish defense organization led by Ben-Gurion, practiced a policy of restraint toward the British during World War II, the Irgun Zvai Leumi (IZL), led by Begin, pursued an activist policy primarily against the British presence in Palestine, and Lechi, known in the English-language press as the Stern gang after the commander, Avraham (Yair) Stern, pursued a policy of terrorism and reprisals against both the British and the Arabs (Niv, 1980; Tzameret, 1983). At one point when Begin and

Stern refused to bring their dissident organizations under the discipline of the elected institutions of the Palestine Jewish community, Operation *Saison* (French for "open season") was implemented. During this operation elite Palmach units of the Haganah tracked down the dissidents, abducted and interrogated them, occasionally resorting to violence. The British were informed of the names and/or hideouts of some of the dissidents, while in other cases they were even turned over to the British. It has been said that "For both camps it was the darkest hour in Israel's battle for independence" (Haber, 1979:217). However, there was an even darker hour yet to follow.

Undoubtedly the single most serious incident that brought the conflict between the two camps to the brink of potential civil war was the *Altalena* affair. The *Altalena*, a ship bought by the IZL and loaded with desperately needed arms and ammunition, sailed from Europe to Israel on June 11, 1948. It arrived during a cease-fire arranged by the United Nations. Ben-Gurion had disbanded the military organizations of the prestate political movements, which were in the process of being merged into the newly created Zahal (IDF; Israel Defense Forces). However, the IZL and Lechi maintained their separate and autonomous units in Jerusalem, because the partition plan of the United Nations had declared it to be an international city.

Since Begin had signed an agreement with the provisional government integrating the IZL units into Zahal, Ben-Gurion expected the arms to be turned over to the latter. When Begin requested that 20 percent of the arms be allocated to IZL units in Jerusalem, his request was granted. However, Begin's proposal to use the remaining 80 percent of the weapons exclusively to arm the IZL units within the Israel Defense Forces was rejected, and the negotiations between the two sides broke down. The events that followed were the most bitter and the most dangerous in contemporary Israeli history. Their interpretation is colored by the partisan positions of those who discuss the events (Brenner, 1978; Nakdimon, 1978).

When Begin defied the government's orders to turn over the arms and began unloading the *Altalena* with the aid of IZL soldiers (many of whom had deserted their Zahal units), a gun battle broke out between the dissidents and government troops. The ship steamed out to sea with Begin on board. The next morning when the *Altalena* docked at Tel Aviv to unload its cargo, the last tragic act of the drama was played out. Hundreds of IZL soldiers and sympathizers had gathered and confronted a much smaller number of Palmach troops commanded by Yigal Allon. The cabinet had met in an emergency session and decided to demand that the ship be handed over to the government, and if Begin refused, force was to be used. A gun battle broke out between the IZL and the Palmach units. A cannon shot struck the ship, a fire broke out, and explosions followed as the ammunition on board was ignited. Fourteen IZL men and one Palmach soldier died; dozens were wounded.

Ben-Gurion and many of the other members of the government and the army high command feared that the dissidents would have used the arms from the *Altalena* to stage "an armed revolt to seize power to establish a separate Jewish state in Jerusalem and Judea" (Bar-Zohar, 1978:171). In fact, Dr. Yisrael Eldad, the leading ideologue of Lechi, proposed the latter idea to Begin during the unloading of the *Altalena,* but Begin refused because he was afraid that this would lead to a civil war.[2] In retrospect it is not unlikely that, had Begin not demonstrated restraint during this crisis, civil war could have been the consequence.

Even after the state of Israel had been established, there were several incidents that challenged the stability of democratic politics. The more serious of these incidents was the crisis generated over the agreement between Israel and the Federal Republic of Germany (with whom Israel had no formal diplomatic relations) in which Germany agreed to make payments of reparations to Israel in compensation for Jewish property that had been confiscated during the Third Reich. There was widespread and highly emotional opposition to the agreement from both the left and the right wings of the Israeli political party spectrum. On January 7, 1952, the opposition culminated in the most serious domestic political crisis in Israel since the *Altalena* affair.

While Prime Minister Ben-Gurion addressed an extremely tense Knesset, Menachem Begin addressed a mass rally at a square a few hundred yards from the legislature. In a highly emotional speech, Begin referred to his restraint during the *Altalena* affair and threatened on this occasion to show no such restraint, saying, "When you fired at us with cannon, I gave an order: No! Today, I shall give the order yes! This will be a battle of life and death" (Bar-Zohar, 1978:197). He continued, "According to reports we have just received, Mister Ben-Gurion has stationed policemen armed with grenades and tear-gas made in Germany—the same gas that suffocated our parents" (ibid.). Declaring his willingness to be sent to concentration camps and to suffer torture chambers, and with the cry of "Freedom or death!" Begin marched off to the Knesset with the mob following him.[3]

The impassioned mob broke through the police barricades and threw stones at the Knesset, breaking many windows. Tear-gas and the shouts of the angry mob entered the Knesset chambers through the broken windows. When the Speaker of the Knesset attempted to prevent Begin from speaking from the podium during the debate, Begin is reported to have said, "If I don't speak, no one shall speak!" (Bar-Zohar, 1978:197; Haber, 1978:355). Ben-Gurion was forced to call in the army to restore order on the grounds and in the vicinity of the Knesset. In a radio broadcast to the nation the next day, Ben-Gurion condemned Begin for having attempted to destroy democracy in Israel. This incident contributed to the successful projection of the image of Begin and his followers by Ben-Gurion as being irresponsible and on the margins, if not beyond the limits of legitimate political activity.

It is generally, although not unanimously, agreed among experts on Israeli politics that in the process of establishing Labor's political and ideological dominance and legitimacy during the critical formative stages of the development of the society and the state, Ben-Gurion (and other leaders of the Labor movement) succeeded in delegitimizing the revisionists, IZL, and the postindependence Herut party led by Begin. Clearly their ideological worldviews were poles apart and there was considerable personal antipathy between the leaders of the two movements. For example, Ben-Gurion repeatedly refused the requests by Begin to honor Jabotinsky's will, which requested that his remains (which were buried in the United States where Jabotinsky died in 1940) be reburied by the sovereign Jewish government in Israel. Even as late as a Knesset debate on May 13, 1963 (a month prior to his resignation as prime minister), Ben-Gurion expressed his obsessive anxiety that if Begin's Herut was to come to power, "he will replace the army and police command with his ruffians and rule the way Hitler ruled Germany, using brute force to suppress the labor movement; and will destroy the state" (Bar-Zohar, 1978:303).

Also by declaring that all political parties were considered to be legitimate potential coalition partners except Maki (communist) and Herut, Ben-Gurion ensured the centrality and dominance of his own Labor party (Mapai). Therefore, the exclusion of Herut was a most effective political strategy, since it made it impossible to form a coalition government without Mapai. A combination of personal, ideological, and practical considerations appear to have influenced Ben-Gurion's policy of politically isolating Herut.

Given the dynamic growth in population, which included immigrants from practically every state in the world, and substantial changes in crucial aspects of the economy, society, and culture, significant political changes were inevitable. In fact, what is surprising is not that Labor lost its ideological and political dominance, but that it took almost fifty years for it to do so. In chapter 1, we saw how societal changes were related to internal party changes: just as Labor gained ideological dominance before it achieved a dominant position in the political system, the loss of ideological hegemony preceded the party's fall from power in 1977.

Normalization

During the period in which Labor's paramount position was being eroded, a parallel process took place through which Herut gradually overcame its isolation and pariah status, and gained increasing legitimacy. Ariel Levite and Sidney Tarrow (1983) have analyzed the strategies pursued by Herut to gain legitimacy. By the mid-1950s Herut began modifying its free-enterprise-oriented socioeconomic platform with a greater openness to welfare programs in order to broaden its electoral appeal.

When Levi Eshkol became prime minister after the resignation of Ben-Gurion in 1963, in defiance of his former mentor's strong objections he acceded to the request to rebury the remains of Jabotinsky in Israel. The state funeral for the late revisionist leader on Mount Herzl at a site reserved for the great leaders of the nation symbolized the beginning of a process through which his disciples and followers gained legitimate status. The institutionalization of charisma symbolized by Eshkol's succession began the process of erosion of Labor's hegemony.

During the seventh party conference in 1963 Herut made a historic decision. It decided to join the Labor-dominated Histadrut in order to undermine it from within. Mapai managed to block these efforts through legal battles until 1965 when Herut formed an electoral alignment with the Liberal party, called Gahal, and in this new form competed in both the Histadrut and the Knesset elections in the same year. The association with the Liberals gave Herut new respectability and paved the way for the next and most crucial stage of the legitimization of Herut—its participation in government for the first time.

The most significant act of political legitimization came during the extremely tense period prior to the outbreak of the war of June 1967 when pressures within the Labor party, the coalition, particularly from the NRP and Rafi (led by Moshe Dayan and Shimon Peres), and from public opinion resulted in the inclusion of Gahal in a broadly based government of national unity. The responsible participation of Menachem Begin and the other Gahal members in close cooperation with Labor for a period well beyond the immediate national emergency of the 1967 war (until 1970) conclusively established the credentials of Begin and the legitimacy of his party for many Israelis.

In addition to establishing a responsible image through participation in the government of national unity, a number of additional factors contributed to the increasing legitimization of the Herut wing of Gahal. Demographic trends worked in their favor. The increasing proportion of younger voters who were not influenced by the earlier period of intense conflict between the two movements supported Gahal in greater numbers than did their parents. This was particularly the case for the second generation of Jews from the Islamic countries of North Africa and the Middle East, who, with their parents, now constitute a majority of the population. The debacle associated with the initial stages of the surprise attacks that launched the 1973 war further undermined public confidence in Labor, which worked to the advantage of the opposition. Labor began to look less invincible, and the opposition broadened its support by recruiting popular generals and other groups with the formation of the Likud in 1973.

The success of Zahal in 1967 resulted in the occupation of territories, particularly the West Bank of the Jordan River, the biblical Judea and Samaria, which made manifest ideological issues that had not been salient since Israel's borders were determined by the 1948 armistice agreements. It raised fundamental questions not only relating to the territorial boundaries of the state, but also pertaining to the very character and meaning of the state.

> Since the Six-Day War . . . we have come to realize that questions we thought decided were not decided. . . . The political debate on the future of the territories in western Eretz Israel occupied in the war became no more than a chink through which the depths of controversy and interpretation, intention and fantasy . . . were exposed once again. [A. B. Yehoshua, 1981:vii].

Renewed Polarization

The crisis of identity that characterized various segments of Israeli society after a lengthy gestation period following the 1967 war was born in the aftermath of the war in 1973. Many of the old symbols and myths lost their meanings for many people, and new ones arose to take their place. One striking characteristic was the increasing penetration of religious symbolism in what, according to some scholars, constitutes a new civil religion or a New Zionism, one based on a nonrational mythical or totemic worldview (Liebman and Don-Yehiya, 1983 and 1984; Weissbrod, 1981; Paine, 1983). The acquisition of the territories also resulted in diametrically opposed perceptions of the nature of the threat to national survival, which had serious political consequences. "Once the threat is differently perceived, it pits against each other those who identify different—often contradictory—ways of meeting perceived dangers" (Isaac, 1981:207).

The Likud's position with regard to the importance of these territories complemented the ideology of the increasingly influential leaders of the young generation of the National Religious party (NRP; Mafdal). The educational institutions of the NRP also spawned Gush Emunim, a religious-political movement with a messianic mission dedicated to settling

Judea and Samaria and incorporating it into the state of Israel. (See chapter 4 for an analysis of the rise of Gush Emunim.) The movement challenged and helped to undermine the authority of the Labor government through demonstrations, illegal settlements, and confrontations with the army (sent to remove them from the sites on which they had squatted), as well as the ideological supremacy of Labor (which was already very much on the wane) by claiming to be the true heirs of pioneering Zionism. The Likud co-opted Gush Emunim and utilized it as an ideological vanguard through which it increased the legitimacy of its policies (Weissbrod, 1982; Aronoff, 1984; Newman, 1985).

It is in terms of these important cultural changes that the political developments including the renewal and intensification of polarization must be understood. Lilly Weissbrod (1981b:539) argues: "If the Likud wanted to be recognized as the political center of Israel, New Zionism had to become the dominant ideology and Likud the dominant party." The attempt by the Likud to establish both political and ideological dominance since its ascendance to power in the government is a key factor in explaining the renewed polarization, as was (to a lesser extent) the ineffectual and occasionally exaggerated response of the Labor party to this challenge.

Although Golda Meir had collaborated with Menachem Begin in governments of national unity, as late as February 24, 1974, she warned her colleagues in a meeting of the Labor party Central Committee: "I do not doubt that if the Government would be led by the Likud, it would be a national disaster" (Aronoff, 1977:153). In the election campaign of 1977 Labor used scare tactics, which attempted to convince the public of the dire consequences of a Likud victory. These tactics were ineffective, if not counterproductive, because they lacked credibility among much of the general public.

Yet the unanticipated Likud victory created a climate of uncertainty and anxiety among wide sectors of the public, which was expressed in editorials of major newspapers. The Likud sought to assuage these anxieties in newspaper notices that promised, "We shall protect the State of Israel to the utmost" (Weissbrod, 1981b:535). The climate of public anxiety undoubtedly influenced Prime Minister Begin's selection of his cabinet, particularly in his choice of Moshe Dayan as foreign minister. Begin's appointment of the former Labor defense minister (whom he greatly respected) provided a symbol of continuation with past governments through which he hoped to derive additional legitimacy, and it signaled the relative "moderation" of his new cabinet. The same objectives were achieved through the retention of civil servants, including many in top positions who had served previous administrations (Torgovnik, 1982).

Similarly, the Likud government moved slowly in making substantive changes in domestic policy (Sharkansky and Radian, 1982). The most significant achievement of the first Likud government, the successful conclusion of the historic peace treaty with Egypt, received stronger backing from the Labor benches in the Knesset than from Begin's own party. This achievement was likely more popular among those who had been most anxious about the election of the Likud than among those who had most strongly supported Begin throughout the years.

Why then was the 1981 Israeli election campaign the most violent in decades? Clearly one of the major reasons was because it was the closest election in Israeli history. It was the first one in which the outcome of the election was not *presumed* to be known in advance. In the previous election, most people (including pollsters and political scientists) wrongly assumed that the Labor party would be victorious. The victors as well as the losers were shocked at the election results. Likud Knesset member Ehud Olmert, in an interview on December 23, 1982, said the veteran leaders were particularly shocked to have won because they could not conceive of anyone but Labor ruling. In 1981, as Israelis went to the polls, most pollsters and pundits predicted the election could go either way. This was a formidable accomplishment for the Likud, since the government that it led had experienced the resignations of Moshe Dayan from the Foreign Ministry in October 1979, Ezer Weizman from the Defense Ministry at the end of May 1980, and *both* Simcha Ehrlich and Yigal Hurvitz from the Finance Ministry as Israel's triple-digit inflation became the second highest in the world. In fact, between October 1980 and January 1981, public opinion polls predicted that the Labor party would receive an unprecedented absolute majority of 61 (of 120) Knesset seats compared to the Likud's predicted 29 seats.

The early predictions of a return of Labor to power made its leaders overconfident, and aroused anxiety in the ranks of the Likud. Begin had alienated some of his most ardent supporters by agreeing to return the Sinai to the Egyptians, which ultimately resulted in the "uprooting" (a term that gained wide use) of Jewish settlements.[4] He was particularly anxious for another term of office in order to implement his plans for the massive Jewish settlement of Judea and Samaria, which he was confident would preclude the return of these territories to Arab sovereignty by any future Labor government. Given his vision of the historic importance of this mission, Begin and his closest colleagues were motivated to win the elections at practically any cost. Analysis of the Likud's electoral strategy and tactics, and particularly of Begin's rhetorical style and the symbolic themes that he invoked, indicates that these factors played a key role in the renewal of political polarization and the escalation of violence that characterized the campaign and the period which followed.

The Likud is by no means solely responsible for the political violence. Nor did it bear primary responsibility for the underlying sociocultural and political tensions. However, the Likud both expressed and exploited deep-seated underlying feelings of frustration, resentment, and even hatred among certain sectors of the electorate. Since Labor dominated the Israeli political system for nearly fifty years, it was credited with many of the achievements of the state, but was also blamed for many failures. Labor neither deserved all of the credit it claimed nor all the blame that it received from its opponents. Begin, a master of rhetorical skills, success-fully articulated the feelings of those who had been excluded from the main centers of power and from the centers of social, cultural, and ideological acceptability (or legitimacy in some cases) during Labor's long reign—his own followers from the revisionists and Herut, the Oriental or Eastern Jews, and to a certain extent the religious Jews.

Labor's self-image as a pioneering vanguard came to be viewed by many who were excluded from the center or were on its margins as elitist arrogance (Aronoff, 1982:97). If America was the melting pot, Labor made Israel a pressure cooker in which the immigrants would be blended to produce a new Israeli created in Labor's own (European) image. Arnold Lewis (1984) perceptively captures the essence of the paternalistic aspects of Labor's approach to the "absorption of immigrants" in his analysis of folk concepts like "primitive," the "Desert Generation," "Second Is-rael," "Levantinization," and "those in need of fostering." He relates these metaphors of social inequality and their impact on the collective dignity of the Eastern Jews to the pattern of Labor's ideological and political dominance in which ethnic politics was contained and con-strained. The defeat of Labor and the rise of the Likud is significant not only because it increases the importance of the Eastern vote in the more competitive system, but also because it allows the Eastern Jews to redefine their collective status in Israeli society. Moshe Shokeid (1984) critically evaluates an example of such collective redefinition in the attempt by a Sephardi intellectual to create a new ethnic myth aimed at legitimizing the rise to power of this formerly marginal social category.

Labor's version of the Zionist interpretation of reality is no longer taken for granted. The definition of ethnic cleavages in cultural terms, a central assumption in Labor's ideology, has been successfully challenged. By emphasizing dedication to the struggle for the land of Israel through Jewish settlement and annexation of the West Bank rather than sociocultural characteristics, Begin has offered the Eastern Jews an effective means through which they can redefine their collective status and, with him, move from the margins to the center of Israeli society. Lewis argues that the Eastern Jews have traded support of the Likud's foreign-policy position for symbolic gains on the domestic front; and he suggests that this alliance may be a transient phase in the developing Israeli political system.

It was not the intellectual appeal of Jabotinsky's ideology that attracted the massive and enthusiastic support that was expressed for Begin during the election campaign. Whereas Shimon Peres, Labor's candidate for prime minister, primarily appealed to the voter's reason, Begin appealed to emotions, particularly patriotism and feelings of social and ethnic discrimination (Yavin, 1981:39). On several occasions, Labor played directly into his hands. For example, two days before the election, at a mass rally in Tel Aviv, the master of ceremonies, Dudu Topaz, a popular entertainer, made a remark about the *chahchahim* (a derogatory euphemism for Eastern Jews), supporters of the Likud, who, he said, serve as noncommissioned officers in service units in the army while the supporters of Labor serve as officers in combat units. The next day at the same spot at a Likud mass rally, Begin responded by shouting, "Ashkenazi?! Sephardi?! Jew!!!" which precipitated a wildly enthusiastic response from his supporters (ibid.).

On another occasion, the prominent Israeli writer A. B. Yehoshua referred to supporters of Begin who were engaging in violence against the Labor candidates and supporters as a mob (*asafsuf*). Begin responded by sarcastically referring to the supporters of Labor as *yefeh nefesh*. This means literally "beautiful souls" but can be translated as "beautiful people" or "bleeding hearts." It was generally used by Begin (and others) to emphasize the elitism and/or the (perceived) "knee-jerk liberalism" of the Labor camp.

Begin was particularly effective in using such rhetorical techniques to appeal to Eastern, traditional, and religious Jews. He successively appealed to them in their own codes by making his symbolic references meaningful to their experiences.[5] The prime minister successfully projected his image as a proud but humble Jew, a man who shared their reverence for Jewish tradition. Begin even managed to maintain his populist antiestablishment image while he was prime minister. Just as he defied the arrogant Labor establishment at home, he stood up to the anti-Semites and enemies of Israel abroad. When he linked the two he ignited the flames of hatred and violence. The central theme of "the few against the many" or "them" against "us" was used by Begin to play on the national insecurity, which for some Israelis approaches paranoia (Gertz, 1983). Begin's rhetorical style frequently relied on the use of such techniques as argument by enthymeme, in which propositions are left implicit or assumed, thereby enabling him to mobilize shared sentiments having high emotional charge (Paine, 1981:9–23).[6] When Begin charged in several major campaign speeches that Labor's "Jordanian option" would lead to an "Arafatist state," he implied that Labor endangered the very survival of the state (Yavin, 1981:39).

In some cases, the exploitation of resentment led to overt acts. For example, local Likud leaders adapted a cartoon depicting subhuman, gorilla-like thugs (which had been originally labeled with the name of Arab terrorist organizations) threatening the development town of Kiriat Shmona by relabeling it "Kibbutz Movement–Alignment." They labeled the pack of rapacious wolves bearing down on the town with the names of neighboring kibbutzim (Dudman, 1981:14). Shortly thereafter Peres, the head of Labor's Knesset list, was prevented from speaking in Kiriat Shmona by Likud supporters chanting, "Begin! Begin!" He was bombarded by tomatoes and was subjected to obscene gestures. Peres aggravated the situation by condemning the obscene gestures, calling them "Oriental movements." When Peres returned two years later, he was again prevented from speaking in the town by an unruly mob of hecklers.

There were many incidents in which Labor rallies were heckled or broken up, cars bearing Labor bumper stickers were vandalized, and a branch office of the Labor party was set afire. It is likely not a coincidence that most cases of violence were directed against the Labor, and that the Likud and other parties were rarely the target of such acts. When such acts occurred, they were almost invariably directed against parties to the left of the Likud, such as several threats to bomb the offices of the liberal Change party. Yossie Sarid, one of the most outspoken doves in Labor at the time (he switched to the Citizens' Rights movement (Ratz) after the 1984 election), received repeated threats on his life.

Two leading members of the Likud national election staff (both of whom are ranking members of the Knesset) told me that whereas they felt that the Likud benefited from the political polarization that characterized the 1981 election campaign, they felt that the physical violence damaged the party's image. One claimed that they made serious efforts to prevent their supporters from engaging in acts of violence and vandalism, but the situation had got out of hand and was beyond their control. He gave, as one example, the order to the local branch of the party in Kiriat Shmona not to interfere with the appearance of Peres at a Labor rally in town a year after the election. The order was disregarded. He remarked ruefully that according to research they had commissioned they had even lost electoral support, particularly among older voters, due to their association with the acts of violence.[7]

The new Likud-dominated coalition formed after the election in 1981 was even more ideologically homogeneous and militant than its predecessor from which the moderate ministers (Dayan and Weizman) had re-signed. The second Likud government pursued with a single-minded purposefulness, which among the more ardent bordered on obsessiveness, the policy of settling Jews in new settlements in the territories. This goal was given the highest priority and received far more attention and re-sources than any item on the government's agenda with the exception of national security. For this government, the issue of Jewish settlement in what they termed Judea and Samaria, which they perceived as the heart of the land of Israel, was inseparably linked with national security. These policies were vigorously opposed by many leaders of the parliamentary opposition as well as the nonparliamentary peace movement led by Peace Now. The conflict over this highly divisive issue perpetuated the polariza-tion and tensions that had arisen during the election campaign.

The expansion of the war that the government launched against the Palestinian bases in Lebanon beyond their initially announced goals added yet another dimension to the divisive political debate in Israel.[8] The unprecedented lack of consensual support for this war dramatically ex-pressed the polarized ideological perceptions of reality of many Israelis. As Lilly Weissbrod (1984) argues, the protest against this war was partic-ularly noteworthy because it was the first time that any significant part of the Israeli public questioned the justice of an Israeli war, especially during the initial victorious stages.

Weissbrod correctly contends that the activities of dissident groups like *Yesh Gvul* (There Is a Limit) and Soldiers against Silence, while limited in support, more profoundly challenged the legitimacy of the Likud govern-ment and its policies than did the more widely backed protest activities of such groups as Peace Now. The present writer differs with Weissbrod's interpretation of the extremely limited nature of the protest activities. My fieldwork on the protest activities of the peace movement, which focused primarily (although not exclusively) on Peace Now, convinces me that the main thrust of their protest extended considerably beyond censure of specific persons in the government (such as the minister of defense, Ariel "Arik" Sharon), or policies relating exclusively to the war in Lebanon.[9] Weissbrod tends to exaggerate the extent to which the Likud has achieved acceptance of the legitimacy of its ideology as opposed to acceptance of the legality of its rule. (See chapter 6 for an elaboration of this point.)

Whereas Peace Now is an amorphous political movement drawing to-gether people with a variety of political viewpoints, the vast majority of leaders and activists at different levels with whom I spoke indicated their strong disagreement with the settlement policies of the government, which they feel threatens both the Jewish and the democratic character of Israel by imposing its rule on one million Palestinian Arabs.[10] They also strongly opposed the trend toward religious nationalism represented in the New Zionism (or civil religion) of the government and its supporters. They desired not only to replace the government, but to change the direction in which society and culture have been moving in recent years. In fact, most of the top leaders with whom the present writer spoke had considerable sympathy for the main criticisms of the government by the dissidents, with whom they differed more in style than substance. The main substantive difference was that the leaders of Peace Now rejected the dissidents' policy of refusing to serve in Lebanon when called up by the army.

The Likud government has not acquired anywhere near the unquestioned legitimacy that Labor had during its long dominance. All of the public-opinion data that Weissbrod cites to illustrate the increase in religiosity, support for settlement in the territories, and for the war in Lebanon, also clearly show that a very significant proportion of the Israeli people do not share these views. Although the polls vary according to how the questions are phrased and when they are asked, the population is divided fairly equally over many of the most pressing questions facing the nation today. The Likud government acts as if it had the overwhelming mandate of legitimacy that is derived from ideological hegemony. By pursuing highly controversial policies that were vehemently opposed by significant sectors of the society, including most of the intellectuals and the media, it contributed directly to the intensification of polarization.

Although the Labor opposition supported the goal of driving the terrorists from artillary range of Israel's northern border—the original reason given by the government for launching the "Peace for Galilee" war—it became increasingly critical as the government expanded the scope of the war beyond 40 kilometers. For example, Labor cosponsored (with Peace Now, Ratz, and Change) the rally that demanded that the government appoint a commission of inquiry to investigate the massacre in the Sabra and Shatila refugee camps. The rally was the largest in Israeli history with claimed estimates of approximately 400,000 participants. (The estimates have been challenged and appear to have been exaggerated, although there is general agreement that it was the largest political rally ever held in Israel.) This led to the accusation by Prime Minister Begin that Labor was aiding the enemies of Israel through irresponsible criticism. Members of the ruling coalition were quick to point out that they had never criticized the government during previous wars when they were in the oppostion. Obviously Labor, as a party to the left of the government, was more vulnerable to such charges than were the constituent parties of the Likud, all of whom are to the right of Labor.

Some of Begin's less judicious supporters in the Knesset went even further and charged that the opponents of the war were traitors. One deputy minister said in an interview with this writer that such critics in the opposition were not only disloyal to the government, but were traitors to the Jewish people.[11] The consistent repetition of such charges and the use of the terms traitor *(boged)*, fifth column, knife in the back of the nation, and supporter of the Palestine Liberation Organization *(Ashafist)* indicated a policy that aimed to make criticism of the government and its policies illegitimate. Such attempts to delegitimize opposition can be seen as part of the effort of the Likud to establish its political and ideological dominance.[12]

In a Knesset debate on September 22, 1982, over the proposal to establish a government commission of inquiry to investigate the massacre in the Sabra and Shatila refugee camps in Lebanon, Begin taunted the Labor benches, saying, "Nobody is afraid of your threats of civil war." He was evidently referring to a newspaper interview in which A. B. Yehoshua (who holds no position in the Labor party) had expressed his fear of the possibility of civil war.[13] Begin went on to attack personally Peres for exploiting the catastrophe when a "blood libel" had been made against Israel.

The opposition frequently countered such charges by accusing the government of demagoguery. The more leftist Knesset members, especially the communists, consistently called the government fascist. The leaders of the Labor party usually used terms like neo-fascist or Peronist when describing the Likud government.[14] Whereas many (although not all) Knesset members could "frame" such name-calling in its "proper" context, and drink coffee with political opponents after parliamentary debates (several indicated to me that it had become increasingly difficult to do so), some of their less politically sophisticated militant supporters tended to take such charges more literally. If the opponents of the war aided the enemy, then they deserved to be beaten up. If they were traitors, they deserved worse.

On February 10, 1983, Peace Now organized a march from downtown Jerusalem to the prime minister's office to demand that the government fully implement the recommendations of the Kahan Commission Report on the massacres of Palestinians in the refugee camps of Sabra and Shatila by Christian Lebanese forces. The peaceful marchers were jeered and taunted with all of the aforementioned epithets including that of traitor. They were pushed, punched, spat upon; rocks were thrown at them. The number of police present was woefully inadequate to contain the aggressive hecklers. At the prime minister's office, there were speeches by Peace Now leaders, and the demonstration concluded with the singing of "Hatikva" ("The Hope"), Israel's national anthem. As the crowd was dispersing, a hand grenade was thrown. It exploded, killing Emile Grunzweig and wounding several others including the son of Minister Yosef Burg. Media reports that groups of young thugs had harassed those who brought the wounded to the hospital could not be positively confirmed, but it was verified that several top leaders of Peace Now were assaulted at one hospital when they went to visit the wounded.[15]

The following evening television news carried alternating pictures of the thousands of mourners at the funeral of Emile Grunzweig, and of Defense Minister Sharon speaking at the association of lawyers where he attacked the Kahan Commission Report, which had recommended that he be relieved of his cabinet responsibilities. The pictures of Sharon laughing and joking while a significant proportion of the nation was mourning the death of a young man whose murder they felt symbolized a threat to Israeli democracy vividly illustrated serious differences in perceptions of reality among some Israelis.

The next Knesset debate illustrated the same point even more elaborately. It was opened by Prime Minister Begin, who expressed his sorrow at the death of Emile Grunzweig and condemned violence. He also announced that Sharon had relinquished the Defense portfolio but would remain in the cabinet. There was considerable criticism from the opposition benches by members who claimed that Sharon's retention in the government violated the spirit of the recommendations of the Kahan Commission. In spite of the agreement among the Knesset parliamentary factions to maintain a "cultured" debate and the genuine concern of many Knesset members about the danger signaled by the unprecedented political murder, the debate illustrated greater polarization than reconciliation. Yigal Hurwitz, former Likud minister of the treasury, expressed the feelings of many other politically responsible Knesset members when he warned both sides of the house of the danger of "this crazy polarization."

The cartoonist Jacob Kirschen poignantly summed up the week through his character Shuldig, who said:

> I've been sick in bed for a week now and I've been tossing and turning and having nightmares. I dreamt we went mad with half of us thinking the other half fascist and the other half thinking that the first half are cowards and traitors. I dreamt about political murder and violent Knesset "debating" about violent street "debating." Phew! I think it's time to stop taking these pills. [*Jerusalem Post*, February 16, 1983].

President Yitzhak Navon, who had called on the government to appoint the commission of inquiry, warned the nation of the grave implications of the political, ethnic, and religious polarization. He asserted that the violence of language had led to physical violence, and now to murder. Claiming that Israel had reached a critical turning point, Navon stressed the need for tolerance and national unity. In an interview for a French periodical, Navon warned of the possibility of civil war in Israel if the direction of increasing polarization did not change.[16]

The former secretary-general of the Labor party, Arieh "Lyova" Eliav, claimed that the process that led to the death of Emile Grunzweig began with the occupation of the West Bank. He argued that the increasing expressions of animosity and violence toward Arabs had been transferred to those people who opposed the government's policies and who were considered traitors by the government's most militant supporters.[17] The view that the occupation and the rule over the Palestinian inhabitants of the territories is corrupting the ethical traditions on which Israeli democracy is based is widely held among the opponents of the government's settlement policies, particularly among intellectuals.

These critics cite the increase in vigilantism by Jewish settlers against the Arabs in the territories (as discussed by David Weisburd and Vered Vinitzky, 1984) as evidence to support their argument. Weisburd and Vinitzky demonstrate that the settlers of Gush Emunim have developed an ideological legitimization for taking the law into their own hands, which has received support from the military authorities. The critics charge that the vigilantes could not possibly succeed in repeatedly breaking the law and getting away unpunished without receiving substantial political support from the highest political echelons, including the government. They argue that the encouragement of such acts of violence and disregard for the law corrupts the democratic foundations of the state, and can be directly related to the increase in violence within Israel as well.[18]

Such views when expressed by opposition politicians, intellectuals, and journalists in editorials of liberal newspapers are perceived by many ardent supporters of the government's settlement policies as being tantamount to treason. This charge can be heard in the Knesset members' dining room, in the fruit and vegetable market in Jerusalem, in the Gush Emunim settlements, and throughout Israel (Oz, 1983). For example, on one occasion the present writer went to Hebron with a new reporter from *Ha'aretz*, an independent newspaper that has frequently criticized the Likud in its editorials. When the reporter introduced himself to leading figures among the Jewish settlers, he was verbally attacked—at times venemously—by people whom he had never previously met and who had never read his articles. The fact that he was from *Ha'aretz* meant automatically to them that he was the "enemy." Yet even those people who were most hostile and refused to grant him an interview ended up talking to him, if only to express their contempt for his paper and the leftist *yafei nefesh*, whom they considered it represented.[19]

On another occasion this writer met an eminent professor, the winner of the prestigious Israel Prize in his field. In the first few minutes of our meeting he asked me whether I was for Begin or against him. Whereas Israelis tend to be blunt and to the point, many use more subtle, indirect, or euphemistic ways of asking the same question. Almost everywhere one turned during the period, one was confronted with a challenge to state one's position; and once having done so, one becomes either one of "them" or one of "us." Once the lines are drawn, the polemic battle begins.

Virginia Dominguez argues (1984) that the terms "left" and "right" are multivocal and multifunctional. Their shifting referentiality can provide a flexible means of establishing solidarity and oppostion. She persuasively argues that the meanings of such terms must be contextually interpreted. Any attempt to categorize Israeli parties along a simple left-right continuum seriously distorts the complexity and the nuances of Israeli politics.

The period of reemergent and deepening polarization had the effect of eliminating flexibility by ignoring these complexities and nuances through collapsing the multivalent and cross-cutting nature of political divisions in Israel into simple dichotomous categories. In such conditions the world is perceived through the prism of binary opposites: "them" against "us" or the forces of light versus the forces of darkness. Paraphrasing James Baldwin, Carey McWilliams (1984:34) points out that in the midst of battle all people speak in slogans and ignore complexities.

Jerrold Green (1984:93–95) stresses that the process of simplification and polarization of politics preceded and facilitated the countermobilization leading to the Iranian revolution. McWilliams (1984:31) has observed: "A house becomes divided 'against itself' when what is *unlike* is regarded as more important than what is *akin*." The question is: Are Israelis beginning to regard their political differences as more important than their shared values and interests?

The reality of Israeli politics is considerably more complex than the dichotomized perceptions distorted by the process of polarization. Not all observers of Israeli politics would agree that polarization in the period between 1981 and 1984 reached as serious proportions as suggested here. Compared with the earlier period when divisions in the *yishuv* and early state period were more intense and pervasive, the present conflicts appear to be more superficial, and possibly transient, in nature.

Avraham Diskin (1983) concludes that serious polarization exists in spite of the absence of extreme ideological distance between the two camps. On some issues ideological differences within parties can be as great as, if not greater than, differences between parties. In fact the policies of the opposing political blocs have converged in some areas and are closer than in the earlier period of conflict. As the two main blocs consolidate and converge, the remaining differences have become exaggerated. Strong, nonrational emotional responses, feelings of frustration, fear, and resentment were evoked through the invocation of potent symbolic messages. The particular confluence of circumstances that came together to ignite political passions in the period under discussion may have been a passing phase in the transition of the political system, but there are conditions that could reignite and intensify political passions and violence.

Return to Normalization?

The retirement from active participation in public life of the leading actor in this phase was followed by a marked decline in bitter polemics and polarization. Menachem Begin resigned from the premiership in the autumn of 1983 amid growing criticism of the war in Lebanon, the collapse of the stock exchange, and a prolonged depression on his part after the death of his wife. Avram Schweitzer (1986:145) stresses the "gravity of the resignation of the man who embodied the authority and democratic legitimacy of the government just at a time of confusion when the political and economic way had been lost." Schweitzer (1986:138) suggests that the fact that Begin's successor, Yitzhak Shamir, invited the Labor party to enter a government of national unity was an indication that the Likud had lost faith in its ability to govern, which paved the way for Labor to force the holding of elections more than a year before the normal term.

The 1984 election campaign was a much quieter one than the previous election. However, the outcome resulted in a deadlock. Since neither Labor nor the Likud could form a stable coalition with minor parties, they were forced to form a unity government composed of both major blocs, and to enter an unprecedented agreement that the leaders of the two blocs would rotate offices after two years. Shimon Peres, the Labor leader, served as prime minister for the first two years, and the Likud leader, Yitzhak Shamir, served as his deputy and as foreign minister. In spite of a number of crises, the rotation of offices took place. During the first two years, Israel withdrew its army from Lebanon except for a several-mile-wide security zone, and successfully implemented a major austerity economic program.

Since political careers of both pragmatic politicians depended on the success of the coalition and their rotation of offices, Peres and Shamir achieved a close working relationship. Peres received widespread respect and public popularity for his performance as premier, and Shamir retained leadership of the Likud in the face of formidable challenges and regained the premiership. Although the unity government achieved popularity, strong internal pressures repeatedly threatened to bring it down. As both sides prepare for the 1988 election, there is a strong probability of increased polemics and polarization. (This is discussed more extensively in the epilogue.)

Conclusions

One of the most important distinguishing features of Israeli society is that the major social, economic, and political institutions and aspects of the political culture were self-consciously created by the leaders of the dominant voluntary associations of the Jewish community in Palestine. Many of these pioneering visionaries lived to realize their dream of an independent Jewish state in their ancestral homeland.

A newly created society, such as Israel, faces particularly acute challenges to the taken-for-grantedness of its visionary political culture from the generation that succeeds the founders. This is especially so when the society undergoes dynamic growth and diversification of its population and of its social, economic, and political institutions. Perhaps inevitably, a disparity developed between the changing social reality and the structure of symbolic meanings that constituted the dominant socialist version of the Zionist civil religion. Contradictions became more apparent and were exploited. With the corruption of previously "sacred" creeds, a new, revitalized alternative interpretation of Zionist civil religion was adopted by formerly marginal groups, which successfully challenged Labor's dominance. Their unsuccessful attempt to establish their own ideological hegemony played a major role in the renewal of polarization during the early 1980s.

All societies require a minimal common symbolic structure of shared meanings to function. In the absence of such a minimal political culture, serious political conflicts may ultimately result in civil war. Israel appears to have a greater need for a collective vision and a sense of mission than do most states whose right to exist is taken for granted by their neighbors and the international community. The ancient myth, which proclaims a national mission that the Jewish state should be "a light unto the nations," was incorporated into the most popular versions of Zionism, secular as well as religious. Irving Louis Horowitz (1974:120) has argued that given the political and military demands of sovereignty this goal is unrealistic for a nation-state; it invites the application of a double standard and the hypocritical criticism of others. The goal and attempt to act as a moral vanguard contradicts another principal Zionist objective of being a normal nation "like all nations." A. B. Yehoshua (1981:63–64) recommends that the claim to "chosenness" be abandoned. That such suggestions have thus far generally fallen on deaf ears may indicate the continuing salience of this myth in Israeli political culture. (This will be explored in more detail in future chapters.)

It is almost as if the very success of the Zionist dream in the first three decades of statehood resulted in disillusionment because the society had fallen somehow short of its self-proclaimed utopian vision of being a moral example for the world. The following passage from Walter Miller's *A Canticle for Leibowitz* (1961:235–36) poignantly expresses such an orientation, or condition:

> The closer men came to perfecting for themselves a paradise, the more impatient they seemed to become of it as it grew in richness and power and beauty; for then, perhaps, it was easier for them to see that something was missing in the garden, some tree or shrub that would not grow. When the world was in darkness and wretchedness, it could believe in perfection and yearn for it. But when the world became bright with reason and riches, it began to sense the narrowness of the needle's eye, and that rankled for a world no longer willing to believe or yearn.

The main difference between Israel and the world of Miller's novel is that there are many Israelis who still believe and probably even more who yearn to do so. The problem, however, is that they appear no longer to believe the same myths, and there is the danger that eventually they may cease to believe that they share the same vision and destiny. Whether or not this happens depends not only on which coalition of parties will govern for the foreseeable future, but to a large extent on the quality of leaders that Israel produces in the immediate future, and whether or not they are capable of projecting a vision that the majority of Israelis share. This vision will have to unite the nation around a common symbolic framework and at the same time not further isolate Israel from the rest of the world. Such a vision will require a creative synthesis of both primordial loyalties and universal values inherent in traditional Jewish culture, which have been vital aspects of Zionism in the past. Only a refurbished and strengthened political culture can provide the essential sense of common vision and destiny that Israel desperately needs to overcome the crisis of political legitimacy that it is presently experiencing. Yet the threat of false messianism is no less dangerous than the cynicism caused by disillusioned idealism.

Notes

1. Dr. Yisrael Eldad, in a personal interview on June 9, 1983, recalled how he used to call Ben-Gurion a traitor, because he felt the *saison*, the acceptance of the partition of the land of Israel, and German reparations were acts of treason. He said, "We were raised in Betar to think in terms of black and white." He

now says it was a mistake to call Ben-Gurion a traitor, but that "demogoguery is an unavoidable part of democracy." Dr. Ezra Mendelsohn, in an interview on June 19, 1983, in discussing the strong influence of Pilsudski and Polish nationalism on Betar in Poland, claimed that the movement "was not adverse to violence, particularly verbal violence," and that the charge of treason against political opponents was not uncommon. He explained that as latecomers to the Zionist movement, they found many avenues blocked, and reacted sharply. This is similar to the explanation given to me by several people I interviewed to explain the charges of treason against Begin's opponents in the contemporary period. It was suggested that attacks on Begin are considered treasonous because such attacks deny the legitimacy of those who see in him the symbol of their own recent social mobility and political legitimacy. Variations of this point were suggested, among others, by Professor Yitzhak Gal-Nor in an interview on June 28, 1983, and Professor Dan Horowitz in an interview on June 26, 1983.

2. Confirmed by Dr. Eldad in the aforementioned interview.

3. Dr. Eldad claims that the mob's reaction to his speech frightened Begin. He said that Dr. Bader, a close associate of Begin's, actually climbed to the roof of the old Knesset building in an unsuccessful attempt to get the mob to disperse.

4. A conference on "Uprooting Settlements in the Sinai" was held at the Hebrew University of Jerusalem on March 10, 1983, in which, among other topics, the ritual-like nature of the evacuation was discussed.

5. Professor Yoram Bilu, in an interview on June 26, 1983, related to me the politicization of the annual religious pilgrimage to the tomb of Rabbi Shimon Bar-Yochai on Mount Meiron. He said practically every tent displayed Begin's picture. He reported the ecstatic enthusiasm of demonstrations in support of him had the characteristics of a political carnival. He also recorded reports of informants' dreams of Begin who appeared to the dreamers with a long beard, wearing the traditional Moroccan robe and resembling the revered sage Rabbi Abuhatzira. Bilu reports informants' claims that "Begin is holy."

6. In an interview on February 2, 1983, the mayor of Jerusalem, Teddy Kollek, credited Begin with being the best polemicist of all Israeli politicians. He emphasized that his ability to insinuate and play with words far surpassed David Ben-Gurion's rhetorical abilities. He suggested that only the late Dr. Moshe Sneh and Pinchas Lavon among Israeli politicians had approached Begin's speaking ability.

7. Interview with Michael Dekel (who was then deputy minister of agriculture [Likud], and at the time of writing is deputy minister of defense) on November 22, 1982, and subsequent interviews on February 8, 1982, and on March 16, 1983. Interview with Ronnie Milo, MK (brother of the son-in-law of Menachem, Begin) on November 30, 1982.

8. Former Foreign Minister Abba Eban, MK (Labor), in an interview on January 4, 1983, gave an indication of the depth of the opposition to the war in Lebanon by explaining that "Begin is taking away things which we [Labor] considered sacred." He cited the notion that Israel fought wars only when it had no choice. The best study of the war in Lebanon to date is Schiff and Ya'ari (1984).

9. The only studies of Peace Now, Bar-On (1985) and Palgi (1979), are available only in Hebrew. My conclusions are based on an evaluation of the professional and popular literature on Peace Now, the publications of the movement,

extensive personal interviews that I carried out with key leaders, and attendance at various types of meetings and rallies of the movement. See chapter 5,
below, for a more detailed analysis of the movement.

10. Among the leaders I interviewed are Janet Aviad (formerly Odea, May 23,
1983); Mordecai "Morale" Bar-On (May 14, 1983, and July 4, 1983); and
Betzalel "Tzally" Reshef (July 4, 1983). I also attended a private meeting
between representatives of major Western newspapers and Aviad, Bar-On,
Resheff, and other Peace Now leaders including Amiram Goldblum and Danny
Zidon on May 19, 1983.

11. Interview with Michael Dekel on November 22, 1982.

12. The Knesset debate on November 24, 1982, of a resolution of no-confidence in
the government sponsored by Labor in reaction to the justice minister's
remarks on the radio in which he accused leaders of the opposition of treasonous behavior is a good example of such polemical rhetoric. The minister was
reacting to an article by Max Frankel in the *New York Times,* in which Frankel
reported that he was told by leading members of the opposition that the United
States government should withhold aid to pressure Israel. This position had
been expressed to me by Professor Amnon Rubenstein, MK (Shinui) in an
interview on October 26, 1982.

13. In an interview on March 8, 1983, Yehoshua explained that he thought that a
kind of civil war was inevitable if there would be a government agreement to
evacuate parts of Yehuda and Shomrom. He claimed that Algeria was a more
appropriate example than the United States Civil War. On March 11, 1983,
Abba Kovner, Israel Prize winner and writer on the Holocaust, announced on
the evening news that he was leading a campaign against violence, because he
feared the possibility of civil war in Israel.

14. In almost any heated Knesset debate at least one of the members of the
Democratic Front for Peace and Equality (Rakach-dominated) warned of the
threat of fascism (e.g., both Meir Wilner, MK, and Tufik Ziad, MK, on October
27, 1982). However, such charges are not limited to the heat of debate. In an
interview on November 2, 1987, Charlie Biton (DFPE) gave me a calm and
lengthy analysis of the growing process of fascism under Begin. Shimon Peres,
MK (Labor), claimed in an interview on January 3, 1983, that although the
Likud government used the tactic of delegitimization of Labor, was rewriting
history, and engaged in character assassination the cult of personality, "it was
not yet fascist."

15. Shulamit Hareven (1983) gives an eyewitness account of the murder of Emile
Grunzweig. In her account she describes the strong feeling that the atmosphere
in the street was on the verge of a civil war.

16. Personal interview with then President Yitzhak Navon (minister of education
and culture at the time of writing).

17. Personal interview with Arieh "Lyova"' Eliav, on May 20, 1983.

18. The main theme of the annual meeting of the Israel Criminological Association
held in Haifa University on May 5–6, 1983, was "Violence in Israeli Society."
The increased violence in various spheres of Israeli society was extensively
discussed. See the excellent study of illegalism in Israeli society by Ehud
Sprinzak (1986).

19. Individual interviews of Miriam Levinger and her husband, Rabbi Moshe
Levinger, and Eliakim HaEtzni, a secular leader of Gush Emunim (among
others), conducted jointly with Reuven Pedatzure (a reporter for *Ha'aretz*) on
July 5, 1983.

3

The Manipulation of Political Culture under the Likud

The romance of politics was best used to numb and quell the fears of the uninformed [Goethe, Aus Meinen Leben].

The Likud came to power in 1977 after an extended period of Labor dominance of the political system. Herut, the dominant party in the Likud alignment, had to overcome the pariah image that characterized it in the early years of statehood (as it had Herut's parent Revisionist movement in the earlier period). During the Likud's reign (1977–84), it unsuccessfully attempted to eliminate the last vestiges of ideological legitimacy that Labor retained and to establish its own ideological hegemony by systematically utilizing the state agencies to propagate the Likud's heroes, myths, interpretations of both history and present realities, and to incorporate them into the framework of the national political culture.

In this chapter I shall analyze some of the ways in which they failed. Our analysis will focus on selected decisions and activities of the Ministerial Committee on Symbols and Ceremonies (MCSC).[1] From the records of twenty years of the MCSC's activities (April 1962–April 1983), I shall examine two cases that are illustrative of the process through which the Likud's leaders, building on past decisions and practices of previous Labor governments, unsuccessfully attempted to shape political culture according to their own unique interpretation of reality.

The first case is the memorialization (and near deification) of Vladimir Zeev Jabotinsky, the ideological guru of the Revisionist movement and of Herut. Jabotinsky died and was buried in the United States in 1940. His remains were reinterred on Mount Herzl in Jerusalem at the decision of Prime Minister Levi Eshkol (Labor) in 1963. The attempt to elevate Jabotinsky to the status of one of the greats of the nation was continued to an elaborate extent under the governments headed by his disciple, Menachem Begin. I shall analyze the symbolic and political implications of the unprecedented festivities and events marking Jabotinsky's 100th birthday anniversary and related memorialization activities.

In the second case, I explore the implications of the elaborate state funeral that was given by the Likud government for the reputed remains of the fighters and followers of Shimon Bar Kochba, the leader of the last Jewish revolt against the Romans. Although David Ben-Gurion (Israel's first prime minister) had initially agreed (with reservations) to the reinterment of these remains, neither he nor any of his Labor successors actually arranged to do so. These cases illustrate how the symbolic and ceremonial presentation of selected historical events and figures is manipulated to provide explanations of current political realities that support government policies. Such tactics increased the legitimacy of the Likud government but failed to establish its ideological dominance.

Background

A dramatic increase in the scope and volume of subjects covered in the MCSC occurred after the Likud came to power. Although over the years that Labor dominated the government, the number of meetings of the MCSC and the decisions made by it increased considerably, there was a substantial growth in both during the Likud-dominated governments. As table 3.1 shows, during fifteen years of Labor rule the MCSC met 134 times and made 429 decisions compared with 87 meetings and 615 decisions during the five-year period of Likud rule analyzed. Leaving out the term of the committee in which the Likud took over from Labor, and comparing the last five full terms of the committee under Labor with five almost complete terms under the Likud, we find that the Labor MCSC met 52 times and made 174 decisions while the Likud MCSC met 82 times and came to 595 decisions. Labor averaged 10.4 meetings and 34.8 decisions per term, while the Likud averaged 16.4 meetings and 119 decisions per term.[2] The Likud MCSC made almost three and a half times as many decisions as did the Labor MCSC. The difference is even greater than appears, because the Likud MCSC adopted the technique of approving en bloc decisions on entire series of stamps for the year, whereas many of the decisions during the Labor period included approval of individual series or even individual stamps. Therefore the actual proportion of decisions made by the Likud MCSC is even greater than the figure indicates.

There are a number of reasons why the MCSC under the Likud-led government was considerably more active than it was under Labor govern-

TABLE 3.1

Comparison of the Number of Meetings Held and Decisions Taken by the Ministerial
Committee on Symbols and Ceremonies during Labor- and Likud-Led Governments

LABOR-LED GOVERNMENTS (1962–77)				LIKUD-LED GOVERNMENTS (1977–83)		
Term of Committee	Meetings	Decisions		Term of Committee	Meetings	Decisions
1) 4/3/62–6/18/62	2	9				
2) 3/18/63–5/6/63	2	7				
3) 10/28/63–5/5/64	5	14				
4) 10/26/64–12/27/65	6	20				
5) 3/8/66–6/20/66	4	11				
6) 11/9/66–8/21/67	7	29				
7) 11/6/67–6/16/68	11	37				
8) 10/27/68–8/18/69	12	40				
9) 10/5/69–9/27/70	17	44		16) 7/26/77–9/4/77	5	20
10) 1/3/71–8/16/71	6	23		17) 9/20/77–9/19/78	18	129
11) 9/26/71–7/17/72	15	51		18) 10/31/78–8/27/79	19	120
12) 10/8/72–8/12/73	12	35		19) 10/15/79–9/8/80	10	68
13) 11/14/73–9/8/74	8	27		20) 10/12/80–6/14/81	9	70
14) 11/19/74–8/20/75	10	40		21) 10/14/81–4/13/83	26	208
15) 10/19/75–8/23/76	7	21				
16) 9/29/76–7/14/77	10	21				
Total	134	429			87	615
Average	8.375	26.81			14.5	102.5
Labor 9/26/71–8/23/76	52	174		Likud 9/20/77–4/13/83	82	595
Labor Average per term	10.4	34.8		Likud Average per term	16.4	119

ments. The two movements and their leaders had strikingly different philosophical attitudes toward symbols and ceremonies. Whereas Labor resorted to ceremonials, it denigrated their importance. Within the Labor movement there was an element of exaggerated opposition to appearance and formality. For example, members of the Palmach (an elite military unit affiliated with the Labor-dominated Haganah defense organization before independence) neither wore insignia of rank nor saluted.

In contrast, the historic leadership of the Herut component of the Likud greatly valued the importance of the symbolic dimension of politics. Liebman and Don-Yehiya (1983:77) claim that "despite their failure to create their own integrated symbol system, the revisionists regarded symbols with even greater seriousness than did the Zionist-socialists." Quoting Jabotinsky's statement, Remba (1964:159) writes that "Almost three-fourths of true culture is made up of ritual and ceremony. Political law and freedom rise and fall through parliamentary ritual and procedure, and the life of social groups would sink into darkness without the primeval ceremonies of culture and custom." Jabotinsky claimed that Jews have a special need to be educated to ceremonials. His disciple and successor, Menachem Begin, exhibited a similar orientation. He was from 1967 to 1969 an active member of the MCSC while he served in the national unity governments led by Levi Eshkol and by Golda Meir. During his tenure as prime minister, Begin not only took an interest in the decisions of the MCSC, but directly intervened on several critical occasions to initiate and/ or to influence decisions. (Table 3.2 lists the responsibilities of the MCSC.)

The last Labor chairman of the MCSC, Shlomo Hillel, felt strongly that there were too many state ceremonials and that their number needed to be reduced in order to maintain their value. The chairman of the MCSC during the tenure of Likud governments under discussion, Yitzhak Moda'i, agreed in principle with this position. However, he was an extremely dynamic and ambitious politician who was attempting to establish his leadership of the Liberal party and a prominent position at the top of the Likud leadership. He served as a minister without portfolio and as minister

TABLE 3.2
Spheres of Responsibility of the MCSC

Protocol
The determination of priority lists of categories of officials invited to state events
The establishment of procedures for state funerals
State visits of foreign dignitaries and heads of state
The display of the flag and the playing of the national anthem
The official status of Jerusalem and its role as the capital of the state

State Recognition and Honor
The awarding of military citations by the state and granting permission to Israelis to receive citations from foreign countries
Memorialization through the naming of places, the holding of state ceremonies, or the creation of monuments
The issuance of stamps, currency, or medals
The authorization of all state memorial days and holidays, for example, Holocaust and Heroism Remembrance Day, Memorial Day, Independence Day, and Reunification of Jerusalem Day (established by Labor)

Anniversaries of Historic Events
Balfour Declaration Day (November 2, 1917)
The anniversary of the United Nations resolution that led to Israeli independence (November 29, 1947)
Tel Hai Day (11th of Adar—discussed below) (established by Labor)
The Peace Treaty with Egypt (March 26, 1979) (established by the Likud)

The Death Anniversaries of National Figures
The first three presidents (Chaim Weizmann, Izhak Ben-Zvi, and Zalman Shazar)
The first four prime ministers (David Ben-Gurion, Moshe Sharett, Levi Eshkol, and Golda Meir)
The father of modern political Zionism, who was the founder and first president of the World Zionist Organization, Theodore Herzl
The founder and head of Revisionist Zionism, Ze'ev (Vladimir) Jabotinsky

of energy at different times during this period. Moda'i utilized his chairmanship of the MCSC to improve his position in his party, in the Likud bloc, and in the cabinet as well as to gain greater public recognition. Therefore, against his own judgment, he gave in to Begin's pressures in the cases discussed below. As a former top business executive he used his considerable administrative skills to further rationalize and institutionalize the procedures of the MCSC. (After the 1984 election led to a grand coalition of Labor and the Likud, Moda'i, who had gained leadership of the Liberals, became finance minister but was forced to take another portfolio after entering into a bitter feud with the then prime minister, Shimon Peres.)

The government's positive orientation toward the symbolic dimension of politics and its recognition of the importance of symbols and ceremonies, combined with the more efficiently run MCSC headed by its ambitious chairman, created an environment in which requests by individual citizens and various groups were given prompt and frequently positive attention. This greater responsiveness of the MCSC, especially to the interests of groups close to it or which it courted, in turn encouraged more groups to turn to it with their requests, thereby increasing the volume of decisions handled by the committee.

Since the ascendance of the Likud to power ended nearly fifty years of Labor dominance of the political system, the new regime was faced with a particularly acute need to create a solid base of legitimacy for its rule. The MCSC became one of the principal (although certainly not the exclusive) means of establishing, extending, and consolidating the legitimacy of the Likud leadership of the nation. The increased number of meetings and decisions of the MCSC resulted in a much larger number of ceremonials having been held during the rule of the Likud than during any comparable period of Labor tenure in office.[3]

The Memorialization of Jabotinsky

When the Likud came to power, Moda'i proposed a single day to memorialize all of the "greats of the nation." However, this idea was opposed by Prime Minister Begin. The initial decision of the MSCS to the request, by the Board of Trustees for the Memorialization of Jabotinsky, for a state memorial ceremony to be held within the framework of the celebration of Israel's thirtieth year of independence was that it should be held within the framework of the Jewish Agency, as were the memorial ceremonies for Herzl and Chaim Weizmann. Upon Begin's insistence, nevertheless, the MCSC decided that the memorials for the three would henceforth be state ceremonies.

Begin was not content with honoring his former mentor through the framework of the Jewish Agency, but insisted on the honor that had been accorded to David Ben-Gurion—a state ceremony. He was sensitive to the symbolic implications in the difference between the two types of ceremonies, and by associating the decision with one involving memorials for Herzl and Weizmann, Jabotinsky was symbolically accorded equal position with the founder of Zionism, and his successor, the first president of the state. The political implications for the legitimization of Jabotinsky's disciple, Begin, and his followers are most significant. This symbolic act was an important step in the process through which the former pariah movement acquired legitimacy as an integral part of the Zionist enterprise and through which its leaders attempted to establish their heroes, myths, and symbols as central to, if not dominant forces in, the political culture of the state.

In his efforts to normalize relations with the opposition (and perhaps to establish his independence from his mentor, Ben-Gurion), Levi Eshkol aided the Herut in several ways—most particularly by reburying the remains of Jabotinsky on Mount Herzl in a state ceremony.[4] Other decisions by the MCSC during the same period contributed to the same process. For example, they stressed that representatives of all Knesset factions, including the opposition, must be invited to all state ceremonies. Since the MCSC stressed that it was the responsibility of the Foreign Office to enforce this decision and that it would check to make sure that the decision was being implemented, it is logical to assume that this practice had not always been scrupulously followed.[5]

The process of legitimization of the Likud was immeasurably strengthened when Gahal (the alignment between Herut and the Liberal party) was co-opted into the government of national unity on the eve of the June 1967 war. Menachem Begin joined the MCSC for the first time on August 21, 1967, and served on it through the meeting on October 5, 1969. Begin's active participation on the committee further facilitated symbolic acts of legitimization of the movement he led. For example, during his tenure on the committee it included the members of the Irgun Zvai Leumi (IZL), which Begin commanded, and Lechi undergrounds for eligibility for citations for Fighters for the Establishment of the State.[6] This act gave symbolic recognition to the important role these organizations played in creating the state. Their role had previously been downplayed, ignored, or delegitimized by emphasizing their dissident character and the terrorist tactics they employed.[7] The decision to issue a stamp bearing the picture of Jabotinsky during the period in which Labor was in power was another example of such a legitimating act.

Jabotinsky's 100th Birthday Celebration

The memorial days for the great leaders of the Zionist movement and the state of Israel were set according to Jewish tradition on the anniversary of their deaths (based on the Jewish calendar). An unprecedented decision was taken by the MCSC, at the strong urging of Prime Minister Begin, to hold elaborate national celebrations in honor of the 100th birthday of Jabotinsky.[8] After the MCSC had responded favorably to Begin's initiative and suggested the appropriate agencies to direct the ceremonies, the committee yielded to the prime minister's request that his office be placed in charge of the events.

The events were scheduled to take place between Jabotinsky's birthday and the anniversary of his death, based on the Hebrew calendar. The activities that were held between October 22, 1980, and July 22, 1981, were unprecedented in scope. When compared with the most elaborate equivalent series of events conducted during Labor's rule, those that memorialized the first anniversary of the death of David Ben-Gurion (who died on December 1, 1973), the Likud's efforts, while following a basic pattern established by previous Labor governments, were far more extensive than were those of their predecessors.[9] It is as if the Likud attempted to outdo Labor by honoring their ideological mentor and leader far more elaborately than Labor had honored Ben-Gurion. The new unity government formed after the 1984 election, headed for the first two years by Labor's Shimon Peres, decided to hold similar celebrations in honor of the 100th birthday of David Ben-Gurion. The major activities for the Jabotinsky memorialization are summarized in table 3.3

The MCSC received reports confirming the implementation of all its decisions regarding the events for the 100th anniversary of Jabotinsky's birth.[10] Whereas the MCSC authorized the expenditure of 320,000 shekels on July 30, 1980, and 800,000 shekels on September 8, 1980, it specified that each agency and institution engaged in the activities, for example, the universities and the Ministry of Defense, would pay its share of the expenses from its regular budget. Also a considerable amount of expenses came from special funds in the prime minister's office (which may be one of the reasons why the prime minister insisted that his office should have direct responsibility). Therefore, the cost of these activities is extremely difficult to estimate. It is obvious that the actual expenses far exceeded the nominal working budget authorized by the MCSC. Referring to the aforementioned procedures whereby the events were financed, the chairman of the MCSC told me, "The practice should be forbidden."[11]

TABLE 3.3
Major Activities of the Jabotinsky 100th Birthday Celebration

1) Symposia in all of the universities and dissertation prize
2) Pamphlets, guide for teachers, special programs in schools
3) Audio-visual programs in the schools (movie, educational television)
4) Special conferences for teachers, youth movement leaders, and students
5) Jabotinsky essays assigned, with prizes for the best ones
6) World Zionist Organization produced materials (including collections of Jabotinsky's writings) in foreign languages for Diaspora schools
7) Pamphlet prepared by the Jabotinsky Institute and poster published and widely
   distributed by the Government Information Office
8) Biographical film, special television and radio programs commissioned
9) Ministry of Defense published book and held seminars in army units led by
   personnel specially trained at the Jabotinsky Institute
10) Sound and Light shows held in ten major cities
11) Settlement, neighborhoods, housing projects, schools named Jabotinsky
12) Special recordings of Jabotinsky's poems issued
13) 100-shekel note bearing Jabotinsky's picture, coins, medallions, and stamps
    with a special cancellation issued
14) A special celebration symbol including Jabotinsky's image commissioned
15) Special tours, lectures, seminars, and conventions held throughout the country

Notes on a Jabotinsky Memorial Ceremony

Whereas most of the aforementioned activities were aimed at the wider public, actual participation in some ceremonies involved primarily the already converted. The following brief summary of the memorial service held for Jabotinsky on July 10, 1983 (taken from the present author's notes) illustrates such an example. Buses rented by Herut branches brought people from all over the country to Mount Herzl. Overseas Betar (Herut's youth movement) youths, looking more militaristic in their uniforms than the more casually clad Israeli Betar youngsters, dashed about as veterans of the "fighting family" (as members of the dissident undergrounds are called) and greeted one another with hugs and kisses. A woman complained to a friend that only one of her grandchildren had joined Betar, and having found it boring, joined Maccabee (the youth movement associated with the Liberal wing of the Likud). She disapprovingly said it was not the same as Betar, and her friend commiserated with her about losing the youth. Members of the honor guard took their places around Jabotinsky's tomb.

As various ministers, deputy ministers, members of the Knesset, and present and former ranking party leaders arrived and took their reserved places on chairs arranged around the grave, people in the crowd called out their names. One could gauge the status and popularity of individuals by where they were seated, who greeted them, and the extent of applause they received from the crowd. For example, Ariel "Arik" Sharon, who timed his arrival after everyone was seated and just before the announced entrances of the Speaker of the House (who was greeted by silence), Prime Minister Begin, and President Herzog, was as warmly received by the crowd as was Begin himself.

The ceremony was formally opened by Eitan Livni, a senior member of the movement. The banner of Betar was raised (with a bugle salute) followed by the national flag and the singing of the national anthem. The memorial torch was lit by two of Jabotinsky's adult grandchildren as taps was sounded. Readings from Jabotinsky's writings were recited, stressing the uniqueness and purity of the land of Israel, the glory of the generation of the revolt, and on the right of the Jewish people to all of Eretz Yisrael, which should never be given up. The traditional mourner's prayer was led by the chief rabbi of Zahal, and the chief cantor of Zahal chanted *El maleh rahamim*. (A young Betar honor guard fainted.) Wreaths were laid by the president, the Speaker of the Knesset, the prime minister (who looked aged, sad, and feeble), by representatives of the World Zionist Organization and the Jewish Agency, Zahal, the Israeli police, the foreign diplomatic corps in Israel, and "Jabotinsky's movement." The ceremony was concluded with the singing of the Betar hymn, which I noted was sung with considerably greater enthusiasm and participation than the national anthem had been sung. [Yitzhak Navon, the former president, had objected to the singing of the partisan song during the state ceremony, and had requested that it be sung after the conclusion of the official ceremony so that he could leave prior to its being sung.] The dignitaries filed by the grave to pay their respects in order of rank followed by the others. At the conclusion of the ceremony the people were invited to go up to Herzl's grave, but I did not see anyone do so.

As people were leaving, I heard a grandfather ask his grandson, "It was impressive wasn't it?" When the boy failed to respond, he continued, "Did I tell you about the time the foreign minister came to me at two-thirty a.m.?" Without waiting for a reply, he continued to relate a tale, which he had likely told many times previously, about Yitzhak Shamir and a gun.

Analysis

Jabotinsky is the central mythical figure in a cult of personality established around him by his disciples and their followers. The 100th birthday celebrations of Jabotinsky were unprecedented in several respects. First, the celebration of the birthday rather than the death anniversary of a deceased public figure was not within the terms of reference of the authority of the MCSC, and had never previously taken place. The decision to celebrate the birthday of their movement's hero was probably a pragmatic one to take advantage of the opportunity of the 100th birthday to launch such a series of celebrations while the party was still in power. However, the celebration of a birthday, rather than a death anniversary, may be suffused with symbolic significance and resonates with meanings—even if not consciously intended by those who made the decision.

The celebration of Jabotinsky's birthday symbolized the rebirth of revisionism through Herut's dominance in the Likud-led government after the symbolic death of its unusually extended period in the political wilderness. Don Handelman (in a personal communication) points out the parallel between these celebrations, which began on Jabotinsky's birthday and ended on his death anniversary, and the Christian celebration of the birth and death of Christ. Following this line of interpretation, the ceremonial deification of Jabotinsky also announces the resurrection of revisionism through the rise to power of Jabotinsky's disciple, Begin. Given his image as the first truly Jewish (i.e., relatively religious) Israeli prime minister, Begin could not utilize the metaphor of resurrection as effectively as did Rev. Jesse Jackson, who, during the Democratic primary in New York that was held on the anniversary of the assassination of the Rev. Dr. Martin Luther King, Jr., dramatically proclaimed, "Today a stone has been rolled away!"

Whereas Labor had memorialized leading Zionist figures including Ben-Gurion, there had never been celebrations of such an extensive scope for any of them. The unprecedented scope of the events that memorialized Jabotinsky, and the conspicuous manner in which they were carried out, were necessary because they attempted to elevate to the universal mythical plane of one of the greats of the nation a previously partisan figure, who had been considered by many-including leading intellectuals and key—figures in the media—to have been a pariah in the Zionist movement.

Colonel Uziel, head of the unit in Zahal that is in charge of symbols and ceremonies, suggested in a conversation, "Jabotinsky and Ben-Gurion are not necessarily national leaders, since not everyone identifies with them."[12] Such an evaluation is an unusual one regarding the status of Ben-Gurion, but not for Jabotinsky. Ben-Gurion has long been regarded by most Israelis as the father of his country (a view fostered by Labor during its years in power). Although he was a most controversial figure who not only clashed with his political rivals and the leading intellectuals of the country but also with leading figures in his own party, he is almost universally considered to have been one of the greatest figures, if not the greatest, in contemporary Israeli history (Keren, 1983). Even some of his most bitter political enemies whom I interviewed referred to him with great respect and even affection.[13]

As much as Jabotinsky was revered by his disciples, he was reviled by his enemies. To be sure, the passing of time and the death of the main protagonists had tempered attitudes. Jabotinsky had yet to approach the degree of universal acceptance in the pantheon of Israel's great heroes that Ben-Gurion had acquired. The celebration of his 100th birthday was designed to rectify this situation, which was viewed by the prime minister as a grave historical injustice. Similarly, the elaborate measures taken to enshrine the heroes and martyrs of the dissident underground movements were aimed at correcting the injustice of their having been ignored or even maligned by the former Labor establishment. For example, the special series of stamps and first-day cover with special cancellation issued in honor of the "martyrs of the struggle for Israel's Independence" (proposed by Begin) prominently featured members of IZL and Lechi among the nineteen men and one woman who were martyred—through hanging, shooting by firing squad, or suicide (to cheat the executioner).

The extent to which partisan political bodies and perspectives were presented as nonpartisan national institutions and views in particularly sensitive areas such as the schools and Zahal is noteworthy. For example, the Jabotinsky Institute (an unquestionably partisan institution) trained lecturers to lead discussions of Jabotinsky in army units. The same institution prepared pamphlets and guides for teachers, which were published by the government and distributed in all Israeli schools. Whereas such things undoubtedly occurred in previous years under Labor governments, both the magnitude and the self-consciously planned nature of this particular campaign by the Likud government were unprecedented. Yet, as I indicated previously, this set a precedent that was followed by the next government in celebrating Ben-Gurion's 100th birthday.

To a certain extent every government attempts to make its own partisan perspectives accepted as being national ones. Politicians may be either sincere or cynical (i.e., as a conscious political strategy to gain greater legitimacy) in so doing. Obviously the two are not mutually exclusive. Usually both factors are operative, as they undoubtedly were in this case. Prime Minister Begin was particularly sensitive, since he had been the object of Ben-Gurion's strategy of projecting Jabotinsky and Begin, revisionism and Herut, IZL and Lechi, as pariahs beyond the pale of legitimate Zionism. That he was committed to rectifying what he obviously perceived to have been a grave injustice is clear. One's evaluation of whether he (and his government) either merely corrected a historic wrong or went well beyond that by rewriting Zionist history and giving an exaggerated importance to the contributions of their leaders, ideology, and underground movements depends on one's values and understanding of history and the contemporary political situation. For example, Labor leaders strongly protested that the Sound and Light pageant that opened the Zionist Congress in 1982 "was a falsification of Zionist history," which exaggerated the role of Jabotinsky and undervalued the contributions of Ben-Gurion.[14]

Moshe Shahal, the parliamentary whip of the Labor alignment Knesset faction, suggested that when Begin looked out from the Knesset podium on the seats of the Labor Knesset members he didn't see them, but instead saw Ben-Gurion. Shahal claimed that Begin sought revenge. "He knows he can't erase Ben-Gurion, but wants to chip away at his image."[15] When asked, Likud leaders emphatically denied such charges. Whether or not Begin was engaged in seeking revenge by delegitimizing Labor and its myths, he was unquestionably engaged in a concerted and even passionate campaign to establish his personal, his movement's, and his government's legitimacy through the resocialization of the Israeli public to gain a new and wider appreciation of Jabotinsky and all that Jabotinsky symbolized. He condemned those who refused to accept this new interpretation of reality, particularly intellectuals and the media.

The acceptance of a movement's heroes is a first step in accepting its values. One of the means by which the Likud government attempted to accomplish this was through the use of ceremony in commemorating historical figures whose heroic acts could be utilized to provide meaningful guides to understanding current problems and dilemmas.

The State Funeral for the Remains of Bar Kochba's Fighters and People

In March 1960 the noted archaeologist Yigal Yadin discovered, in a cave in the Judean desert, bones and artifacts from the period of the second Jewish revolt against Rome led by Shimon Bar Koziba (popularly known as Bar Kochba) in A.D. 132–35. This discovery set off a lengthy chain of events that eventually led to an elaborate state funeral, on May 11, 1982, in which the remains were reinterred in a place near where they had been discovered. We shall briefly outline the main events as they relate to the discussion of the role of the MCSC in the efforts to extend the Likud's legitimacy and to impose its interpretation of reality.

Different issues complicated this case from the beginning. First, the determination of the probability that the remains were Jews brought pressure from religious figures, led by Colonel Shlomo Goren (who was at the time the chief rabbi of Zahal), to rebury them. It was first suggested that they be buried in a military cemetery in Jerusalem. Second, the attorney general claimed that, given the age of the bones, the Department of Antiquities had authority over them, which created a jurisdictional dispute.[16] To complicate matters, Professor Yadin informed Dr. Kahana, who was director general of the Ministry of Religious Affairs at the time, that it could not be certain that the bones were those of Jews rather than Romans.[17]

Prime Minister David Ben-Gurion appointed a committee headed by Rabbi Goren to investigate the situation. The committee determined that the bones, which included those of women and children, were the remains of Jewish refugee families from the Bar Kochba period, since they were found with Jewish artifacts and there were indications that they had been buried according to Jewish custom. The committee determined that they should be reburied according to *Halachah* (Jewish law), and considered several possible sites including Mount Herzl. It finally recommended a site near the cave where they had been discovered and suggested that a monument be constructed expressing the heroism of the uprising of the people and the connection between the heroism of that period and the present. Ben-Gurion wrote in a memo, "I authorize the recommendation of the committee to establish a memorial *(yad)* for the slain of Bar Kochba. *I have some doubts regarding the recommendations. . . .* I would like to know the opinion of Yigal Yadin" (italics added).[18]

Rabbi Goren told me he knew nothing of any reservations expressed by Ben-Gurion regarding the committee's recommendations contained in the aforementioned memo. When asked to account for the fact that the committee's recommendations were never implemented, he responded, "Ben-Gurion became busy with other matters and Yadin and the [other] archaeologists stole the bones."[19] This writer was unsuccessful in verifying the nature of Ben-Gurion's reservations regarding the committee's recommendations, although we shall explore a possible explanation below. Clearly, Ben-Gurion had more important priorities.

Since Ben-Gurion expressed a desire to discuss the matter with Yigal Yadin, it is noteworthy that Yadin refused to attend the state funeral in 1982. He publicly declared that he could not vouch for the Jewishness of the nineteen skeletons he discovered, and expressed political, ecological, and professional objections to the ceremonies that were held (cited below).

Rabbi Goren, by then chief Ashkenazic Rabbi of Israel, had become embroiled in a conflict with the nation's archaeologists when he sided with ultra-orthodox Jews who violently protested the excavations taking place in David's city, along the external perimeter of the walled part of Jerusalem, because they claimed the archaeologists were desecrating an ancient Jewish cemetery (a charge that the archaeologists vehemently denied). Rabbi Goren explained to the present writer that, after keeping quiet all these years, the controversy over the excavations in David's city gave him the opportunity to reopen the issue of the reburial of the bones discovered by Yadin and others twenty-three years earlier.

When Rabbi Goren approached Minister Moda'i with his request for a state funeral for the Bar Kochba remains, Moda'i refused his request because he opposed state ceremonies for such historic cases. He feared there would be no end to such requests if the precedent were to be established. Goren then approached Prime Minister Begin, who enthusiastically agreed and, overriding Moda'i's objections, obtained MCSC decision 17 on November 10, 1981, to hold a state funeral ceremony for "Bar Kochba's fighters and people."

In this decision and two subsequent ones (54 on March 31, 1982, and 60 on April 25, 1982), the following policies pertaining to the ceremony were established. The Ministry of Defense and the Ministry of Education and Culture were instructed to hold informational and educational activities on the period of Bar Kochba's revolt stressing the tradition of heroism. This complemented the decision to make the theme for the celebrations of Israel's thirty-fifth year of independence the "Year of Heroism." The MCSC delegated authority for all final decisions relating to the ceremony to the prime minister (including the location for the ceremonies), and delegated responsibility for the implementation of the ceremonies to Rabbi Goren and Zahal. In decision 60, on April 25, 1980, they approved the final plans, which were carried out to the letter.

The funeral took place on May 11, 1982, at 10 A.M. at Nahal Hever in the Judean desert 500 meters from the camp from which the cave had been besieged by the Romans. The remains of the fighters (men), women, and children were buried in three separate, identical wooden caskets brought from Tel HaShomer cemetery by honor guard in helicopters to the burial site. Military chaplains acted as pall-bearers. Prayers were recited by the chief military chaplain, including one especially composed for the occasion, which berated the "evil" Romans. Psalms (pirke t'hilim) were recited by the chief Sephardic rabbi. The chief Ashkenazic rabbi recited the traditional mourner's prayer (kaddish). The prime minister gave the eulogies. The chief cantor of Zahal chaplaincy for burials recited bakashat mechila (request for forgiveness). State wreaths were placed and the honor guard fired honor shots. The full ceremonies were covered by Israel's only television channel as well as by radio broadcasts, thereby reaching a wide section of the population.

One hundred-fifty official guests were brought by helicopter. The guest list included the president, the prime minister, the Speaker of the Knesset, the president of the Supreme Court, the two chief rabbis, cabinet ministers, the chairman of the Jewish Agency, deputy ministers, the attorney general, the state controller, the governor of the Bank of Israel, the chief of staff of Zahal, the commander of the police, the secretary of the cabinet, former presidents, heads of the Knesset party factions, deputy Knesset Speakers, Knesset committee chairmen, former ministers, a limited number of Zahal generals, a limited number of police commanders, the president's and the prime minister's military secretaries and the sergeant of arms of the Knesset, the prime minister's security personnel, and the archaeologists who excavated the site (who boycotted the ceremony).

The budget for the ceremonies was 7,158,000 shekels, which came from a special fund for state funerals in the prime minister's office. An additional 450,000 shekels was allocated for a tombstone, which was authorized in decision 120 of the MCSC on November 17, 1982. Estimates by the press that actual costs were in the vicinity of $250,000, which included the cost of bulldozing helicopter landing pads that brought protests from the Nature Reserve Authority, because the government failed to follow the legal procedures for obtaining the proper permits, and the damage to the delicate desert ecology was extensive.

In fact, various types of protest against the ceremonies were expressed in different ways and for different reasons. Professor Yadin expressed a preference for burial on Mount Herzl, saying, "There are political implications here. And secondly, the landscape is too beautiful and it's a shame to ruin it. But the main problem is that in the end they utilized this event as a means of demonstrating against the archaeologists. And it had a somewhat overly nationalistic flavor to it."[20] Other leading archaeologists who did not attend the event evidently agreed with Yadin, that the ceremonies were being used by Rabbi Goren as a symbolic attack on the archaeologists. (From my conversation with Rabbi Goren, I had the distinct impression that this was one of several motivations. I discuss another, which was equally if not more important, below.)

A group of twenty-four protestors wearing Roman-style togas and helmets and carrying spears, chanted, "You're making a laughing stock out of history." They sang a Hanukkah song about chasing darkness from the land as Rabbi Goren emerged from a helicopter. Police and soldiers destroyed their protest signs and removed them from the area.[21] Shlomo Hillel, former Labor chairman of the MCSC, called the ceremony "crazy" and *avoda zara* (the worship of false gods).[22] Rabbi Menachem HaCohen, a Labor Knesset member (who is a personal friend of Rabbi Goren), claimed that the ceremony perverted and carried to "grotesque extremes" the meaning of the custom of the reburial of bones in Jewish tradition.[23] Obviously opponents of the government and its settlement policies opposed the political implications of the ceremony, but there were also members of the government who were less than enthusiastic about the event. For example, one senior cabinet member (who asked not to be quoted by name) said he did not attend the ceremonies because he thought the whole affair was a farce. He noted that it had particularly appealed to the prime minister, and elliptically concluded that the exaggerated emphasis on Bar Kochba "can be very dangerous." Moda'i criticized the failure "to distinguish between state ceremonials and the personal feelings of leaders. They wanted to emphasize the historic connection with the hills of Judea. In my opinion this was not the correct instrument."[24]

To understand the controversial nature of this event, several aspects of the ceremony must be examined in greater detail. It was decided that the ceremonies would take place on the traditional holiday of Lag ba-Omer, the thirty-third day of the counting of the "Omer" (a period of forty-nine days between Passover and Shavu'ot). This day is characterized by bonfires, weddings, and a mass pilgrimage to the northern village of Meron, near Safed, to the tomb of Rabbi Shimon Bar Yohai. Significantly, it is also an occasion in which children engage in games of acting out Bar Kochba fighting the Romans.

By way of sharp contrast, the committee appointed by Ben-Gurion had chosen the sixteenth of the month of Av, which, according to Talmudic tradition, is the appropriate day for the burial and mourning of those who died fighting with Bar Kochba. This day is preceded by the Ninth of Av (Tish'ah be-Av), the most important fast and day of mourning for the destruction of both the first (586 B.C.E.) and the second (70 C.E.) temples in Jerusalem. The day became a symbol for all the persecutions and misfortunes that befell the Jewish people throughout history. Since Rabbi Goren had chaired the earlier committee, and he, with the prime minister, played the dominant role in the planning and implementation of the latter ceremonies, why was the more appropriate day in the month of Av not chosen? They probably wished to disassociate the acts of herosim, which they clearly wished to emphasize, from both the destruction of the second Temple in Jerusalem during the Great Revolt and from the consequences of Bar Kochba's revolt, that is, the loss of Jewish independence and the beginning of 2,000 years of the Diaspora.[25] When Rabbi Goren descended on a cable from a helicopter while looking for a suitable burial site, he candidly admitted that he was "seeking a new symbol of national heroism." He also expressed the hope that the new focus on the area precipitated by the funeral would lead to "the creation in the area of Jewish settlements."[26]

David Rapoport has pointed out that the deep-seated Jewish ambivalences to what is known as the *Hurban* (destruction), has led to conflicting interpretations of the political consequences of this major catastrophe in Jewish history.[27] He argues that the several revolts against Rome varied considerably in their consequences, including the physical destruction they wrought. Whereas the Great Revolt led to the destruction of the Temple, Bar Kochba's revolt against Hadrian eighty-two years later, according to the Roman historian Dio Cassius, led to the death of approximately 600,000 Jewish soldiers, the destruction of more than 900 villages, the banishment of the Jews from Jerusalem, the selling of many thousands of Jews into slavery and prostitution, and the beginning of the 2,000-year dispersal of the Jewish people from its ancient homeland. Rapoport suggests that the conflicting interpretations of the political implications of the revolts are reflected in the contrasting emotions evoked by the two Jewish holidays identified with it, Tish'ah be-Av, the day of mourning and fasting for atonement for the loss of the Temple, and Lag ba-Omer, in which the ritual games played by children symbolize Jewish power, self-confidence, and heroism.

Rapoport claims that Ben-Gurion, as chairman of the executive of the Jewish Agency in the 1940s, was obsessed with the meaning of Masada, which he understood as the inevitable culmination of senseless decisions by a reluctant Jewish settlement compelled by religious terrorists to launch a suicidal rebellion. He argues that this understanding motivated Ben-Gurion's policies against the Jewish dissidents, who, he felt, made a political solution impossible; and that a contradictory lesson drawn from the same historic events convinced Menachem Begin, as commander of the Irgun, that a political solution was insufficient in order to regain the self-respect the Jews had lost through the exile and the Holocaust.[28]

This perspective was clearly reflected in the eulogy for the reinterred, in which Prime Minister Begin frequently referred to the liberation and unity of Jerusalem, and emphasized the link between the Bar Kochba revolt and the rise and expansion of the Third Jewish Commonwealth. He reminded his audience that it had been the Roman emperor Publius Aelius Hadrianus who had given Judea the name Palestine, "a name that still haunts us."[29] He declared, "Our glorious fathers, we have a message for you: We have returned to the place from whence we came. The people of Israel lives, and will live in its homeland of Eretz Israel for generations upon generations. Glorious fathers, we are back and we will not budge from here."[30]

The obvious political implications of the eulogy added to the ceremony's controversiality. Even foreign journalists noted the Israeli obsession with the story of Bar Kochba. The national debate over whether Bar Kochba's rebellion was justified kindled passions because it is "a metaphor for Israel's contemporary quandary" (Friedman, 1982: 22E). One indication of the interest generated over the subject was a conference on Bar Kochba sponsored by the Van Leer Institute of Jerusalem in January 1982, which was attended by hundreds of Israelis. It was noted that whereas the Talmud and traditional sources referred to Bar Kochba as a cruel, imperious leader and as a false messiah, one stream of contemporary Zionism viewed him as a heroic freedom fighter. That particular stream of Zionism, having attained power in the state, was now trying to impose its interpretation of history and contemporary reality on the entire nation.

The leading critic of the use of Bar Kochba as a mythical hero is Professor Yehoshafat Harkabi, former head of military intelligence and presently a professor of international relations. In two books, Harkabi (1982 and 1983) argues that Bar Kochba waged an unrealistic policy, which directly led to the decimation of the Jewish people. He suggests, "The problem is not how Bar Kochba erred, but how we came to admire his error and how this influences the manner of our national thinking. By admiring the Bar Kochba revolt, we are forced into the position of admiring our destruction and rejoicing over a deed amounting to national suicide."[31] He charged that current Israeli policy relating to the settlement of occupied territories and their de-facto annexation, including over a million Palestinian Arabs, was unrealistic and could lead to disastrous consequences.

On the one hand, the debate over the burial of the bones, based on contradictory interpretations of the lessons drawn from Bar Kockba's revolt, reveals the existence of highly polarized ideological interpretations of the Zionist vision. On the other hand, the fact that secular scholars like Harkabi and Yadin (both played major military roles in earlier periods) engage in public debate with the prime minister and the chief Ashkenazic rabbi over the consequences and implications of events that took place 2,000 years previously implies that they share an underlying Zionist/Israeli worldview that makes the debate over such a root cultural paradigm both possible and significant. (We shall elaborate on this point in chapter 6.)

Conclusions

To explain fully the implications of these cases it is necessary to clarify the relationship between the main values and symbols of the dominant element of the government and the ceremonial activities discussed in the chapter. Israeli political culture is generally characterized by the utilization of both history and mythology in the interpretation of contemporary political situations and events.[32] While this is true for Labor as well, it particularly applies to the followers of Jabotinsky and to the religious ultranationalists who strongly emphasize the understanding of contemporary events through historic analogies, and the understanding of the present as a phase in a historic process.[33] For example, they call the present state the Third Commonwealth, thereby stressing historical continuity with the previous two periods of independent Jewish national existence. Jewish statehood, poetically expressed through the biblical term

Malkhut Yisrael (kingdom of Israel), was (and is) the supreme and sacred value to the revisionists, Jabotinsky coined the term "monism" to express his opposition to the adulteration of Zionism by adding on to it other ideologies, and to emphasize the supremacy of Zionist nationalism above all other values.

Heroism, especially self-sacrifice through the military fighting spirit, is practically worshiped in the movement. In its extreme form the exaggerated adulation of military might led to the cultivation of a cult of power by Brit Habiryonim (named after the zealots who fought the Romans) in the early *yishuv*, by Lechi in a later period, and by their contemporary descendants among the extreme ultranationalists. The name of the youth movement, Betar, refers to, and merges, two symbols of heroism: the site of Bar Kochba's last stand, and the heroic image of Joseph Trumpeldor, a leader of Jewish self-defense during the period of Ottoman rule over Palestine.[34]

Heroism is expressed in many symbolic forms, especially in the poems, songs, and stories of the underground. Tales of the martyrdom of those who went to the British gallows, or who blew themselves up with a grenade prior to their hanging, are revered as sacred martyrs. Their former prisons have been turned into permanent exhibitions testifying to their heroism, and at annual memorial ceremonies the feats of their heroism are retold. Among the mythical heroes selected from Jewish history, the Zealots, who were the most radical and controversial activists in the Jewish revolt against Rome, are particular favorites of the revisionists. Similarly the sites of heroic battles are important shrines for pilgrimage and memorial ceremonies. Among the more important are Tel Hai (where Trumpeldor died), Masada (where the Zealot defenders committed communal suicide rather than fall prisoners to the Romans), Betar (where Bar Kochba fell), and Yodefat (another stronghold of the Bar Kochba rebels). Significantly, the theme for Israel's thirty-fifth year of independence celebrations was declared to be the "Year of Heroism" by the MCSC.

Since the period of the British Mandate, revisionism preached activism and adventurism as opposed to restraint and self-defense practiced by the Labor movement, which to the revisionists too closely resembled the passivity of the Diaspora Jew. Because this activist adventurism led to actions that were opposed by the main Zionist authorities as well as considered illegal by the British Mandatory government, conspiracy was a hallmark of the dissident underground movements. This left an indelible stamp on the character of the movement and its adherents for many years thereafter. The suspiciousness of outsiders, defined as all who disagree with the movement, is passed on from generation to generation.[35]

The youth are taught the revisionist interpretation of the biblical reference to Israel as "A nation that dwells alone," namely that "all the world is against us." The general tendency of Israelis (and Jews in general) to be sensitive to anti-Semitism reaches paranoic proportions among the more militant supporters of revisionism and Herut (as well as among those of Gush Emunim and other ultranationalist parties). Given the level of insecurity and sense of isolation expressed in this worldview, it is not surprising that such strong emphasis is given to military heroism. Although even paranoics may have real enemies, the more militant go as far as to charge those who disgaree with their policies as being either anti-Semites (if non-Jewish), self-hating Jews (if Jewish, particularly in the Diaspora), or traitors (generally reserved for Israeli opponents).[36] Brit Habiryonim "portrayed labor Zionists as traitors to the national cause" (Liebman and Don-Yehiya, 1983:64), and the contemporary descendants of the former call the descendants of the latter a "knife in the heart of the nation," and various other epithets.

The sacred right of the Jewish people to the entire land of Israel *(Eretz Yisrael)* has been a central and consistently maintained ideological principle, and the Bible is invoked to give legitimacy to this claim. Liebman and Don-Yehiya (1983:66–70) suggest a number of other factors that drew revisionism close to traditional Judaism. The principle of monism precluded drawing from alternative symbol systems. The revisionists, rejecting the universalistic humanism of Labor (which they condemned as a foreign ideology), relied on the more particularistic interpretation of Jewish tradition (reflected in the aforementioned stress on "A nation that dwells alone"). They attracted many religious Jews whom they accommodated by adopting a more favorable attitude toward tradition. The militant antisocialism of the ideology and the religious traditionalism of several top leaders were also influential. Finally, European romantic nationalism, particularly Polish nationalism, which lauded religion as an authentic expression of national spirit, influenced the appreciation of the contribution of religion to nationalism.

"Jabotinsky's intense regard for ceremony found expression in the concept *hadar* (literally: splendor, majesty, glory, beauty) which was used to describe the pattern of behavior appropriate to the members of Betar" (Liebman and Don-Yehiya, 1983:77). He stressed noble and princely manners, in the image of the European gentleman. Samson was the ideal man according to Jabotinsky (who devoted a novel to the biblical figure). He represented Jewish adventurism, activism, and love of Eretz Yisrael. He was a hero who fought Israel's enemy and sacrificed his life for his people. He personified the beauty of body and mind expressed in *hadar*. He was handsome, wise, esteemed and respected. In short, Samson represented the opposite of Jabotinsky's image of the Diaspora Jew.

Shochat found a strongly mystical element in revisionist writings and ceremonies. Repeated themes were expressed in symbols of blood, death, redemption, renaissance, and rebirth linked to messianism.[37] Jabotinsky was a poet and he expressed his ideological worldview in highly poetic terminology and imagery. Jabotinsky deliberately emphasized nonrational elements in an attempt to create a revisionist man whose character and worldview was largely instinctive and dependent upon feelings. He felt that Zionism should be instinctive. In his first speech at the Zionist Congress, Jabotinsky emphasized the importance of symbols and ceremony for teaching the values of a worldview. Jabotinsky's disciples learned their mentor's lessons well, and applied them when they finally gained positions of national power.

Political positions are repeatedly posed in such terms as our holy historic rights, our holy graves, our precious inheritance, and the holy blood of our soldiers. Shochat suggests that the concept *tagar* in the Betar hymn written by Jabotinsky represents a call to activism as a character trait and a way of life, rather than a solution to concrete political problems. Widespread manifestations of such an orientation, particularly in the form of government policies and actions, led Robert Paine (1983) to suggest that a form of totemism, namely, nonrational eschatological politics, has become the dominant political worldview in contemporary Israel. Although he concedes it is not the only one, he implies that it is the most influential one during the Likud's reign.

The mystical orientation toward nonrational symbolism and ceremonial both discouraged ideological innovation and change in Jabotinsky's movement and compensated for the lack of the same. With the death of Jabotinsky and his subsequent near deification by his disciples, his recorded words became like Holy Writ and, therefore, were not subject to challenge or to change. The one innovation that took place was the subtle dropping of the emphasis on both sides of the Jordan, and the focusing of Zionist activism and adventurism on the settlement activities in the territories, referred to by them by the biblical names of Yehuda and Shomron. The shared mystical and messianic orientation, and preoccuption (almost to the point of obsession) with settlement of the historic Eretz Yisrael led the disciples of Jabotinsky in the government, and the disciples of Rabbi Kook, who formed the militant leadership of Gush Emunim, into an alliance (which we shall explore in chapter 4).

The state funeral for the reputed remains of Bar Kochba's fighters and followers symbolically incorporated all of the aforementioned key ideological elements. The burial of the bones has deep resonance for religious Jews because it is necessary for the conservation of souls for the Day of Judgment. The burial site linked historic biblical rights to present political claims. The ritual associated mythical heroes to present leaders. It asserted historical continuity and justified present policies in terms of one interpretation of ancient history.

Begin utilized the MCSC in an unprecedented campaign to attempt to elevate revisionism's venerated leader to the pantheon of Israel's greatest mythical heroes. Through an elaborate, unprecedented state funeral ceremony he unsuccessfully attempted to impose a partisan definition of contemporary reality through the invocation and dramatization of a controversial mythical interpretation of history. Although Begin built upon past practice, he carried the deliberate manipulation of political culture to unprecedented extremes.

Begin's failure to achieve his goals can be explained by two major factors. The majority of the nations's educational and cultural elite and leading figures in the media are among the substantial number of Israelis who do not share the cultural definition of political reality staged by the Likud in such ceremonies. In addition, the blatant nature of such manipulation also helps account for the failure of the Likud to establish ideological hegemony. The very obviousness of such manipulations called attention to the socially constructed and artificial symbolic edifice being built. The parody of the ceremonies conducted by the toga-clad Peace Now demonstraters dramatically made this point clear. Such examples of the invention of tradition are not uncommon. Although by no means exclusive to them, this kind of cultural manipulation is particularly characteristic of new nations. Hobsbawm (1983:14) points out the paradox: "modern nations and all their impedimenta generally claim to be the opposite of novel, namely rooted in the remotest antiquity, and the opposite of constructed, namely human communities so 'natural' as to require no definition other than self-assertion." The heavy-handed, exaggerated, overuse of ceremonials and symbolic politics detracts from their effectiveness and undermines the frail fabric of authority.

Notes

1. I am particularly indebted to Minister Yitzhak Moda'i and Deputy Cabinet Secretary Aaron Lishansky for their cooperation and help in gaining access to the data for this essay. I also wish to thank Professor David C. Rapoport and Orit Shochat for their permission to cite their unpublished work.
2. The terms, which varied in actual length of time, are based on the system used by the government, which presumably corresponds with the terms of the Knesset.
3. This was attested to by Yaacov Shatz, director of the Government Information Office (*Merkaz Hazbara*), the body that implements most of the decisions of the MCSC dealing with ceremonies and other forms of symbolic activities, in an interview on December 28, 1982.

4. When Arieh "Lyova" Eliav informed Menachem Begin of Levi Eshkol's decision, Begin broke into tears and hugged Eliav with joy. Reported by Eliav in an interview on May 20, 1983. Professor Shlomo Avineri, in an interview on January 24, 1983, told me that David Ben-Gurion had the remains of Moses Hess, an early exponent of socialist-Zionist ideology, reinterred in the region of the Kinneret in Israel.

5. The informants interviewed gave conflicting accounts on this topic. For example, Dr. Bader, Herut's former top economic expert in the Knesset, claims (in an interview on June 3, 1983), to have been invited to more state occasions when Labor was in power than since the Likud came to power; while others claimed that Begin was excluded from some functions. It seems likely that leaders of the opposition who were on friendly personal terms with the leaders of Labor were invited, while others who were on less amicable terms with them were sometimes excluded from such invitations.

6. The proposal, made by the director of the Government Information Office, was supported by the Labor chairman of the MCSC, Shlomo Hillel.

7. Rael Jean Isaac (1981:47), a scholar with obvious sympathies for the Likud, has gone so far as to argue: "It was the underground organizations that developed from the Revisionist perspective which made the most substantial contribution to winning the independence. . . ." Such historical revisionism is very much in the spirit of the ceremonies discussed in this chapter.

8. Interviews with Yitzhak Moda'i on January 12, 1983, and with Aharon Lishanksy (secretary of the MCSC) on July 26, 1983, confirmed that the decision to hold the events was Begin's idea. Moda'i said the committee agreed to Begin's request that his office be in charge of the events in recognition of Begin's strong personal interest (kirva nafsheet, literally "spiritual closeness").

9. The details of the plans for the Ben-Gurion memorial were outlined in MCSC decision 23 on August 12, 1974. Details of the Jabotinsky memorial appear in the government decision 350 on January 13, 1980, and in MCSC decisions 9 (December 17, 1979), 24 (February 24, 1980), 53 (June 22, 1980), 58 (July 30, 1980), and 68 (September 8, 1980). The aforementioned decisions deal only with those events officially connected with the celebrations, and do not include such items as the request by the Likud youth to name the new government circle in Sheik Jara (East Jerusalem) after Jabotinsky.

10. Confirmed in an interview with Aharon Lishansky on July 11, 1983.

11. Interview with Yitzhak Moda'i on January 12, 1983.

12. Interview with Colonel Uziel on December 29, 1982.

13. Interview with Yochanan Bader on June 3, 1983. Bader was one of several former political foes of Ben-Gurion to express such feelings.

14. "It's Jabotinsky versus Ben-Gurion at the pageant," *Jerusalem Post,* December 8, 1982, p. 2.

15. Interview with Moshe Shahal on December 7, 1982.

16. Document dated July 7, 1960, from Rabbi Goren's file.

17. Document dated November 24, 1963, from Rabbi Goren's file.

18. Documents dated July 7, 1960, November 17, 1960, March 29, 1961, April 25, 1961, and September 21, 1961, from the files of Rabbi Goren.

19. Interview with Rabbi Goren on July 26, 1983.

20. David K. Shipler, "Israel Buries Bones of Ancient Warriors," *New York Times,* May 12, 1982, Sec. A3.

21. Ibid.
22. Interview with Shlomo Hillel on May 3, 1983.
23. Interview with Rabbi Menachem HaCohen on June 7, 1983.
24. Interview with Yitzhak Moda'i on January 12, 1983.
25. See Zeruvabel (1980) and (1980 unpublished b).
26. The first quotation is from Jane Friedman, "For Israelis, Bar Kochba Isn't Ancient History," *New York Times,* January 31, 1982, Sec. 22E. Yadin speculated that this was because Masada had been tarnished by its suicidal image; the second quotation is from the *Jerusalem Post,* May 9, 1982.
27. David C. Rapoport, "Responses to Questions for I.S.C.S.C. Catastrophe and Political Consciousness Colloquiums," May 28, 1982, Pittsburgh, Pa. Unpublished written notes, p. 13.
28. Ibid., pp.14–15.
29. *Jerusalem Post,* May 12, 1982.
30. Shipler. *Op. Cit.* (1982).
31. Friedman quotes from *Facing Reality: Lessons from Jeremiah, the Destruction of the Second Temple and Bar Kochba's Rebellion.* Similar views can be found in *The Bar Kochba Syndrome: Risk and Realism in International Politics* (New York: Rossel Books), e.g., p. 105.
32. For an interesting discussion of the distinction and the relation between myth and history, see Karin R. Andriolo, "Myth and History: A General Model and Its Application to the Bible," *American Anthropologist* 83, no. 2 (June 1981).
33. Among the several sources utilized in this discussion, I found particularly useful the unpublished graduate seminar report of one of my former students, Orit Shochat, on "Symbolism and Ritual in the Herut Movement." This report was based on her extensive fieldwork on the Betar youth movement (both the national leadership and local branches), and on the Arieh Ben-Eliezer National Seminar (*midrasha*), which involved participant observation and interviewing. She also conducted a content analysis of two years of the periodicals *HaUma* and *Maoz,* and relevant literature by members of the movement. Chap. 3, "Revisionist Zionism as a Civil Religion," in Liebman and Don-Yehiya (1983) also contains a most useful discussion of similar material and themes.
34. They even changed the spelling of Trumpeldor's name, replacing the Hebrew letter *tet* with a *taf,* thereby making Betar an acronym for Brit (covenant) Trumpledor.
35. Shochat gives several examples that illustrate the continuation of a conspiratorial character. Her informants refused to discuss their relations with Gush Emunim. Their plans for demonstrations, settlement activities, and prayer on the Temple Mount were carried out with the greatest of secrecy. I found a certain degree of suspicion of outsiders in the Labor party (Aronoff, 1977: Acknowledgments and p. 58). For example, almost all Labor politicians carefully shred the notes they pass to one another after reading them. However, I found far more suspiciousness among Herut politicians. Even among individuals with whom I established cordial personal relationships, such as with a former student, there was a level of distance and suspicion of outsiders that was more pronounced than I found with politicians from any other Israeli political party, including Herut's Liberal partners in the Likud.
36. See Amos Oz (1983:87–100) for an extreme example of this type.

37. When militant followers of Jabotinsky broke away from Begin's party in protest against the signing of the peace treaty with Egypt and the evacuation from the Sinai, they named their party "Techiya," which means "renaissance" or "rebirth."

4

The Revitalization of Political Culture: Gush Emunim

We—and only we—are continuing the true Zionism [Rabbi Yochanon Fried].

Introduction

Gush Emunim (Bloc of the Faithful) is both a product of, and an active participant helping to shape the most significant changes in, contemporary Israeli political culture. It is a movement that has sought to achieve religious ends through political means; and that has justified extraparliamentary and illegal political actions (including the use of violence) through the evocation of religious sentiment and authority. The analysis evaluates the role of Gush Emunim in effecting as well as reflecting important changes in Israeli society, particularly in the context of Labor's loss of dominance and the Likud's unsuccessful attempt to reestablish a dominant party system in Israel.

This chapter will focus on the process of institutionalization through which Gush Emunim passed from a spontaneous, charismatic, loosely organized extraparliamentary pressure group on the margins of the political system, to a well-organized and functionally differentiated network of related institutions that were incorporated within the national ruling establishment under the Likud governments (1977–84). However, the implications of a countertrend are also examined with the emergence of a Jewish underground terrorist organization, which drew heavily from the ranks of Gush Emunim. Finally, changes in the movement under the Labor-Likud national unity government formed after the 1984 election are examined, including the emergence of a parliamentary caucus drawn from several political parties in the eleventh Knesset dedicated to furthering the goals of Gush Emunim.

69

Background

The ideological vacuum created by the erosion of the authority of the Labor party, particularly in the last decade prior to its electoral defeat (discussed in previous chapters), provided the general context that paved the way for the emergence of Gush Emunim (among other movements). Labor's historic partner in every coalition cabinet (with absences in 1958–59 and 1974), the National Religious party (NRP; also known as Mafdal), provided the more specific political and cultural context that gave birth to the new revitalization movement. Just as the loss of its independent socialist school system contributed to the undermining of Labor's dominance, the recognition of a separate state religious school system in 1953 under the control of the National Religious party contributed to the development of a generation with a unique subculture from which Gush Emunim emerged.

The leaders, activists, and supporters of Gush Emunim are mostly graduates of the extensive network of institutions of the state religious educational system and related bodies.[1] The new generation of leaders of the NRP and of Gush Emunim were trained in high school yeshivot (which combined secular and religious curricula), especially those of B'nei Akiva. As Danny Rubenstein (1982) observed, life in the single-sex religious boarding schools, like that of the agricultural schools of the socialist camp in an earlier period, produced strong social bonds among those who emerged in the 1950s and 1960s as the new generation of national religious elite.[2] This new generation of national religious leaders, their unity symbolized by the knitted skullcaps they all wear, see themselves as leading a moral renaissance of the entire country.

The founder-leaders of Gush Emunim are graduates of the Yeshivat Merkaz Harav and are disciples of the late Rabbi Zvi Yehuda Kook, interpreter and exegete of his father, Rabbi Avraham Yitzhak Kook, the first chief Ashkenazi rabbi of Palestine. Having come to the yeshiva to continue their higher religious education after the completion of their army service, they developed close social bonds with one another and a reverent devotion to their teacher. Rabbi Kook was considered to be naïve and unrealistic by the veteran Mafdal leadership. Danny Rubenstein suggests that the fact that Rabbi Kook was the complete opposite of the typical religious party politician may have made him attractive to his idealistic students. Rabbi Kook ascribed to the state mystical and holy authority as precursor of the messianic redemption.

Most of the studies of Gush Emunim mention a speech given by Rabbi Kook at a reunion of his former students on Independence Day 1967. In the midst of his lecture, Rabbi Kook dramatically altered his style of delivery as he told his students how he sat in mourning when the United

Nations resolution on partition of the land of Israel was announced. He lamented, "Where is our Shechem? Where is our Jericho? Where is our Jordan?" Shortly thereafter, as his students participated in what they perceived to be the liberation of these integral parts of the historic land of Israel, they interpreted their rabbi's speech as having been a case of true prophecy.

The wars of June 1967 and of October 1973 were important milestones in the development of Gush Emunim. Shortly after the 1967 war, a convocation of graduates of Yeshivat Merkaz Harav met and discussed issues related to the newly acquired territories. They decided to establish *yeshivot hesder* (which combine higher religious study and military training), which they hoped would be located by the army in the territories to prevent Israeli withdrawal from them. They asked hundreds of rabbis for their interpretation of religious law pertaining to the land of Israel and whether it was permitted to withdraw from it for any reason. Whereas there were rabbinic opinions that specified conditions under which it was acceptable to return territories (except for Jerusalem) in exchange for peace, Rabbi Kook and those associated with him declared there were no authorized circumstances under which it was acceptable to sacrifice any part of the Holy Land.

The October war of 1973 was called an earthquake in Israel. It was a traumatic event that catalyzed conditions that eventually led to major political changes. National morale was at an all-time low following the war. The unprecedented crisis of confidence in the government led to a proliferation of protest movements and demonstrations that, combined with internal party pressures, led to the resignation of Prime Minister Meir and Defense Minister Dayan. In contrast to the triumphant self-confidence and ecstasy that resulted from the Six-Day War, the post-Yom-Kippur-War period produced doubt and agony. Gush Emunim was a response to this general social malaise, and to the weakness of governmental authority that resulted from this situation, which Gush Emunim criticized and exploited (Avruch, 1978–79).

After a series of preliminary meetings among the founding leaders, Gush Emunim was formally established at Gush Etzion in February 1974. Although originally established as a faction within the NRP, when the parent party eventually joined the government formed by Yitzhak Rabin (after the resignation of Golda Meir) without succeeding in gaining their demand for a government of national unity that would include the Likud, Gush Emunim soon severed its official ties with the NRP. However, as we shall see, the close symbiotic relationship that remained between the two was of considerable importance to both groups.

Ideology and Worldview

Although Gush Emunim is characterized by a unique religious political worldview, it has never clearly formulated a comprehensive general ideology. The basis for its worldview can be found in the teachings of Rabbi Avraham Yitzhak Kook as expounded and interpreted by his son, Rabbi Zvi Yehuda Kook. Further elaborations have been developed by the younger generation of rabbis trained by Rabbi Kook in his yeshiva. Rabbi Kook, the elder, saw in the modern Zionist movement the precursor and harbinger of the messianic process of redemption. The "liberation" of Judea and Samaria was interpreted by his son as ushering in the next stage of the process of moral and spiritual redemption. The true believers of Gush Emunim are completely convinced of the historical inevitability of the process (Weisbrod, 1982). They firmly believe in the mystical unity of the entire historic land of Israel and the Jewish people. Given what they perceive to be the miraculous liberation of the very heart of the Holy Land, they believe it is the sacred duty of every Jew to inhabit and repossess every portion of the ancestral inheritance. They relate this mystical tie of the people to the land to the central traditional Labor-Zionist value of settlement. In so doing they claim to be the true successors of the pioneering Zionist settlement,[3] calling themselves a movement for the renewal of Zionist fulfillment. Sprinzak (1981:37) observed: "It is apparent from all its operations and activities that it sees itself as a movement of revival, whose task it is to revitalize historic Zionism that died out in the Israel of the fifties and sixties."

> Its complaint is that the state has veered from the self-confident and determined past that marked its earlier success. Instead, it has been overtaken by a lack of resolution and self-doubt. Defined in both secular and religious terms, willingness to sacrifice territorial integrity for vague promises of peace is both blunder and moral sin. The consequent policies supported by the movement are annexationist bordering on irredentism [Schnall, 1979:139].

Rubenstein (1982:126–30) relates how Gush Emunim effectively manipulated key symbols of the earlier pioneering era and timed some of its demonstrations to coincide with important nationalistic anniversaries (e.g., the demonstration at Sebastia was held on Tel-Hai day). He describes the physical appearance of the Gush Emunim demonstrators, which hearkened back to the veteran pioneers of a previous era: mustachioed men, and women wearing long hair in braids, shirttails out, sweaters tied around the neck, sandaled feet, knapsacks and weapons hanging at their sides. Many observers of Gush Emunim have commented on its character as a movement of sociopolitical reform and of cultural renewal that confronted an unacceptable reality by nostalgically returning to the sources of what it considered to be good and beautiful in the Jewish and Zionist past. Whereas Janet O'Dea suggests that Gush Emunim is a type of religious sect, Avruch (1979) and the present writer have characterized it as a revitalization movement.[4]

> The frame of reference in which the issue of the territories is perceived is determined by the deeply rooted prototype of "Jew versus world." . . . They have withdrawn from a world, which in the past oppressed them and in the present would press upon them intolerable compromises. Gush Emunim approaches mundane politics . . . with a "trained incapacity" to disentangle real from symbolic. . . . The fierce defensiveness of Gush Emunim is founded upon profound national, social and religious antipathy to the non-Jew, and equally upon fear of the possible unsettling or disintegrative effects of western culture [O'Dea, 1976:46].

Given this worldview, it is not difficult to understand the movement's position on relations with the Palestinian Arabs. Although infrequently mentioned in their publications, their position is fairly clear. As Sprinzak (1981:38) succinctly summarized, the Palestinians living in Judea and Samaria should be given the choice: to recognize publicly the legitimacy of Zionism and enjoy full rights as citizens; to obey the laws without recognizing Zionism and enjoy all but political rights; or, with economic incentives, to immigrate to Arab countries.[5]

Gush Emunim's attitude toward democracy, the state, the rule of law, and modern thought are the subject of considerable controversy and disagreement among those who have written on the subject. Whereas originally Sprinzak was relatively sanguine about Gush Emunim's respect for the secular institutional expressions of Israeli sovereignty, after the arrest of the Jewish terrorist underground his position has reflected growing concern with the threat that elements within the movement aligned with other extreme groups pose to Israeli democracy.[6] According to Gush Emunim, democracy is an acceptable system only as long as it remains within a "proper" (as interpreted by Gush Emunim) Zionist framework. Even if a majority of the Knesset were to rule against settlement in Judea and Samaria, by definition this would be an illegitimate act that should be opposed at all costs. Danny Rubenstein and Raanan, both of whom take a more engaged and therefore polemic stance, express great anxiety about the threat that Gush Emunim poses to Israeli democracy. Ian Lustick (forthcoming), writing later after details revealed in the trial of the Jewish terrorist underground became known, is even more emphatic about these dangers.

Tactics

Ever since its formal founding in the spring of 1974, *Gush Emunim* has been marked by its extra-parliamentary style. The *Gush* was not prepared to confine itself to the framework of the law and the accepted rules of the Israeli political game. From the outset it adopted an extremist style of political action that included demonstrations, protests, unauthorized settlement and the like [Sprinzak, 1981:28].

Whereas each of these tactics had been used individually and sporadically by previous groups, Gush Emunim developed them in combination systematically with such effectiveness that some observers conclude that the rules of the political game in Israeli politics have been permanently altered. They became professionals who developed their own political style and special techniques over the years. They adapted their techniques to changing political conditions, the most important of which was the change from Labor governments, which were essentially hostile to their goals, to governments dominated by the sympathetic Likud in 1977. They effectively exploited rivalries within the Labor governments (between Moshe Dayan and Yigal Allon, and between Yitzhak Rabin and Shimon Peres), and received consistent support from the Mafdal ministers. From the beginning they enjoyed easy access to many government ministers, members of the Knesset, and other high-ranking officials of government and other public agencies.[7]

A few weeks after the 1967 war, Kfar Etzion was established west of Hebron, with the government's blessing, at the initiative of a group of predominantly religious settlers, some of whom were members or descendants of members of the original settlement, which had been captured and destroyed during the war for independence. One of the settlers, Hanon Porat, became one of the most active and visible leaders of Gush Emunim. Another future leader, Rabbi Moshe Levinger, led a group that celebrated Passover in a Hebron hotel in the spring of 1968. A series of events, such as squatting and refusing to leave, negotiations with various cabinet members, and demonstrations, forced the Labor governments first to agree to the establishment of a yeshiva in Hebron (June 1968), and later to allocate 250 housing units (March 1970), which led to the creation of an urban Jewish town (Kiryat Arba) on the outskirts of Hebron, something the government had not intended. Later, under the Likud governments, Gush Emunim began to build a Jewish presence in the former Jewish neighborhoods of central Hebron.

Gush Emunim began its first phase of major protests against the interim agreements with Egypt and Syria in the spring of 1974, reached a peak with several mass rallies, and dwindled after the signing of the agreements.

These activities were followed by large demonstrative marches in the territories, usually coinciding with school holidays to ensure a large contingent of religious youths. Such demonstrations created considerable excitement in religious neighborhoods.

The activity for which Gush Emunim is best known is the initiation of settlements across the Green Line (the armistice lines of 1948). The first such settlement established in the Golan Heights, Keshet, was actually initiated by members of a kibbutz movement affiliated with the Labor party. Thereafter, Gush Emunim took the initiative in forcing the government to recognize scores of settlements that had been established against the government's wishes. In almost all cases, the government initially agreed to a seemingly modest demand (such as the establishment of a yeshiva in Hebron) that was over time expanded into an urban settlement. The government was pressured into agreeing to the establishment of a camp for workers in the planned industrial zone east of Jerusalem (January 1975), which eventually became the town of Ma'alei Adumim. A similar camp established east of Ramala in March 1975 became the settlement of Ofra. The most dramatic of all was the group led by Benny Katzover and Menachem Felix, which attempted eight times to settle at Sebastia near Nablus. Each time they were forcibly removed by the army. The final confrontation forced the Rabin government to compromise and allow the settlement of Kadum. The same leaders forced the government to allow the establishment of a "field school," which became the settlement of Elon Moreh.

One of Menachem Begin's first acts before he assumed office after the victory of the Likud in May 1977 was to attend a ceremony in which a Torah scroll (containing the five books of Moses) was placed in the new synagogue at Kadum. He signaled his full support for the settlement efforts of Gush Emunim by declaring (with characteristically dramatic rhetoric) that "we will have many more Elon Morehs." And yet the Likud government continued the previous government's practice of disguising settlements, especially by attaching settlers in military camps, some of which were set up especially for the settlers. The settlement that became Shilo was initially called an "archaeological camp."

Rubenstein (1982:74) notes that it was as if the government wanted to establish settlements but was afraid to do so. He claims that the disguised decisions and euphemisms were signs of weakness that were more self-deceptive than attempts to fool others. This weakness of government, he argues, increased the self-confidence and the missionary feelings of the settlers. Although this conclusion blurs important differences between the motivations of Labor and the conditions in the Likud governments, the general point is well taken.

The internal strains within the Labor governments, particularly the one headed by Yitzhak Rabin, severely weakened them and made them incapable of decisively resolving the conflicting external pressures (particularly from the United States) and internal pressures (from Gush Emunim). To a somewhat lesser extent the same was true for the initial half of the Likud's first term in office. The liberal-moderate forces within the ruling coalition were initially weakened by the split in the Democratic Movement for Change when Professor Amnon Rubinstein led his faction into the opposition. With the resignation of Moshe Dayan as foreign minister in October 1979 and Ezer Weizman as defense minister in May 1980, and with the former Liberal ministers within the Likud coalition following the more hawkish Herut line, the forces of moderation were dealt a mortal blow, and the government thereafter was much more homogeneous. Gush Emunim no longer needed to engage in public demonstrations to accomplish its goals with a government dominated by Begin, Shamir, and Sharon.

However, before this happened, Gush Emunim was dealt a near-fatal blow by Sadat's famous visit to Jerusalem and the drastic change in national perceptions of the possibility for peace that it precipitated (Lewis, 1979), the Camp David Accords, the peace treaty, and the autonomy plan. Gush Emunim failed to mobilize support for demonstrations against Sadat's visit, and the mass support it anticipated in support of its physical resistance to withdrawal from the town of Yamit in the Sinai failed to materialize (Aran, 1985). The establishment of Atzmona in the northern Sinai in March 1979 in protest against the peace treaty with Egypt was a desperately defiant act of a highly demoralized movement. Ironically, it was during this period of greatest demoralization and the low point of public support that Gush Emunim made its most dramatic stride in accomplishing its goal of creating new Jewish settlements in Judea and Samaria, and it did so with the complete cooperation and active support of the government, the army, and the Jewish Agency.

Settlement Activities

In the ten years of military occupation of the territories, the Labor governments established twenty-four settlements on the West Bank, with 3,500 residents mostly in the sparsely populated lower Jordan Valley. Settlements established by the Likud governments, reflecting the goals of Gush Emunim, were established mostly in the heart of areas most heavily populated by Palestinian Arabs. By 1987 there were over 150 settlements with approximately 60,000 residents. One of the leading experts, Meiron Benvenisti, estimated government expenditure for West Bank settlement in 1982 was $100 million (Richardson, 1982).

The settlements have been linked together and to Israel proper through extensive new networks of highways, and they have also been linked to the Israeli national electric grid and water supplies. The West Bank has also become economically integrated with half the employed labor force working in Israel (more than half of whom are employed in construction). Likud leaders argued that the Green Line had been effectively abolished. The extensive expansion of Jewish settlements on the West Bank was carried out at the initiative of Ariel "Arik" Sharon, who served as minister of agriculture and chairman of the Ministerial Committee on Settlements (and later as defense minister), and Matityahu Drobles, co-chairman of the Settlement Department of the World Zionist Organization, with the active support of the military government and an extremely sympathetic chief of staff, Raphael (Raful) Eitan, whose views were very close to those of Gush Emunim. During the same period Zahal was deployed more extensively on the West Bank.

Citing two critical military orders that laid the legal basis for creating and determining the boundaries of the Jewish regional councils and that established the civilian administration for the territories, Benvenisti convincingly argues that a de-facto dual society has been created: "These are two separate systems. One for the Jews, now run by Gush Emunim and other settlers, and one for Arabs. . . . The pattern's establishment makes disengagement from the territories more expensive, and the progression is geometric. . . . In the end, disengagement may only come about through trauma or catastrophe" (Richardson, 1982:7). The domestic and regional implications of these trends are profound.[8]

Social Base and Relationship with the National Religious Party

Both Raanan (1980:13) and Sprinzak (1981) have called Gush Emunim "the tip of the iceberg," to indicate that it is based on a much broader sociocultural subsystem in Israeli society. As mentioned previously, the creation of a separate state religious school system under the control of the National Religious party resulted in the development of a new and distinct subculture in Israeli society, the renaissance of the "knitted-skullcap" generation. The sociocultural environment of these national religious schools, yeshivot, youth movement, and associated institutions led to the emergence of newly synthesized and formulated values that became articulated by the new leaders of the Tze'irim (youths) faction of the NRP and of Gush Emunim. This sociocultural base produced the leaders and activists of both the Tze'irim faction of the NRP and of Gush Emunim, and has remained their most important base of political support (Don-Yehiya, 1981).

The nature of the relationship between Gush Emunim and the NRP has been both complex and critical for the success of the former, and in significantly changing the religious as well as political character of the latter. The Tze'irim emerged in the 1960s from a young-adult auxiliary of the NRP. It is composed primarily of native-born, urban, middle-class graduates of the aforementioned socialization system, particularly the Bnei Akiva high school yeshivot (Zucker, 1973). Having abandoned the kibbutz orientation of the Bnei Akiva youth movement, the faction emphasized "the preparation of religious young people to fulfill key positions in the state," including the government, the army, and the economy (Schiff, 1977:63). Competing for the first time in internal NRP elections in 1968, the Tze'irim received 22 percent of the vote, which led to the entry of the faction's two main leaders, Zevulun Hammer and Dr. Yehuda Ben-Meir, into the Knesset, and eventually into government posts.

Gush Emunim was created by a small homogeneous group of a dozen or so leaders who, in addition to sharing the general characteristics of the new religious elite previously mentioned, graduated during overlapping years from the Yeshivat Merkaz Harav in Jerusalem. They favored efforts within Mafdal to insist that a government of national unity be established that would include the Likud, in order to prevent withdrawal from the occupied territories. In spite of lively debates in the party's Central Committee, the traditional leadership of the NRP won out and the party joined a coalition with the Labor party. This decision led to the severing of the formal affiliation of Gush Emunim with the NRP. However, the informal relationship that remained was critical in shaping the development of both institutions. Like a rebellious teenager, Gush Emunim criticized and fought with its parent body, and yet continued to receive sustenance from it that enabled it to grow and to develop. Reciprocally, the parent party was reinvigorated by the youthful dynamism and religious-political revival and ideological reformulation that took place through the influence of the Tze'irim and their allies in Gush Emunim. After unprecedented pressure from the party's youth movement, B'nei Akiva, the NRP placed Rabbi Haim Drukman, one of the top leaders of Gush Emunim, in the number-two position on its list of candidates for the Knesset in the 1977 election, and it gained two additional mandates.

The process of secularization, which has particularly affected the Oriental Jewish community in Israel, has contributed to the decline in the NRP's share of the school's population from 29 to 24.7 percent between 1968 and 1974. The NRP's long identification with the ruling "establishment" detracted from its public image as well. As Isaac (1981:85) perceptively observed, the territorial issue not only "gave the Mafdal renewed dynamism, it also threatened to split it." The issue has greatly increased ideological tension within the party. The creation of the Techiya (renais-sance) party in 1979 by prominent leaders of Gush Emunim and secular ultranationalists with whom they had cooperated in the Movement to Stop Withdrawal from the Sinai (former members of the Greater Land of Israel movement [Isaac, 1976]) and former members of Herut (who opposed the peace treaty with Egypt) split the Mafdal vote and created serious divisions within Gush Emunim.

> The absence of unity on an issue held by some religious members to be of central importance suggests that the religious bloc might lose its chief strength— a common definition of the targets of the state. The intrusion of what is simultaneously a secular-national issue into the religious domain has opened the religious parties to the same possibilities for fission and fusion that confront the secular parties [Isaac, 1981:85].

Sprinzak correctly stressed that much of Gush Emunim's influence, at least in the early stages of its development, was based on its political support in the NRP. He argued, "Paradoxically, this also explains why there is little chance that Gush Emunim will become an adventuristic movement" (Sprinzak, 1981:45). Later developments, discussed below, tend to refute this optimistic prediction.,

The political rift (after the formal split) between Gush Emunim and their patrons in the NRP, Zevulun Hammer and Dr. Yehuda Ben-Meir, deepened when the latter, as members of the government, supported the peace treaty with Egypt and the evacuation of the Sinai, which the militant members of Gush Emunim vigorously opposed. Dr. Yehuda Ben-Meir was forced to change his telephone number because of harassment from militant members of Gush Emunim who considered the NRP's support of withdrawal as treason. Ben-Meir and Zevulun Hammer began to see the extremism of Gush Emunim as dangerous.[9]

An interview given by Minister of Education and Culture Hammer on an evening news program, on September 29, 1982, sent shock waves through the Gush Emunim settlements. Hammer indicated that his political thought had been undergoing change. He expressed regret that the nation-alist emphasis on the land of Israel had overshadowed the religious emphasis on the Torah, which had always been an important part of his party's mission. He expressed his desire to see more balance in the future (Segal, 1982:5).[10] Reaction was immediate as several Gush Emunim settle-ments canceled visits that Hammer had been scheduled to make—in effect, declaring the minister persona non grata. Others did not cancel his visit but gave him a cool reception, and subjected him to intensive cross-examination about his political positions. Rabbi Haim Drukman, MK, said he was "astounded and taken back"; and Rabbi Moshe Levinger called on

Hammer to resign "in view of his about-turn and treason to the idea of Eretz Yisrael" (Honig, 1982:1–2). Hammer's close ally, Deputy Foreign Minister Yehuda Ben-Meir, replied to the attacks on Hammer by launching an all-out attack on Gush Emunim. He charged that it "would lead us to eternal war."[11]

There are several possible explanations for these developments. First, there were political factors. Through the influence of Gush Emunim and the Tze'irim, the NRP's political policies became practically indistinguishable from those of the Likud, to whom it had lost considerable electoral support. The creation of the ultranationalist Techiya further eroded support from the NRP, particularly among the militants in Gush Emunim. The splitting away of the Mafdal's young Oriental leader, Aharon Abuhatzeira, who created the ethnic Tami party, further eroded support. Consequently, the NRP lost half of its Knesset seats in the 1981 election. Its leaders were aware of the need to carve a new definitive niche for the party in the Israeli political arena. Hammer, in facing the approaching internal party elections, realized that many of the Gush Emunim activists who had been the mainstay of his support had left the party or at least no longer supported his faction. He therefore needed to attract a new party constituency.

Second, the war in Lebanon and its aftermath, including the massacre by Christian forces of Palestinians who were ostensibly under Israeli protection, profoundly influenced many religious as well as secular Israelis. Close associates of Hammer claimed that he was particularly influenced by the high casualty rate suffered in the war by soldiers from the Hesder Yeshivot. A crack appeared in the hawkish views of some of these nationalist religious youth. In television interviews, young Hesder soldiers expressed for the first time the view that it might be worth making territorial sacrifices for peace. Knitted skullcaps appeared in public protests demanding an investigation of the slaughter of the Palestinians by Lebanese Christian forces in the refugee camps. Rabbis Yehuda Amital and Aharon Lichtenstein of Har Etzion Yeshiva (among others) brought Jewish ethics to bear in their condemnations of these events. Elhanon Noeh of the Hebrew University observed:

> Yamit was perhaps the first indication that the all-embracing messianism has been undermined. The general religious community was not willing to go to Yamit. . . . Moreover, they were angry with Gush Emunim for pitting Jew against Jew. They weighed it in commonsense, non-messianic terms. I think it was a turning point. The war in Lebanon perhaps continued the process [Furstenberg, 1982:9].

For all of these reasons the unique symbiotic relationship between Gush Emunim and the NRP, and especially its Tze'irim faction, came to an end.

The breakdown of the symbiotic relationship contributed to the weakening of both, but particularly the NRP. It contributed to the decline in the NRP's Knesset representation from twelve in 1977, to six in 1981, to four in 1984. It also led to the restriction of *direct* representation of Gush Emunim in the Knesset to parties in the opposition after the formation of the National Unity Government following the 1984 election.

Parliamentary Activity

The decision of prominent leaders to run for the Knesset provoked heated debates in Gush Emunim, which decided to allow individuals to do so, but without officially affiliating the movement to any political party. Some activists withdrew from involvement in the movement in protest against the appearance of movement leaders on parliamentary lists during the election campaign. Rabbi Haim Drukman split from the Mafdal and set up an independent faction called Matzad during the tenth Knesset. Matzad merged temporarily with the renmants of Poalei Agudat Yisrael to form Morasha in the 1984 election, and during the tenure of the eleventh Knesset the two Knesset members elected on the Morasha ticket split into their original constituent units, and Drukman eventually realigned his one-man faction with the NRP.

The party with which Gush Emunim has become most closely identified since the break with the NRP is Techiya. Formed by activists in the Movement to Stop Withdrawal from the Sinai, it received 44,700 votes in the 1981 election. Of its three Knesset members, Hanon Porat had played a leading role in Gush Emunim. Porat joined with Rabbi Drukman's Matzad faction of the ill-fated Morasha and was not reelected. However, Hatechiya, after co-opting former Chief of Staff Rafael Eitan's Tsomet movement, gained five seats in the eleventh Knesset.

Techiya is an alliance of three different social groupings. Former stalwarts of Herut who left the Likud in protest against the Israel-Egypt peace treaty are represented by Geula Cohen, a fiery former spokeswoman for Lechi. Her intellectual mentor is Dr. Israel Eldad who helped found the movement. The movement is also composed of militant followers of Gush Emunim who are directly represented in Techiya's Knesset delegation by Rabbi Eliezer Waldman and Gershon Shafat. Approximately a fourth of the Gush Emunim settlers voted for Techiya (half voted for the Likud). The third element is from the veteran Labor settlements who had supported the Greater Land of Israel movement, through the Ein Vered Circle. Although not directly their leader, given the similarity of background Yuval Ne'eman (professor of physics) nominally represents this constituency in Techiya's Knesset delegation. However, Ne'eman told the present writer in an interview on July 4, 1983, that he sees the settlers of Gush Emunim as "my constituency," and that they "have my ear." Former Chief of Staff Rafael Eitan's Tsomet movement, which was temporarily co-opted into Techiya, attracts many of its followers from those who came out of the Labor movement and who were associated with Eitan in the Zahal. Eitan split from Techiya prior to the 1988 election. A poll commissioned by the *Jerusalem Post* (May 9, 1987) indicated that had the election been held in April 1987 Techiya would have received eight Knesset seats. Techiya (like the Citizens' Rights movement) has made the most headway among Israel's youngest voters.

The leaders of Techiya have strong ties with leading figures in Herut, particularly with Arik Sharon, Yitzhak Shamir, and Moshe Arens. Professor Ne'eman was closely associated with the late Moshe Dayan, and continues to have cordial social relations with the two most prominent leaders of Labor, Shimon Peres and Yitzhak Rabin. As Rosenbaum (1987) points out, unlike Meir Kahane's Kach, which is considered a marginal movement, Techiya's leaders are members of the Israeli political elite. It is clearly a leading candidate for a major role in a future Likud-led coalition that excludes Labor, since many, if not most, Labor Knesset members would refuse to support a government in which Techiya participated, and Techiya would never agree to a freeze on settlements, which would be demanded by Labor.

The most striking change in Gush Emunim's political fortune has been that it has lost its previous position of influence in the Likud governments headed by Prime Minister Menachem Begin and Yitzhak Shamir. The government formed after the 1984 election excluded the parties that had elected leaders of Gush Emunim. However, Ariel "Arik" Sharon acts as their unofficial cabinet patron. Estimates of representation of, and support for, Gush Emunim in the Knesset vary. One needs to distinguish between noted leaders of Gush Emunim who represent the movement in the Knesset, Drukman, Waldman, and Shafat, their committed secular allies in Techiya, a patron such as Sharon, and mere sympathizers who might vote with them on given issues. Given the high degree of party discipline in the Knesset, it is unlikely that Knesset members would vote against the leadership on important issues. From twenty to twenty-four Knesset members might be considered sufficiently sympathetic to support Gush Emunim on certain issues.[12]

Leadership and Organization

Whereas there has been striking continuity in the top leadership of Gush Emunim, there has been a marked differentiation and institutionalization of their spheres of activity, and a recent competition for leadership of the movement. For example, in the beginning Hanon Porat directed all settlement activity. In the summer of 1976, with the decline in the importance of demonstrations and the increasing importance of initiating settlements, Amana was established as the major settlement movement. Amana became the main institution through which Gush Emunim's settlement activities were sponsored. Several leaders of Gush Emunim found employment on Amana's full-time paid staff. As settlements were established they elected secretaries to administer their affairs and representatives to regional councils. With the active support of the Likud governments the number of settlements proliferated, and the regional councils were united under the Council of Jewish Settlements in Judea, Samaria, and Gaza (Yesha), which has gained considerable political/administrative importance. Under the leadership of Israel Harel (from Ofra), Yesha has broadened Gush Emunim's authority and facilitated its bureaucratic incorporation into the institutions of the state.

Gush Emunim's main spiritual leader was the late and revered Rabbi Zvi Yehuda Kook. The former chief Ashkenazic rabbi of Israel, Shlomo Goren, and Rabbi Moshe Zvi Neria are also influential spiritual leaders. The younger generation of rabbis tend to combine active political roles with their religious functions. Two are Knesset members (Drukman and Waldman), while others, such as Moshe Levinger, concentrate their political activities outside the parliamentary arena. Others such as Yochanon Fried and Shlomo Aviner have devoted their energies more to educational activities.

The routinization, bureaucratization, and diversification of Gush Emunim's activities had led to the specialization of its leaders in different organizational spheres. Some are primarily engaged in settlement activity and others in their administration, which has been institutionalized, legalized, and legitimated through Amana. The Yesha Council carries out some of the political functions, particularly in representing the settlements in dealing with government agencies. Additional lobbying and political party activity are coordinated through an informal Knesset caucus (known as "the Lobby"). To a large extent Gush Emunim became incorporated into the main institutional framework of Israeli society. Whereas it appears to have been transformed from a militant, extraparliamentary, antiestablishment political and religious revitalization movement into an institutionally diverse and integral part of the Israeli institutional establishment, there is another, less apparent side.

Militancy Revived: Resistance, Vigilantism, and Terrorism

The fact that the routinization of Gush Emunim is incomplete became apparent through its role in resistance to the implementation of the Israel-

Egypt peace treaty, vigilante activity, and the emergence of a Jewish terrorist underground. Gush Emunim played an active leadership role in the Movement to Stop Retreat in the Sinai. Engaging in acts of controlled and ritual-like violence, members confronted Israeli troops in their vain efforts to prevent the withdrawal of Israel from the Sinai in compliance with the peace treaty signed between Israel and Egypt (Aran, 1985; Wolfsfeld, 1984).[13]

The growth of vigilantism on the part of Jewish settlers on the West Bank has been justified by the movement as a necessary means of self-defense. "These vigilantes are 'agents' of the Gush Emunim community as a whole. They carry out a strategy of control that is broadly discussed and supported" (Weisburd and Vinitzky, 1984:82). The progression in types of vigilante activity eventually escalated in degree of violence as well as in scope of activity.

On April 27, 1984, the first of a series of arrests took place, which led to the trial and conviction of twenty-five Jewish settlers for membership in a terrorist organization and for having participated in six violent attacks on Arabs over a period of four years. Among those convicted were a number of prominent leaders and activists of Gush Emunim. The assaults included the planting of bombs that maimed two Arab mayors of West Bank cities in 1980; a machine-gun and grenade attack on the Islamic University in Hebron in July 1983 that killed three and wounded thirty-three, the planting of bombs on five Arab buses that were disarmed before they exploded, and a plot to blow up the Dome of the Rock in Jerusalem (the third holiest shrine in Islam).

Three of the Jewish settlers convicted of murder, Menachem Livni (the leader of the group), Shaul Nir, and Uziah Sharabaf (son-in-law of Rabbi Moshe Levinger), were prominent in Gush Emunim. Gush Emunim spokesmen claimed that the Jewish settlers were forced to take up arms to protect themselves because of the "security vacuum" in the territories. They condemned the courts for refusing to allow the accused to explain their motives and called for a general pardon for the convicted. A number of prominent politicians of the ultranationalist right supported this demand.

During the eleventh Knesset the parties linked to Gush Emunim were in the opposition, and they and Gush Emunim were considerably less restrained in their criticism of the national unity government's policies. The release of over 1,000 Palestinian prisoners convicted of various acts of terrorism in exchange for three Israeli soldiers held by the PLO precipitated protests of outrage and increased pressures to pardon the convicted Jewish terrorists on the part of Gush Emunim and its political allies. The demonstrated willingness and ability of key elements within Gush Emunim to take armed action in pursuit of its policies constitutes a direct challenge to the authority of the government and to the rule of law. The sympathy and support that they have received from the more militantly nationalistic elements of the population indicate the extent to which they are the "tip" of a larger iceberg. (The political implications of this development are discussed in the concluding analysis, below.)

Gush Emunim as a Revitalization Movement

In his classic essay on the subject, Wallace (1956:265) says, "A revitalization movement is defined as a deliberate, organized, conscious effort by members of a society to construct a more satisfying culture." He particularly stressed that the dissatisfaction with significant aspects of the cultural system, and the conscious effort to initiate broad cultural innovations, takes the form of *reviving what are thought to have been traditional cultural patterns.* Gush Emunim perfectly fits this description. In an interview with this author, Rabbi Yochanon Fried, one of the founders of Gush Emunim, stressed that "We—and only we—are continuing the true Zionism." Without prompting from this writer, he stated that Gush Emunim was a "revitalization movement."[14] Gush Emunim's attempt to project its image as the modern Maccabees fighting Hellenism and as the legitimate heirs and successors to labor as the pioneering vanguard perfectly symbolize the revitalization character of the movement.

There are many different kinds of revitalization movements. Millenarian movements emphasize supernatural apocalyptic world transformation. Messianic movements emphasize the personification of a divine role in bringing about such world transformation. Charismatic movements revolve around leaders with unique qualities whom the followers consider to have been divinely inspired and/or selected. Gush Emunim shares characteristics of all of the above types, which it combines to form its own unique corporate persona.

It outspokenly rejects many significant aspects not only of modern secular Israeli culture but of religious Orthodox positions as well. Gush Emunim rejects modern Western secular culture for its spiritual barrenness and for corrupting core Jewish and Zionist values. Both Lustick's (forthcoming) study of Jewish fundamentalism and Rosenbaum's (1987) analysis of Techiya stress atavistic qualities in this reaction to the secular modern world and to the changes that have transformed Israeli society. It condemns the lack of Zionist fervor in the ultra-Orthodox community and the political pragmatism and lack of vision of the veteran leadership of the national religious community. While drawing from the springs of Jewish mysticism in the Cabala, its version of messianism and redemption deviates markedly from tradition in its concentration on nationalism and practical politics.

Raanan (1980: chap. 6) points out that the "political theology" of Gush Emunim completely changed the priority of the three pillars of religious Zionist faith—the people of Israel, the land of Israel, and the Torah of Israel—by stressing the primary importance of the land, or Eretz Yisrael. He argues that Gush Emunim successfully crystallized around a wide range of frustrations that were felt deeply in many sectors of Israeli society: despair that the "ingathering of the exiles" had not brought more immigrants to Israel's shores; the lack of the realization of the dream of the Greater Land of Israel; despair over the possibility of attaining peace; the continuation of anti-Semitism after the creation of the state of Israel; disappointment due to the gap between the myths of the "new Jew" and the new Israeli society as a "light unto the nations" and reality; and despair with the direction of the development of Israeli society and culture as it was influenced by postindustrial Western culture. Gush Emunim capitalized on the aforementioned despair within a segment of the subculture of the national religious camp—despair among idealistic youths who had become disillusioned with the veteran leadership for what was perceived by the youths to be the failure of the leaders to practice the principles they preached.

Weber's concept of charisma is one of the most widely abused and misapplied concepts in the social science literature. Therefore, it is with considerable care that I apply the term to the spiritual leader of Gush Emunim, the late Rabbi Zvi Yehuda Kook. At first glance he would appear to have been an unlikely candidate to become a charismatic leader, and, in fact he became one only in the last stage of his long life. Even his former students admit he was barely articulate, and that both his speeches and his writings were hard to follow. When a documentary on his life was shown on Israeli television they had to use printed subtitles, since the rabbi's Hebrew was so difficult to comprehend. Yet he clearly cast a spell that created, first of all, a coterie of devoted desciples, and through them a much larger following. As in similar cases, the reciprocal relationship between the charismatic leader and his disciples is critical for explaining the mobilization and expansion of a revitalization movement. When Rabbi Kook died at the age of ninety-two in 1982, he was mourned by hundreds of thousands who expressed the depth of their grief at his loss.

With the death of Rabbi Kook, the process of the institutionalization of charisma, which was already under way, intensified. The leadership of Gush Emunim became more differentiated, tending to specialize in one of the various spheres of activity carried on through the network of institutional frameworks that the movement has spawned. The lack of an individual successor or of one homogeneous leadership group has had significant ramifications, including a struggle for leadership of the movement. Lustick analyzes the division in the movement between the more moderate "consensus-builders" who emphasize a policy of attempting to educate and to mobilize the public at large, and the more militant "vanguardists" who perceive that direct action is required to fulfill the redemptive process. The later group, generally associated with Techiya, has been most active in seeking a presidential pardon for the members of the Jewish terrorist underground. In May 1987 a rift in the movement was narrowly averted as a compromise was worked out after moderates led by Yoel Bin-Nun challenged the leadership of Secretary-General Daniella Weiss, a member of the vanguardist militants. "Bin-Nun and other secretariat members criticized Weiss's militant style and said it had alienated the public from Gush Emunim" (Greenberg, 1987:4).[15] Although Weiss retained her position, her powers were curtailed by the appointment of a four-man administrative committee. It was also decided that an assembly of between 200 to 300 rank-and-file members would be established (but it was never implemented). Whereas the differences between these tendencies or factions tend to be tactical ones, these tactical differences have extremely important political implications. For example, the movement to alter the status quo on the Temple Mount has emerged as an issue that directly threatens regional stability.

Conclusions

Having begun as a movement on the margins of the political system, Gush Emunim was co-opted and incorporated as an integral part of the ruling political establishment during the Begin era. Although it was somewhat less central with the advent of the unity government, particularly during Shimon Peres's two-year tenure as prime minister, Gush Emunim continued to have parliamentary representation (through Techiya and Morasha), considerable support from Knesset members representing several other parties, and institutional power through its affiliated settlement movement and the Yesha Council. In addition the more militant wing revived and intensified the extraparliamentary and illegal activities, which reached a peak with the emergence of the Jewish terrorist underground.

It is difficult to evaluate exactly what the impact of the movement has been on the political system and the political culture, because it reflects changes and it has also contributed to them. Gush Emunim exploited the ideological and political weaknesses of the last two Labor governments and contributed to Labor's downfall. It is unlikely that such a movement would have been successful had Labor been in its prime. As I have suggested, Gush Emunim was born in social conditions created by the loss of Labor's Zionist vision and political leadership. The successes of the Likud were even more important than were the activities of Gush Emunim in toppling Labor. In fact it was the coalition of interests and efforts of the secular-nationalist right (which mobilized the discontent of Eastern Jews among others) with the religious nationalists (who are predominantly of European background) that built the new political center that replaced Labor. However, Begin's populist folk religiosity was insufficient without the added ideological legitimacy his policies acquired through the co-optation of Gush Emunim as a vanguard playing the role that the kibbutz movement had played in the pioneering days of Labor Zionism.

It is difficult to evaluate exactly how influential Gush Emunim was in the implementation of settlement policy during the latter period of Likud rule. Gush Emunim's influence in pressuring the reluctant Labor governments and even the first Likud government (which included Dayan and Weizman) is easier to evaluate. However, the second Likud government seemed to pursue its own settlement policies.[16] With the apparent depletion of the reserves of Gush Emunim's idealistic pioneers, economic inducements were used to attract a different kind of settler to the larger urban communities built in close proximity to Tel Aviv and Jerusalem. Gush Emunim's single-minded obsession strengthened the resolve of a government that was already strongly committed to Jewish settlement of all of the land of Israel.

Gush Emunim's influence in strengthening the self-confidence of the national religious subculture has been very significant. As the most radical expression of nationalist sentiment in the religious camp, it mobilized support for a more militant foreign policy and, through its alliance with the Young Guard of the NRP, played an important role in moving religious Zionism to the forefront of the leadership in the most crucial issues facing the nation. Gush Emunim played an active role in moving the religious camp from their defensive posture of self-segregation, which has had profound social, cultural, and political consequences. Even though the leadership of the Tze'irim moderated its stand, and a new movement of dovish religious Zionists called Netivot Shalom (Paths to Peace) has countered Gush Emunim's hawkish stand, these phenomena reflect the long-term influence of the latter in contributing to a new self-confidence of religious Jews in Israel.[17]

Gush Emunim's most dangerous influence has been in contributing toward the undermining of the respect for the law through the legitimation of illegal activities, vigilantism, and violence, and in helping to abort the peace process. Some of the Jewish underground members were convicted for plotting to blow up the el-Aqsa Mosque (the third holiest shrine in

Islam). Lustick suggests that the Temple Mount issue has come to occupy a central place in the mainstream of Gush Emunim, which aims dramatically to alter the present status quo. The threat by leaders of Gush Emunim to offer armed resistance and the possibility of at least a limited civil war are powerful constraints, which make it extremely difficult for any government, much less the present one, to keep the peace process alive.

Notes

1. For an analysis of the relationships between the religious majority and the secular minority in Gush Emunim, see Bauer (1985).
2. See Bar-lev (1977). References to Hebrew sources are paraphrased from my own translations.
3. Raanan (1980:133–62) elaborates the substantial differences between the traditional Labor-Zionist concept of settlement and that of Gush Emunim.
4. Kevin Avruch suggested the applicability of the term in a version of his essay, which I had not seen when I published the earlier version of this essay.
5. Lustick (forthcoming), Raanan (1982), A. Rubenstein (1980), D. Rubenstein (1982), Sprinzak (1981), and Weissbrod (1982) give extensive accounts of various aspects of Gush Emunim's ideology.
6. The postscript Sprinzak added to the previously cited essay when it was republished in Newman (1985) already expressed this concern. Later publications, e.g., Sprinzak (1986), and his ongoing research focuses greater attention on the role of violence and terrorism in Gush Emunim and other extremist groups in Israel. It should be noted that there is a long association between religious extremist groups and violence. Dr. Joseph Burg (National Religious party), who was at the time both minister of the interior and minister of police, in an interview on July 22, 1983, told me of incidents in Jerusalem dating back to 1887. He dissociated himself from religious extremist groups, both Gush Emunim and Neturei Karta, which perpetrated acts of violence and terrorism. Lehman-Wilzig and Goldberg (1983:6–7) have shown that while religious protest constitutes only 13 percent of all protests over a thirty-year period, 38.4 percent of protests over religious issues involved violence.
7. Danny Rubenstein (1982:81–82) estimated that 350 families in Kiryat Arba were supported through public funds.
8. Benvenisti's interim report was published in 1982 and a later survey was published in 1984. For an excellent discussion of the West Bank in Israeli politics, see Lustick (1984).
9. Interviews with Eli Yerushalmi, administrative assistant to Dr. Ben-Meir, on November 23, 1982, and with Dr. Yehuda Ben-Meir, deputy foreign minister, on November 30, 1982. Dr. Mordecai Bar-Lev reported (at a conference on "Religious Parties and Movements in Israel" at Bar-Ilan University, on December 30, 1987) that at the fiftieth convention of B'nei Akiva there was an unsuccessful attempt to break away from the NRP in protest over the peace treaty with Egypt.
10. Hammer elaborated on these and other points in an interview with me on May 25, 1983. Hanon Porat, MK (Techiya) in an interview on November 8, 1982, suggested that Hammer changed his position for political reasons. He claimed

that when religious people disguise the mystical quality of their beliefs to appear less strange to the secular people, they are only ritually religious—not really religious. The implication was clearly that this was the case of Hammer as far as Porat was concerned.

11. He further claimed that "the Gush is now advocating that Israel stay on in parts of Lebanon, because these are the lands of the biblical tribes of Naftali and Asher" (Honig, 1982:2).

12. Rick Hasen (forthcoming), relying on the estimates of Otniel Schneller, secretary of the Yesha Council and one of the founders of the so-called Lobby, estimated support in the summer of 1985 to be 38 members of Knesset (30 Likud, 5 Techiya, 2 Morasha, and 1 Mafdal). Including unaffiliated cabinet ministers (Shamir, Sharon, Levy, and Arens), and MKs like Meir Kahane, he estimates total support to be approximately 50 Knesset members. This estimate is exaggerated and unreliable. Perhaps only half this number could be counted on for reliable support, and even then such support would depend on the specific issues and on the specific context in which they arose. For example, support for continued settlement on the West Bank (without progress made toward a peace settlement) would likely be supported by such a large number, whereas support for the actions of the Jewish terrorist underground (particularly if there was progress towards further peace negotiations) would not likely receive the support of anywhere near that number.

13. In an interview on March 16, 1983, Michael Dekel, who was at the time Sharon's deputy minister, confirmed that Sharon was in close contact with the leaders of Gush Emunim during this period and implied that there was tacit coordination and cooperation between them. It seems clear that the government used the opposition to withdrawal from the Sinai for its own purposes of dramatizing the price it had paid for peace and indicating that any future withdrawal from the West Bank would be politically out of the question.

14. Interview with Rabbi Yochanon Fried on December 6, 1982. Fried, a moderate, ceased active involvement in protest against the increased political party involvement and violent activites of Gush Emunim. He told me of his shock of acting like members of Neturei Karta when they took to the streets. He said even his manner of speaking changed when he addressed crowds of 50,000 people. It gave him such a sense of power that he lost his moderation of speech and found himself shouting slogans. He said this was a bad educational example to set for the youth.

15. Also see Greenberg's interview with Bin-Nun in "Split in the Bloc" (1987:7).

16. Michael Dekel, MK (Likud), deputy minister of agriculture, (November 22, 1982) credited Gush Emunim for having played an important role in the early stages of settlement, but insisted they became more marginal as Minister of Agriculture Sharon took almost single-handed control of settlement policy. This evaluation was corroborated by Knesset member Ronnie Milo (Likud) in an interview on December 6, 1982. On the other hand, Rabbi Eliezer Waldman, MK (Techiya), in an interview on July 11, 1983, argued that without Gush Emunim's pressure the government would not have built as many settlements as it did. He also credited Sharon.

17. Rabbi Menachem HaCohen, MK (Labor), recounted (in an interview on December 6, 1982) an incident that is highly revealing of the self-consciousness of religious youth in an earlier period. He and religious friends in an army Nachal unit (which combined farming and military service) were singing

religious songs while driving in their jeep. However, when they reached a predominantly secular Israeli town, they started singing army songs. He claimed that it was not until the Six-Day War that national religious youth began to gain a sense of pride in their identity. For a good, brief discussion of Gush Emunim as an expression of the frustration and resentment aroused among Orthodox Jews by the secular environment, see Schweitzer (1986:85–91).

5

Protests for Peace: Peace Now and Two Smaller Peace Movements

We are the expression of a mood—that is Peace Now [Mordecai Bar-On].

Introduction

Ten thousand Peace Now demonstrators piled out of buses on a cold and rainy day atop Mount Bracha overlooking the Arab city of Nablus (Shechem, in Hebrew). It was April 18, 1983—Israel's independence day, which the Ministerial Committee on Symbols and Ceremonies had declared "The Year of Heroism." The occasion was a Peace Now protest against the government for holding a ceremony to launch the establishment of a new and highly controversial Jewish settlement overlooking this major Arab city on independence day. They felt that the holding of the controversial ceremony on a day that was supposed to emphasize the unity of the Israeli people was a deliberate provocation.

Like a Scottish bagpiper accompanying marching troops, an accordianist from Kibbutz Negba played and sang songs from the war of independence as the demonstrators moved down the police-cordoned line to face the Gush Emunim demonstrators on the other side. While popular songs blared on the loudspeakers, the Peace Now demonstrators sang peace songs and chanted slogans like "Conquest No! Peace Yes!" During a rousing rendition of "We Shall Overcome" (in English no less!) the demonstrators overwhelmed the few soldiers who stood in the quickly disappearing no-man's land between the two sides. The volume of the loudspeakers was turned up in an attempt to drown out the peace songs.

The atmosphere was surprisingly low key. Soldiers flirted with demonstrators. A few religious hecklers unsuccessfully attempted to rile the peace demonstrators. Peace Now ushers joined hands to prevent the two sides of demonstrators from intermingling. Small groups of religious men said their afternoon prayers. A group of yeshiva students danced—young men and women separately. The Peace Now demonstrators (who greatly outnumbered those who were there in support of the government) sang the "Song of Peace" and waved Israeli flags and banners (one read "Burying the Peace—Dividing the People"). They then started chanting "We want David Levy" (the minister of housing who was to be the main speaker). While the radio announced that the ceremony had been canceled because of the bad weather, it was learned that there was a secret ceremony held indoors to avoid the embarrassment to the government by the overwhelming numbers of hostile demonstrators. Peace Now released two crates of doves, and sang, "We Bring Peace Unto You" and "Hatikva" (the national anthem), then boarded the buses and returned to their homes. In several respects the leading actor in the peace camp, Peace Now (Shalom Achshav), is similar to Gush Emunim, and in other important respects it can be seen as its mirror image. An outsider observing representatives of both movements at the aforementioned rally would have a difficult time telling the difference between them. The only visual clue for differentiating between them would be the predominance of knitted skullcaps on the heads of the men and scarves on the heads of the women of Gush Emunim, and the rarity of the same among Peace Now activists. Also, many of the Gush Emunim demonstrators carried weapons, whereas none of the Peace Now demonstrators were armed.

The adherents of both movements are overwhelmingly native-born Israelis of Western (Ashkenazi) backgrounds, middle to upper-middle class, and with higher education. Most activists range in age between twenty and forty years. Peace Now, like its ideological rival, is characterized by the enthusiasm and idealism of its membership. While Gush Emunim relies on key rabbis for spiritual guidance, Peace Now has a large number of professors from whom it receives ideological guidance and support. Whereas both started out as spontaneous voluntary movements, Peace Now has undergone much less institutionalization than has Gush Emunim. Many of the key leaders of Gush Emunim have jobs that allow them to engage in full- or nearly full-time activity on behalf of the movement, which is not the case with Peace Now except for the very few members of the Kibbutz Artzi movement who are given full or partial release for activity in Peace Now.

Background

Brit Shalom (Covenant of Peace), the first peace movement in Israel, was founded in 1925. However, until the founding of Peace Now on April

8. 1978, the peace movement in Israel was highly fragmented and was generally considered to be on the fringes of the poiiticai sysieui.' The major catalyst that began the chain reaction leading to the formation of Peace Now was the historic visit of Egyptian President Anwar Sadat to Jerusalem. Mordecai Bar-On (1985:13) asserts that Sadat's visit brought about a revolution in Israeli consciousness by exploding the myth of "no choice" (*ein breira*).[2] Ayre Palgi (1979:19) claims that Sadat's visit exploded the consensus that there was no Arab leader with whom Israel could talk.

Palgi vividly portrays the dynamics of raised hopes, and then the anxiety that a historic opportunity might be lost, which prompted a group of reserve officers to formulate a letter that they circulated among acquaintances (gaining 348 signatures) and sent to Prime Minister Begin.

> March 7, 1978 . . . A government that will prefer the existence of Israel in borders of the greater Israel to its existence in peace in the context of good neighborly relations will arouse in us grave misgivings. A government that will prefer the establishment of settlements across the "green line" to the ending of the historic conflict and to the establishment of a system of normal relations will raise questions about the justice of our course. A government policy that will lead to the continued rule over one million Arabs is liable to damage the Jewish democratic character of the state, and would make it difficult for us to identify with the basic direction of the State of Israel. . . . The strength of the Israel Defense Forces lies in the identification of its soldiers with the course of the State of Israel. We call upon you to choose the path of peace, and through this choice, to strengthen our faith in the justice of our cause.[3]

Although none of the original organizers of the letter dreamed of founding a mass movement, the dynamics of the spontaneous response to their initiative and the attention that it drew in the media led to this unanticipated consequence. In fact, when Israel television called to ask that a spokesperson for the group appear on the evening news, none of them would volunteer to do so. Two were finally drafted to make the appearance. During the broadcast they gave the private telephone numbers of several members and the phones did not stop ringing all night. The letter to Begin obviously struck a responsive chord among thousands of Israelis (including many serving on active military duty) who shared in their anxiety and wanted to know what they could do to make sure that the opportunity for peace was not lost.

By the end of the month the organizers of the letter held a press conference and announced the opening of a campaign of public struggle to achieve the goals articulated in the letter. The next day (March 30, 1978) they held their first demonstration in front of the prime minister's house. They carried signs reading "Peace is Greater than Greater Israel," "Begin,

We Are Worried!'' ''Better Live Sons than Ancestors' Tombs'' (which rhymes in Hebrew), and ''Peace Now.'' On the first of April the first mass rally in Tel Aviv drew between 30,000 and 40,000 supporters. A week later the founding of the movement was announced.

Peace Now succeeded in consolidating a number of already existing groups in the three major cities and mobilizing new ones throughout the country. A Jerusalem group known as the Movement for a Different Zionism had focused its opposition against the initiatives of Gush Emunim to establish illegal settlements, and another small group from Tel Aviv had published announcements using the name Peace Now.[4] With minimal institutionalization, the new group, which adopted the name Peace Now, has played a vital and vibrant role in the Israeli political system in the first decade of its existence.

Peace with Egypt

Peace Now's first major political campaign was its most conspicuous success. It played a major role in mobilizing Israeli public opinion and in maintaining the momentum of public support for the negotiations that led to the peace treaty between Israel and Egypt achieved at Camp David. Within half a year of its founding, Peace Now sponsored thirty major demonstrations and events, in addition to the circulation and publication of petitions, and the lobbying of members of the government (including meetings with the prime minister) and of the opposition in support of the negotiations and a peace treaty with Egypt.

Many of the activities were highly original and were sophisticated in their appeal to the media and the public, and in the logistics required to carry them out successfully. There was a relay involving some 3,000 participants who ran up the Jerusalem road and passed from hand to hand a telegram to the prime minister. Eight conferences were held simultaneously throughout the country. Demonstrations were held outside the prime minister's house and the Knesset. A marathon of performing artists was held. Perhaps the most novel, and certainly the most difficult, project was the erection of a large peace sculpture at the entrance of an unauthorized Gush Emunim settlement on the West Bank.[5] The activities culminated in a mass rally in Tel Aviv (on September 2, 1978) attended by 100,000 demonstrators who called on Prime Minister Begin to return from Camp David with a peace treaty. Peace Now activists welcomed Begin with flowers and placards reading ''We are all with you on the road to peace'' upon his return both at the airport and at the entrance to Jerusalem.

The peace treaty with Egypt was ratified by the Knesset by a vote of 84 in favor, 19 against, and 17 abstentions (on September 27, 1978). The majority of support came from the opposition benches (particularly Labor), and the majority of abstentions and negative votes came from the Likud and its allies. Seven months had passed from the time that the "officers' letter" to Begin was sent until the ratification of the treaty. Peace Now played an important role in preventing the more militant and reactionary forces within and allied to the Likud government from aborting the peace process. However, the movement was less conspicuously successful in achieving the goals it set itself after this initial mission.

Autonomy versus Settlement of the West Bank

On December 5, 1978, a major meeting of activists in Jerusalem adopted major policy goals. They condemned Menachem Begin's interpretation of the autonomy plan, arguing it aimed at ensuring continued Israeli settlement and a creeping annexation of the territories. Peace Now offered its own interpretation of the autonomy plan, which it urged the government to adopt. It stressed the temporary nature of the plan as a way toward a permanent solution to the Palestinian problem. It called for a declaration that Israel had no claims of sovereignty over the territories and was ready to negotiate withdrawal to borders exclusively based on security considerations. It called for a freeze on all settlement and for recognition that peace cannot be achieved without satisfying "the legitimate rights and justified claims of the Palestinian people . . . [who] are entitled to participate in the determination of their future."[6]

The passage of the Jerusalem law (initiated by Geula Cohen of Techiya), the imposition of Israeli law on the Golan Heights, and (upon expiration of the moratorium), the continuation of Israeli settlement in areas with dense Palestinian populations on the West Bank essentially aborted the autonomy talks. Bar-On suggests that this was the period during which Peace Now was transformed from a temporary protest movement into a permanent political movement. This occurred when Peace Now decided to campaign against the notion of a separate peace with Egypt that would allow the Begin-led government to pursue a policy of de-facto annexation of the West Bank. He claims that the battle over the attempts by Gush Emunim to establish the settlement of Elon Moreh became a symbol around which Peace Now mobilized its opposition to this policy. Thirty Knesset members from different parties appeared at the rally in Jerusalem sponsored by Peace Now against the settlement policy.

Peace Now sponsored a wide range of activities and events during this period. For example, when in May 1979 Jewish settlers from Kiriat Arba uprooted a couple of thousand seedlings from Arab property, Peace Now activists and their families together with local Arab residents planted new seedlings. Until this point Peace Now had assiduously refrained from personally criticizing Menachem Begin. But the realization that the prime minister's political ideological position was a serious obstacle blocking the peace process led to their demand that the government be replaced. In June 1980 they erected a giant sand clock opposite the prime minister's office symbolizing that time was running out. They carried signs demanding that the government go home. Later in the month another demonstration involving 40,000 demonstrators called on the government to resign.

Peace Now intensified its activities in response to the heightened violence in the occupied territories. Bar-On reports a meeting in January 1982 at Kibbutz Ga'ash in which the movement's positions were examined and reformulated, focusing on the need for peace with the Palestinians and the need to intensify opposition to the settlements.[7] This was particularly critical given the growing tension in the territories. For example, a group of ranking reserve officers affiliated with Peace Now held a press conference in which they condemned the government's policies in the territories that compelled soldiers to use harsh methods. They also revealed that they had reported the names of soldiers and officers who had exceeded their authority in the mistreatment of residents of the territories.

Establishing Contacts with Palestinian Leaders

Peace Now assiduously maintained its image as a serious, responsible, Zionist movement, progressive yet within the national consensus. In two interviews with this author as well as in his book, Bar-On discussed the crisis that developed in the movement in October 1980 over the meeting between two Peace Now activists and the (moderate) PLO representative in Europe, the late Dr. Issam Sartawi (who was later gunned down by assassins reputedly belonging to the group of terrorists led by Abu Nidal), in Vienna. A similar crisis occurred when Bar-On met with Abu Iyad (second in command of Fatah after Yassar Arafat) in Budapest.[8] Whereas many favored such contacts, most feared the loss of public support that might result from them. Bar-On claims that the consequent crisis of confidence resulted in the departure of four leading activists from the movement. At the end of the month a special conference involving 3,000 activists met in Jerusalem and formulated the movement's Zionist identity. Peace Now declared its readiness to meet only with Palestinians who recognize Israel's right to exist and renounced violence as a means of achieving their national aspirations.[9]

Following this decision, Peace Now focused on contacts with Palestinian leaders resident on the West Bank. These were mostly with intellectuals, professors at West Bank universities, journalists, lawyers, and mayors of

West Bank communities. As a spokesman for Peace Now, Tzally Reshef, explained, these were not considered negotiations but a form of self-education.[10] However, such meetings sometimes had more than merely symbolic significance. For example, Mayor Natche of Hebron contrasted the activities of Peace Now with those of the settlers of Gush Emunim in his town. He told me that after the destruction of electric pylons and young trees by the settlers, they were replaced by Peace Now.[11]

Elections and the Dilemma of Party Affiliation

Another crisis was posed by the dilemma that the movement faced at the approach of the 1981 elections: whether to become a political party and compete in the election for representation in the Knesset, to affiliate itself with an already existing party, or, as it ultimately decided, not to play an official role at all in the campaign. Three parliamentary parties were closely identified with the positions of Peace Now: the Citizens' Rights movement (CRM or Ratz), Change (Shinui), and Mapam (which at the time was part of the alignment with Labor). The dovish wing of Labor was very sympathetic to the movement, as was the Zionist majority of Sheli, which lacked parliamentary representation. There was also support for the movement among a minority of dovish members of the National Religious party (mainly from its kibbutz movement and intellectuals). As a single-issue movement it decided to encourage its members to vote for those parties that accepted its principles.

An interparty Committee on Activities was appointed, which met with representatives of various parties. Bar-On (1985:44) reports on its unsuccessful meetings with the hawkish chairman of labor's platform committee, Yisrael Galili, and the encouragement they received from the dovish "77 Circle" of university professors who joined the party, after its defeat by the Likud, to invigorate it and breathe new ideological life into Labor. The movement also initiated two meetings with dovish representatives of the opposition parties to coordinate their efforts. Those Peace Now activists who neither belonged to nor wished to join a political party rallied around the slogan "Only Not the Likud!"

A crisis of belief (or trust) occurred within the movement when a group of central activists in Peace Now (who had previously met with Dr. Sartawi of the PLO) decided to join and devote their efforts to the Citizens' Rights movement (as occurred in Gush Emunim when several leaders joined Techiya). Consequently the Citizens' Rights movement officially became the Citizens' Rights and Peace movement (still known as Ratz for the Hebrew acronym prior to the addition), and two of the Peace Now recruits were placed in respectable positions on the party's list of candidates to the

Knesset. Given the close identity of the positions of Ratz and Peace Now, and the appearance on its list of two individuals prominently associated with the movement, there was concern in Peace Now that the public would identify it exclusively with Ratz. Obviously those peace Now activists who were affiliated with other parties or who proudly defended their lack of partisan affiliation strongly objected. This soured relationships among some activists for a considerable period.

Parliamentary Links

Whereas Peace Now essentially ceased to function as a movement during the 1981 election campaign, during the 1984 election it continued its activities as usual. Leading Peace Now activists played prominent roles in the campaigns of the Labor alignment (which included Mapam), Change (Shinui), and the Citizens' Rights movement (Ratz). In fact, two peace activists were elected to the Knesset on the Ratz ticket. The involvement of key Peace Now leaders in Ratz is similar to that of Gush Emunim activists in Techiya. Similarly the support and guidance given to Peace Now by Mapam (particularly its Kibbutz Artzi) is analogous to that given to Gush Emunim by the NRP. Just as Gush Emunim maintains critical ties to leading hawks in the Likud, Peace Now has its links with ranking doves in Labor.

Peace Now is closely identified with an informal Knesset alliance between Mapam (with six Knesset seats), and the Citizens' Rights movement (five Knesset seats). Whereas Mapam has a strong organizational and financial base in the Kibbutz Artzi movement, its long subordination to Labor in the Labor alignment (Ma'arach) led to a weakening of its independence, ideology, and leadership. Mapam is likely to lose heavily in the next elections, particularly to the more dynamic Citizens' Rights movement. A poll commissioned by the *Jerusalem Post* (May 9, 1987) indicated that the Citizens' Rights movement would receive six Knesset seats, while Mapam would drop to a single mandate.

The CRM's founder, senior Knesset member, and most prominent figure is Shulamit Aloni. A former Labor Knesset member, Aloni founded Ratz in 1973 after repeated clashes with Prime Minister Golda Meir made her position in labor untenable. Aloni is a civil rights lawyer and a leader in the struggle for civil rights (including Arab and women's rights). She is a strong opponent of religious coercion. Mordecai Bar-On, former chief education officer of the Israel Defense Forces and assistant to then Chief of Staff Moshe Dayan, is closely identified with the Peace Now movement. Bar-On resigned his Knesset seat in midterm (the end of November 1987). He was replaced by David "Dedie" Zucker, the general secretary of the

CRM and one of the original founders of Peace Now. Like Bar-On, Zucker is completing a doctoral dissertation. Iraqi-born Ran Cohen, the only member of the CRM Knesset faction not born in Israel, was one of the founders of the defunct Sheli party and is a peace activist. A member of Kibbutz Gan Shmuel, Cohen is a colonel in the active reserves. The disenchanted Labor dove Yossi Sarid, a protégé of the late Pinchas Sapir, was the youngest Labor MK when he entered the Knesset. A member of the Knesset Foreign Affairs and Security Committee, Sarid is an experienced parliamentarian, having served in parliament since 1973. During the summer of 1987 Mordechai Virshubski, who had been one of the founders and one of the two veteran Knesset members representing Change, joined the CRM. He is one of the most respected parliamentarians in the Knesset.

Peace Now had always had excellent relations with Virshubski and with Professor Amnon Rubinstein, the leader of the liberal Shinui (Change), Knesset members who frequently vote with Mapam and the CRM on issues when their votes do not violate their alliance with the Labor party in the present coalition. (Rubinstein is heading a new alliance with two other small liberal groups called the Centre Movement, which will submit a joint list in the next Knesset election). The Knesset bloc of Mapam and the Citizens' Rights movement could be an influential force in any future narrower coalition government led by Labor. Although there may be a significant redistribution of mandates within this camp (particularly given the boost that the co-optation of Peace Now leaders and Mordecai Virshubski seems to have given to Ratz), it is likely to at least maintain its present strength and may grow slightly. Bar-On (1985:116) reports that twenty to thirty Knesset members from four political parties regularly support various Peace Now initiatives.

The War in Lebanon

Unlike previous wars, which had united Israel, the war in Lebanon deeply divided the population and aggravated the political polarization that had intensified during the preceding election campaign.[12] Bar-On notes that the intentions of Defense Minister Sharon were not a secret and that on May 16, 1981, a year before the war broke out, 3,000 Peace Now adherents demonstrated against the possibility of war in Lebanon during the crisis over the Syrian emplacement of advanced missiles in Lebanon. In spite of their strong opposition to it, when the war broke out most of the male activists were mobilized and fought in Lebanon. Both in personal interviews and in his book, Bar-On noted that one of the first victims of the war was identified with Peace Now.[13]

In a number of different contexts the present writer has heard leaders of

Peace Now compare and contrast their position during the war in Lebanon to those slightly to their left and to their right. They stress that while Labor had joined them in warning the government against involvement in Lebanon, Labor changed its position and supported the initial officially announced goal of the government (of establishing a forty-kilometer defense perimeter north of Israel's border) once the war broke out. Peace Now consistently opposed the war, although it waited ten days into the war before going public in its official condemnation of the war, and waited until the first temporary cease-fire to hold a mass rally (on June 26) against the war, which was attended by 120,000 demonstrators. However, unlike more radical groups they neither supported unconditional unilateral withdrawal, nor did they support the dissident movements that encouraged soldiers to refuse to serve in the war.

Peace Now's stand on unequivocal opposition to the war, but willingness to fight in the war when mobilized, was a carefully balanced position. They insisted on playing by the democratic rules of the game. As Danny Zidon put it, "If we divide the army between those willing to serve and those not willing it would be disastrous for Israel. I am willing to dirty my hands. . . . It is not wise for a political movement to oppose the law if your goal is democracy . . . . Still I don't try to convince those who refuse to serve, because I know personally how hard it is."[14] Bar-On added, "The question is where to draw the line. As a movement Peace Now opposed disobedience, which is what we tell the youngsters about to serve in the army. If we don't do it we could expect others to refuse to dislodge settlers from the West Bank."[15] He explained that when he had served as chief education officer in the IDF, he argued that a soldier was obliged to disobey an illegal order. The response of Peace Now to Elie Geva's request to be relieved of his command rather than lead his men into an attack on Beirut was to condemn the government for having put him in such a position and to express the hope that others would not follow his example. Janet Aviad said, "Once people start choosing which war they will serve in, it will be disastrous. We are effective because we don't take extreme positions . . . . We aren't a left-wing movement as are Yesh Gevul and the Committee for Beir Zeiyit University."[16] She pointed to areas of agreement with such groups, but stressed that they took care to prevent being associated with them in order not to curtail their effectiveness. Bar-On (1985:73) says that they try to march in the front rank and to keep a half-step ahead, since to get too far ahead of the general public would undermine their political effectiveness.

The great care taken by Peace Now in formulating balanced and moderate positions within the democratic rules of the game, and which they viewed as being well within the national consensus, precipitated violent attacks from ardent supporters of the government. In many ways Peace Now was a more important target for delegitimation by charges of treason than were the more extreme dissident groups. Because the dissidents were perceived as being politically marginal they did not constitute a serious threat to the government. However, the activists of Peace Now were viewed as the offspring and heirs of those who had only recently lost political dominance, and who yet retained leading positions in the social and cultural elites. Baram (1985:84) stresses the loyalty of Peace Now, saying not only are its members not antiestablishment, but that they considered themselves to be the "true establishment." Their positions and opposition therefore constituted a far greater danger. For they had credibility and threatened to call into question not just the wisdom of the war in Lebanon, but the assumptions upon which were based the new political and cultural realities defined by the Likud. This seems to be why they were targeted for such a vicious campaign of delegitimation.

The massacre by Christian forces of Palestinian refugees in camps under the military control of the IDF aroused the deepest sense of moral outrage among a large section of the Israeli people. For the first time Peace Now cooperated with the Labor party and other parties in the opposition in sponsoring a mass rally demanding the government appoint an independent investigating commission to examine Israel's responsibility and demanding the resignation of the government. The largest number of Israelis who ever attended a political rally and who expressed their moral outrage testified poignantly to their support for an alternative morality and worldview to that represented by the leadership of the government at the time. This most impressive expression of public conscience and belief was persuasive evidence that the Likud had not succeeded in establishing the hegemony of its worldview.[17]

Peace Now can justifiably claim a share of the credit for mobilizing public opinion and helping to apply political pressure, which ultimately forced the reluctant prime minister to appoint a judicial commission of inquiry headed by the president of the high court of justice. After the report of the findings of the Kahan Commission (which took three months) Peace Now again mounted a demonstration to demand the implementation of the commission's recommendations—most particularly the removal of Arik Sharon from office. The Peace Now demonstrators, who marched from the Jerusalem town center to the prime minister's office, were forced to run a gauntlet of both verbal and physical abuse from scores of ruffians who were supporters of Begin and Sharon. It was during the singing of the national anthem, "Hatikva" ("The Hope"), by the peaceful demonstrators at the end of their rally that the hand grenade was thrown that killed Emile Grunzweig and seriously wounded several others.

The murder of the young Peace Now activist, who had served as an officer in a combat unit in the war in Lebanon, precipitated a reaction in which some of the most vociferous opponents of Peace Now attempted to engage in a dialogue with them. Perhaps most noteworthy was Gush-Emunim. Tzally Reshef claimed that having overplayed their incitement against Peace Now, Gush Emunim felt the need to establish rules for political fighting. Reshef was pessimistic about the possibility of their reaching a genuine understanding. "They wanted to talk of violence, but we feel that violence is part of their ideology. It is the only way to control one and a half million Arabs. Across the Green Line their violence is legitimate in their eyes and is totally illegal in our eyes. They said, 'Let us issue a statement against violence.' We see the Arabs on the West Bank as human beings," who also needed to be protected from violence.[18]

Tzachi HaNegbi (son of Techiya leader Geula Cohen) had organized the demonstration in support of the government, which urged Prime Minister Begin not to make any changes in the government in response to the Kahan Commission recommendations. After the murder of Emile Grunzweig, he publicly urged both sides to pull back from the brink. He considered everything that happened on the day of the murder to be "writing on the wall." He told this writer that, since the 1981 election, the mutual delegitimation of and by the opposing camps had led to polarization, which threatened both the security of the state and democracy in Israel. He explained that the murder was the catalyst that prompted him to appear on television where he argued that each side needed to recognize the legitimacy of the other.[19]

Not everyone was moved to moderation as a result of these events. A symposium on political assassination was held in memory of Emile Grunzweig at the Van Leer Institute (where several of the key leaders of Peace Now work) in Jerusalem on May 19, 1983. Outside, two men asked passersby to sign a petition expressing the right of the Jewish people to the land of Israel, which declared: "We will not surrender, nor move from our position in spite of the pressure from 'beautiful souls'—the traitors and PLO supporters."[20] As the participants in the symposium left, they engaged in heated debate with the petitioners. Fifty thousand people attended the memorial ceremony commemorating the first anniversary of Grunzweig's death.

Leadership and Organization

The structure of Peace Now is characterized by extreme informality. Although Bar-On stresses the spontaneity, lack of formal leadership, structured decision making, and institutionalization, the movement is anything but disorganized. Palgi claims that the original group that founded the movement was based on personal-friendship networks, groups that got together socially on Shabat. Bar-On (1985:67) compares such groups, which continue to be important constituent components of the movement, to the political salons in France prior to the revolution. Clearly the spirit of comraderie and togetherness engendered through mutual participation in the activities of the movement reinforced the solidarity of such friendship networks and contributed to the creation of new ones. Palgi (1979:43) compares the mutual trust that developed among many in the movement to that which arises among fellow combatants.

In the three major cities, in the towns, and in kibbutzim there emerged informal leadership groups among the activists who regularly engage in the planning and the implementation of Peace Now's activities. With the formal declaration of the movement a national coordinating committee was established. It initially included a few representatives from the major constituent groups from which the movement was constituted: Jerusalem, Tel Aviv, Haifa, and the Kibbutz Artzi. Subsequently, as groups were formed in other towns, for example, Ashkelon and Be'er Sheva, their representatives were added. The coordinating committee meets biweekly. There are never formal votes, since all decisions must be taken only after a consensus has been reached. This gives every major branch a veto over the activities of the movement as a whole.

Since activity is voluntary, the consensus of all representatives of the key branches ensures that the issue is likely to be sufficiently salient to mobilize wide support. Bar-On calls Peace Now a movement of unending referendum, since its activities constantly test public sentiment on a variety of issues. Unlike the more institutionalized veteran political parties, Peace Now encourages a maximal participation from its supporters, and its informal structure and decision-making process made it highly responsive to its supporters. Bar-On (1985:69–71) contrasts the alienation between leaders and rank-and-file members characteristic of most Israeli parties with the responsiveness of Peace Now to its constituency.

In addition to the two dozen or so leaders who participate in the national coordinating forum, between 250 and 300 key activists are the heart of the activities of the branches in the major cities and the kibbutzim. Bar-On estimates that between 5,000 and 8,000 activists participate in almost all of the movement's activities. The spokesperson and the treasurer are the only two formal positions in the movement. Many others assume informal leadership in the different spheres of activities in which the movement is involved. Once the national coordinating forum agrees on a project it is implemented by a special ad-hoc committee composed of activists with experience in the particular sphere of activity.

Activity among the Youth and in "the Neighborhoods"

Peace Now focused its major efforts on mobilizing public opinion and parliamentary support for peace with Egypt, an agreement with the Palestinians, and opposition to the war in Lebanon. However, it has consciously focused on two long-range projects that it considers to be of particular importance—attracting more support from among the youth and from among the Eastern Jewish community. It also engages, at a much lower level of activity, in developing ties with sympathizers abroad—particularly in the United States.

For example, at a fairly typical meeting of the Jerusalem branch, which this writer attended on May 22, 1983, the three major subjects of discussion were youth activities, meetings with neighborhood leaders, and the campaign against the war in Lebanon. The latter entailed two weeks of activities focusing around a march from the Lebanese border to Tel Aviv, culminating in a mass rally. They also planned the construction of an environmental sculpture with images representing each Israeli who fell in the war.

There was a lengthy and enthusiastic report on the national rally attended by approximately 5,000 high school students from all over the country in Tel Aviv in May 1983. (Since my daughters had attended the rally with their friends I had already received their enthusiastic reports). Given the success of this rally, it was decided to hold them three times annually. They also debated the desirability of establishing a national youth movement and a youth newspaper. The general feeling seemed to be that they should work through the existing youth movements rather than attempt to replace them.[21] During the discussion it was stated that the youth rally "gave supporters the feeling that they weren't alone and that Techiya is not dominant in the high schools."

The high schools were no more free from the political divisions than any other sphere of society. On the contrary, both the ultranationalist Techiya and Shulamit Aloni's Citizens' Rights movement are more popular among high school students than among the electorate in general. Given the above-average support for two parties at the opposite ends of the two major political blocs, political confrontation during this period was frequently quite intense. For example, in the Hebrew Gymnasium of Jerusalem heated debates over the war in Lebanon disrupted classes so frequently that the principal held a special symposium on the war with the stipulation that thereafter classes would again be devoted exclusively to academic subjects and not to political debates.[22] Since this was an academic high school in an established middle- to upper-middle-class and predominantly Ashkenazi neighborhood, the support for Peace Now was much greater than in poorer neighborhoods where most residents are predominantly of Middle Eastern background.

In order to correct the ethnic imbalance of their movement, Peace Now volunteers began to seek contact in the poorer ethnic neighborhoods. The residents of these neighborhoods were universally mistrustful of these volunteers and in many cases were hostile to them. It was extremely difficult to establish the trust of the people in the *schunot* (neighborhoods). Having learned through prior bitter experience, they were skeptical of the intentions of outsiders, whom they suspected of wanting to manipulate them for their own political purposes. In this case, given their image of the critics of the popular Prime Minister Begin with whom they identified, Peace Now had a particularly difficult task in overcoming suspicion and hostility in order to build bridges of trust and cooperation.

It was decided that the most effective means of establishing contacts in these neighborhoods was to try to form working coalitions of cooperation with already established local groups and with groups and leaders identified with the Eastern Jews on a national level, such as the Ohel (tent) movement of North African Jews (led by university students) and Saadia Marciano, leader of one of the factions of the former Israeli Black Panthers. A number of activists in the movement have expended a considerable amount of time and energy in this area. The initial initiative for such meetings came from a group in the Muswara neighborhood of Jerusalem. Through meetings with another group in Jerusalem's Bucharin neighborhood, Avishai Margalit discovered that in spite of their love for Begin, people in the neighborhood were not at all ideologically committed to his programs.[23]

There were dozens of meetings between Peace Now and "neighborhood" activists during the period in which this writer conducted research. Let us briefly summarize the highlights of one such meeting, which took place in Tel Aviv on June 11, 1983, to give a sense of the kind of interaction that took place in such meetings. The first part of the meeting was an analysis by Dr. Avi Gotlieb (Tel Aviv University) of Project Renewal, a major urban-renewal program carried out under the Likud-led government (initially under a Shinui [Change] minister). Morris, a community activist from Kiriat Menachem (Jerusalem) responded to the scholarly presentation by giving his own explanation for the failure of Project Renewal to accomplish its ambitious aims. He said, "The plans came from above. They never asked the locals what they wanted."

As the discussion focused on what role Peace Now could play in the "neighborhoods," Yigal, who grew up in *shechunat* Hatikva of Tel Aviv and obtained a Ph.D. from the Weizmann Institute of Science, suggested that Peace Now activists should volunteer to teach in the neighborhoods and work with local leaders. He said, "You can only succeed when you see my problem as your problem. Suspicion derives from the fact that people don't make long-term commitments." He cautioned the Peace Now activists that if the problem of the neighborhoods was not sufficiently important to make a long-term commitment to working in them, they were wasting their time. He also cautioned them not to expect miracles. "The fact that you are not seen as an enemy is a gain!"

The second major presentation was a lecture by Professor Sami Smooha (Haifa University) on "The End of Ashkenazi Hegemony in Israel." The Iraqi-born scholar is one of Israel's leading experts on ethnic relations. Smooha argued that the tendency for Eastern Jews to identify Peace Now with Ashkenazi political dominance explained the ethnic tone to attacks on it. He suggested the attitude of Eastern Jews was: "You Ashkenazim had a [political] monopoly for many years and you were the patriots and beautiful people. Now we are the patriots." He argued that the majority of Eastern intellectuals are doves, but the Likud became the means through which Easterners broke Ashkenazi dominance. "The secret of the Likud's strength is that it tells the Easterners they are Israelis in every respect." He advised Peace Now that it made a mistake in assuming those who support the Likud will not support peace. He insisted that the Easterners were not attracted to the Likud because of its foreign policy. Smooha argued that since Peace Now is not a political party, they should not care which party they vote for as long as they support peace. He claimed that Peace Now's anti-Likud stance offended Easterners who see their advancement in Israeli society as being linked with the Likud. He concluded that the Eastern Jews support the Likud as an instrument for social change, not because of its greater-land-of-Israel ideology.

Michael Atlan, a Peace Now coordinator of relations with neighborhoods in Jerusalem, agreed with Smooha's claim that the people in the *schunot* lacked ideological commitment to the Likud. He said Peace Now's identification with Labor in the public mind hurt them among the Eastern Jews, and that they need to stress the difference between Peace Now and Labor. Asher Levy, the director of the Tel Kabir Community Center, claimed that "the edot mizrach [Eastern Jews] see Zahal as theirs now and they see us as attacking it." He said the obstacles to communication were formidable, given the lack of trust. He admitted that "only after working in the community center for three years did I dare to put a Peace Now sticker on my car. They were shocked, but they excuse me."

On this occasion, as well as many others, people who identify with Peace Now told me of their reluctance to argue their views with others— particularly when on active reserve duty or in the markets, where there frequently is a large proportion of Eastern Jews. The threats of violence against those who identify with Peace Now led many to avoid political confrontations and this has resulted in people tending to interact socially with only those who hold similar views. Clearly in the effort to delegitimize the opposition to the Likud, Peace Now became a primary target, since it was in the vanguard of public confrontation with the government on the war in Lebanon and in opposition to its settlement policies. The efforts of Peace Now to build coalitions with leaders of local groups in neighborhoods populated by Jews whose origins are in the Middle East is a long-range project and the results have thus far been very modest.

East for Peace: "Not Hitchhikers on Zionism"

East for Peace was founded on May 29, 1983, by a group of twenty-five to thirty intellectuals of Middle Eastern background, from the three major cities, who had been meeting together for several weeks. The initiative came from a group of Jerusalem educators, journalists, and students representing a variety of political persuasions. Dr. Shlomo Elbaz (Hebrew University), one of the founders of the movement, explained that a highly offensive essay attacking Eastern Jews in the liberal *Ha'aretz* (by a columnist named Amnon Dunkner) was the last straw that brought the group together. He claimed that several of the founders of East for Peace had been actively involved in Peace Now, *"but we weren't seen!"*[24] He claimed that they wanted once and for all to break the common stereotype that Easterners were an obstacle to peace. They aspire to be more than just a Sephardic Peace Now, since they intend to change Israeli society by fostering Jewish values and Eastern tolerance and understanding. The aims of the movement are to encourage the peace process in the Middle East; to combat allegations that Oriental Israelis are extremist, violent, and hostile to peace; to further the political consciousness of the Oriental masses, who have been subject to political manipulation, and to support their struggle for the realization of their true social and cultural rights; and to help to achieve the political, economic, and cultural integration of Israel within the Middle East.[25] The movement's manifesto proclaimed the importance of the role the Oriental Jew must play in the peace process; faith in the possibility of coexistence with the Arabs; a denunciation of prejudice against the East and prejudice against Arabs; opposition to settlement and condemnation of acts of terrorism and fanaticism; a call for dialogue and a just solution to the Palestinian problem; and a call for the promotion of social, educational, and cultural equality for all.[26]

The movement is founded on six guiding principles:

1) The state of Israel is an integral part of the East. . . . we shall act to achieve political, economic and cultural integration of Israel within the region. . . .

2) The establishment of a just society, based on human values, in the spirit of the prophets of Israel is to be considered as a basic Zionist principle and a prime objective of the State of Israel.

3) The yearning for peace is a fundamental and permanent principle of Judaism. It is incompatible with acts of settlement which endanger chances for peace.

4) The physical borders of Israel shall be determined in such a way as to maintain its Jewish nature and democratic character, and to preserve the legitimate rights of all peoples in the area, including the Jewish and the Palestinian.

5) The advent of Peace in the Middle East will create appropriate conditions for Israel's economic, cultural, and spiritual growth and development.

6) The "East For Peace" movement, which is not a political party, is open to all citizens of Israel who identify with its guiding principles. The Movement is voluntary and all the expenses are covered by donations of its members and supporters.[27]

Moroccan-born journalist Jules Daniel, another founder of the movement, believes that Eastern Jews were forced into a more hawkish political position, which was alien to them, out of a sense of inferiority.[28] Since they were perceived by the Ashkenazim as being so much like the Arabs, they adopted extreme anti-Arab positions to prove their "Zionist" credentials. He suggested that once the Eastern Jews regain pride in their cultural traditions they can act as a bridge to the Arab world.

Like Peace Now, East for Peace is dominated by intellectuals, and like the older peace movement they are actively engaged in dialogues with neighborhood activists. Shelley Elkayam, a seventh-generation Israeli and a poetess, claims they have a much better reception in the neighborhoods than do the activists of Peace Now: "They accept us as their representatives because we are part of them. We don't patronize them or tell them what to say. We discuss with them as equals and listen."[29] It will be interesting to see whether or not the common ethnicity between the East for Peace activists and the neighborhood leaders will enable them to overcome differences in education, class, and political worldview and to establish meaningful avenues of political collaboration.

The leaders of East for Peace, like the Peace Now activists engaged in dialogues with neighborhood leaders, are convinced that support for Begin in the neighborhoods does not mean support for revisionism. In fact Elbaz goes even further, suggesting that Zionism was largely an Eastern European creation. "The Europeans are undergoing a crisis. Their dreams are shattered, they are tired. We never had the dream, so our batteries are still charged up. They have never been used."[30] He passionately asserted, "We don't want to be hitchhikers on Zionism! We think we are the new vision and the future of Israel. We are the center of development, not the periphery. . . . We want to value the East which has been devalued."[31] Former kibbutznik Shelley Elkayam echoed this sentiment, arguing that the new centers are the former peripheries, that is, the ethnic neighborhoods and development towns from which many of the new political leadership has come. She claims that "Israel has been facing the west too long. It is time for a change of direction."[32]

Eli Eliachar, who represented the small aristocratic Sephardi community in Jerusalem, expressed views similar to those of East for Peace for decades. Gavron (1983:4) points out that the new movement represents the mass immigration of the 1950s, "the 'second Israel,' which is at last starting to find its voice." He concludes: "Only time will show whether we are seeing the emergence of just another marginal protest group, or a dynamic movement which will turn this country on its head."

The Religious Peace Movements

Oz v'Shalom (Strength and Peace), the older of the two religious peace movements, is made up primarily of intellectuals centered around a group of dovish professors at the religious Bar-Ilan University. It is more of an ideological circle that occasionally takes public stands on issues relating to the peace process, and it is considered to be a part of the dovish liberal/left in Israel. Netivot Shalom (Paths to Peace) was formed as a direct response to Gush Emunim. Unlike Peace Now, which deliberately avoids public debates with Gush Emunim (they argue that their main opponent is the Likud), Netivot Shalom eagerly takes on its main ideological opponent within the national religious camp. Unlike Oz v'Shalom, and like Peace Now and Gush Emunim, Netivot Shalom takes to the street and demonstrates it point of view in public acts. Ideologically Netivot Shalom is to the right of Peace Now.

According to Dr. Gerold Cromer, a leading activist in Netivot Shalom, many of the founders of the movement are alumni of the Yeshivot Hesder (higher religious academies combined with military service), and are the analogues of the officers who originated Peace Now with their letter to Prime Minister Begin.[33] The main spiritual leaders of the movement are Rabbi Yehuda Amital and Rabbi Aharon Lichtenstein. Netivot Shalom is not opposed to all settlement across the Green Line, but opposses settlement in areas densely populated by Arabs that are aimed at the annexation of the West Bank. Rabbi Lichtenstein says that it is not that we love Eretz Yisrael (the land of Israel) less, but that we love Am Yisrael (the people of Israel) more. Netivot Shalom favors settlement in the Galilee region of northern Israel. The movement has been in close consultation with Zevulan Hammer in efforts to move the National Religious party away from the extreme nationalism to which its courting of Gush Emunim had led it.

The violent opposition of Gush Emunim to the evacuation of Yamit in the northern Sinai in compliance with the Camp David Accords was a turning point for many moderates within the national religious camp, and it brought them "out of the closet."[34] For many others the massacre of Palestinian refugees at Sabra and Shatila (and the appearance of Rabbi Drukman on television after the New Year) was the initial incident that brought together observant Israelis to demonstrate their support for the appointment of a commission of inquiry.

Netivot Shalom self-consciously attempts to demonstrate an alternative to the secular image of the religious Orthodox Jew as ultranationalist, and to offer an alternative to the religious youth other than Gush Emunim, on one hand, or Peace Now, on the other. Here let me briefly cite two examples from my field notes of the type of activities in which Netivot is most actively engaged.

On April 26, 1983, Netivot Shalom sponsored a conference on "Relations with Non-Jews." The large auditorium at the journalists' house, Beit Agron, in Jerusalem was filled to capacity and the overflow had to be accommodated in other rooms connected by loudspeakers. The format was two major scholarly lectures, one by Professor Efraim Urbach and the other by Rabbi Aharon Lichtenstein, with the audience breaking up into several discussion groups between the lectures. The audience was made up equally of men and women, who sat together. Most men wore knitted skullcaps, and the women tended to wear long dresses. Their ages ranged from the twenties through the thirties, and many appeared to be university students. The majority appeared to be Ashkenazi and there were a noticeable number of American accents in the Hebrew discussion period. The discussions were lively, and the discussants appeared to be well informed in the traditional texts as well as modern sources ranging from Dostoevsky to Max Weber.

Professor Urbach explained the division between the Jewish people and others and how the insularity of the Jewish people is related to the task of guarding monotheism. Citing the prophets and religious sources, he argued that universalism and particularism go hand in hand in Judaism, and that universalism was perfectly compatible with the concept of chosenness. Acknowledging that there are many contradictory passages, he suggested that these contradictions cannot be ignored. He argued emphatically that it was a desecration of the Lord (*chelul HaShem*) to disregard moral norms and the rights of others. He said that a struggle, in a respectful manner, must be waged with other groups (an indirect reference to Gush Emunim) over the treatment of non-Jews.

Rabbi Lichtenstein unpacked over a dozen books from his bursting briefcase and launched into a scholarly analysis of the concept of chosenness and a nation that dwells alone. The rapt attention that he received from the overflow audience would be the envy of any lecturer (especially before an Israeli audience). Quoting Rabbi Nathan on Hillel, Rashi, and a host of other authorities, Rabbi Lichtenstein discussed the different Jewish views of the godliness of humankind, the sanctity of humankind, and the perspective that is necessary to see the height and the nature of the walls separating Jews from non-Jews. He distinguished his interpretation from that of "circles who follow Rabbi Kook," stressing the need to see the importance of the holiness of humankind along with the aloneness of the Jewish people.

In the parking lot after the meeting, Professor Menachem Friedman told me that he goes to these meetings to meet people who think as he does so that he will not become a rhinoceros. He said that when he goes to the synagogue or is with family, all he hears is the greater land of Israel. He said that those who hold these views are in power, and when they all tell you that you are crazy, you begin to wonder whether you are or not. That, he explained, is why he goes to see "beautiful people" to reinforce his own perceptions and values. The plight of Menachem Friedman points out the difficulty of being a politically liberal Orthodox Israeli Jew during the height of the Likud's power and influence. If it served no other function, Netivot Shalom filled an important void in Israeli society for many people like Friedman.

Unlike Peace Now, Netivot Shalom eagerly took on Gush Emunim in public debate. In one such encounter at the Jerusalem Tzavta Club on July 13, 1983, Rabbi Eliezer Waldman (who the following year was elected to the Knesset on the Techiya slate) and Hanan Porat (who represented Techiya in the Knesset at the time) represented Gush Emunim, and Professor Uriel Simon and Dr. Avi Ravitsky represented Netivot Shalom. The small auditorium was filled beyond capacity and the debate was moved outside to the courtyard in order to accommodate the overflow crowd. The representative of the club (which is affiliated with Mapam) remarked that the attendance was unprecedented for such an affair. He said that the felt need for such a dialogue was a consequence of the tragic death of Emile Grunzweig.

The tactic of the Gush Emunim speakers was clearly nonconfrontational. They tended to stress values that they felt were held by the members of the audience who were religious. (Not all of the audience was religious, but all of those who were religious wore the knitted skullcaps of the national religious camp. There were no ultra-Orthodox people in the audience.) Hanan Porat was the first speaker and he stressed the spiritual experience from which their nationalism derives, the organic unity of the Jewish people, the holiness of the ingathering of the exiles as part of the redemption.

The tactic of the speakers for Netivot Shalom was more confrontational. Avi Ravitsky joked that for the first time in his life he found himself in complete agreement with Porat (whom he addressed familiarly by his first name). He continued in the same humorous vein that if the spiritual message he had just delivered was the main part of Porat's political ideology he (Ravitsky) would be willing to follow him in Techiya. Netivot Shalom, he claimed, offered a choice between secular liberal humanism and religiously based nationalism. He stressed the need to confront what happens when a people returns to its land and finds another people living there for generations. He asked rhetorically what should be done with them, "Expel them? Suppress them?" He claimed there was a choice between the holiness of life and the borders of Eretz Yisrael. Referring to Kiriat Arba, he asked, "How did we return and how did we behave?" He stressed the love of justice, which had traditionally characterized the national religious movement, but which had been ignored because of the overemphasis on the borders of Eretz Yisrael as if that were the only issue. He asked, "Who are the successors of the prophets?"

Ravitsky noted that King Solomon had traded cities, and asked, "Did that make him a traitor?" Quoting different religious sources he agreed that there were legitimate differences in interpretation. However, he argued emphatically that "To be a Zionist is to take a historical responsibility not to be oppressed, but there is another side, God forbid, not to become an oppressor! . . . not to become drunk with power." He concluded by quoting a pagan king who said that when you will become like other people you will act like other people.

Rabbi Eliezer Waldman, picking up on the last statement, said that the Jews in Israel were returning to their nature. "We aren't a normal people, but we are returning to our nature, which was destroyed in the Diaspora . . . in the galut [Diaspora] we lacked a political experience." He then explained the Gush Emunim interpretation of the signs of the redemptive process being expressed through the unfolding of contemporary history. He argued that the world would enjoy the blessings of Eretz Yisrael as a light unto the nations. As did Porat, Waldman presented his most moderate side to the audience, only slightly hinting at the other more militant side when he claimed that there was "no balance in rights of people to the land of Israel . . . it only belongs to the people of Israel."

By sharp contrast Professor Simon launched into a major attack on the political positions of Rabbi Waldman. He said, "I prepared my response to Rabbi Waldman on the basis of his writings in *Nekuda* [the major publication of Gush Emunim]. After reading them I wanted to rush to the mikve [ritual bath] to purify myself." He sarcastically said that it was a riddle how remote their speeches that evening were from the problems confronting the nation. When members of the audience applauded, he asked them to refrain from doing so, claiming that it was extremely difficult for religious people to confront each other before secular people. They prefer to discuss among themselves.

He claimed that it was necessary to decide among values, and gave the example that saving a life had such priority that it justified the desecration of the Sabbath. He argued that there was a conflict between peace and making operational the claim to all of the land of Israel. He asserted that the wholeness that Rabbi Waldman sought would come only with the Messiah. He claimed that it was impossible to realize the wholeness of all, for example, the land of Israel, the people of Israel, and the Torah, at this time. Switching from the religious themes he discussed the threat to democracy and the tremendous polarization of Israeli society during the preceding year. He condemned Rabbi Waldman for his insensitivity to the lives of Arabs. Simon quoted the chief of staff of the IDF, Eitan, as having reputedly said, "If you want to understand how an Arab thinks—open his head." He reported that his son returned from a political rally and told him that Rabbi Dov Lior (one of the most militant of Gush Emunim activists) had said, "In order to prevent the death of one [Israeli] soldier, I am willing to destroy all of Beirut."

Professor Simon quoted racist comments he had heard among religious youth who communicated in a secret code using religious terms that secular people (not to mention Arabs) could not understand. He said that Rabbi Waldman had publicly attacked those who questioned the conduct of the IDF. Simon said, "I learned that a society purifies itself by punishing those who do wrong!" He claimed the word "justice" did not appear in any of Waldman's articles he had read. He quoted an article of Waldman's that said that the people of Israel is the only one who can make order in the world. Professor Simon sharply retorted, "Everyone knows who said he would make order in Europe. Therefore, when the head of a yeshiva says we shall make order in Lebanon it hurts me. I don't know if he would write it today." Waldman replied that he would. Simon continued, "Are we making order in Kiriat Arba and Hebron? Is this the light [unto the nations]?" He concluded with a plea to live for justice.

Hanan Porat condemned Professor Simon's sarcastic style and his not having communicated with Rabbi Waldman to get him to clarify his position. He argued that the media constantly distort their positions, ignoring the fact that Simon had quoted only articles that Waldman had written himself and that were published in Gush Emunim's own magazine.

In addition Waldman had verbally confirmed that he still held to several positions that evening. For the first time losing his calm composure, Porat said, "When you show a tone—which I don't say, God forbid, is hatred—in the wider circle [among secular people], from the bottom of my heart I think you need to search your souls!"

Avi Ravitsky replied that his heart was heavy that Hanan could think that either he or Professor Simon could hate because they disagreed with their positions. He expressed his shock that religious Knesset members voted against the appointment of a commission of inquiry to investigate the massacres that took place in Sabra and Shatila. He argues, "Bnei Akiva has changed, not us!" Ravitsky responded to Porat's challenge that they had said only what they were against and not what they stood for by charging they stood for the classic national religious position from which Gush Emunim had deviated. He said that when you "demand totality which deprives others of their rights, you are sharpening the conflicts." He revealed that the massacre at Sabra and Shatila prompted him to demonstrate for the first time in his life. He argued that they were no longer in the Diaspora. "We are today the rulers and we must take the full ethical responsibility."

Rabbi Waldman said that he "painfully must condemn the lack of morality of Professor Simon for presenting the views of another as absurd so as not to relate to them seriously." He claimed that one of the articles was written a year previously and the other a half-year previously. However, he did not say that they no longer represented his positions. Instead he accused Simon of unethical behavior. Waldman said, "I don't accept the conclusions of the Kahan Commission, since it did not keep the proper perspective." He claimed that the *New York Times* wrote that Israel is seeking its salvation by revealing its shame. He shouted emotionally, "That is how the goyim want to see us—as Nazis—to purify their consciences!" Professor Simon apologized for having spoiled the atmosphere, but claimed that his opponents had more than returned in kind his criticism. He explained, "We came here to speak about things that hurt us, not generalities on which we agree." He said they (Netivot Shalom) feel that the policies of the religious ultranationalists will bring disaster. Simon argued that the violence used by Gush Emunim to resist the evacuation of Yamit influenced the violence that ultra-Orthodox Jews used against the archaeologists who were excavating the ancient city of David. He claimed that his deep frustration made it difficult for him to speak politely. He indicated that he did not think it necessary to apologize for quoting a man who was present and could respond, and that he did not feel he had needed to visit him at his home prior to quoting him. However, he was deeply concerned about the need to keep the unity of the people (as had been expressed by members of the audience). He stressed the importance of keeping the rules of democracy, and concluded that the problem of Gush Emunim was not its words but its actions. At this point the police requested they end the debate since it was late and, being outdoors, it disturbed residents of the neighborhood.

Whereas the symposium on relations with non-Jews had been attended almost exclusively by religious people sympathetic with the positions of Netivot Shalom, the debate with Gush Emunim included not only supporters of both movements, but a significant proportion of nonreligious Israelis. Because of this, the tactic of the Gush Emunim spokespersons was to speak in generalities and to focus on points that they thought would be the least controversial. They attempted to delegitimate the points raised by the spokespersons of Netivot Shalom by accusing them of violating ethical rules by using a confrontational style. In fact they failed to refute directly the charges of their protagonists. Professor Simon's admission of discomfort in holding an open public debate in front of a (partially) secular audience was most revealing. Even he, an intellectual who is used to interacting in a scholarly world in which the majority are not religious, felt uncomfortable in publicly attacking the views of fellow observant Jews. Yet it was clearly one of the major goals of Netivot Shalom to show to the general Israeli public that not all members of the national religious camp shared the ultranationalist views of Gush Emunim. As in the case of East for Peace, they wanted to break a popular stereotype, in this case one that associated the knitted skullcap with militantly hawkish views and intolerance toward Arabs.

Conclusions

Gush Emunim is a revitalization movement that attempts to create and establish the hegemony of a new cultural paradigm patterned after what is perceived to be a traditional theme. Peace Now seeks to maintain the vitality of a worldview that has lost its dominance, and appeared (during the period under discussion) to be fighting a rearguard action against the ascendance of the new one(s).[35] Since Israeli political parties are not organized around the issue of the territories, relations with the Arabs, and war and peace, Peace Now was an important nonpartisan focal point around which to mobilize public opinion and bring it to bear on the government and the opposition.

According to Bar-On (1985:111) Peace Now focused on three major goals: (a) to maintain the minority who are willing to make significant compromises; (b) to arouse those who in principle are willing to compromise, but are suspicious of extreme steps; (c) to attempt to broaden the circle of those who believe in the possibility of compromise and of peace with the Palestinians, and to isolate the extreme nationalists and help return moderates to government.

Peace Now was most effective in the mobilization of opinion in support of the Camp David peace agreement with Egypt. It broke the consensus of support for the war in Lebanon and mobilized opposition to its expansion and excesses. It played a key role in pressuring the reluctant prime minister to appoint the Kahan Commission to investigate the massacres at Sabra and Shatila. It was in the forefront in breaking the consensus against talking with the Palestinians. Whereas it was able to publicize some of the extreme hardships imposed on the Palestinian residents of the West Bank by the occupation (such as through the testimony of six officers who filed charges against their comrades), it was not effective in slowing the pace of settlement, which was a top priority for the government.

Peace Now acted as a moral voice, keeping those who strongly disagreed with government policy from despairing. As Janet Aviad said, "The only alternatives to working for peace are to leave the country or to cultivate your own garden."[36] The actions of Peace Now have also been important for friends of Israel abroad who strongly disagreed with the policies of the government. The massive demonstration of Israelis demanding the appointment of a judicial commission of inquiry restored the confidence of many abroad who were appalled by Israel's invasion of Lebanon. Peace Now played an important role in legitimizing criticism of the Israeli government's policies among American Jews who were extremely reluctant to do so—particularly in public.

To be sure Peace Now has plenty of critics, even from among those who are basically sympathetic with their goals. For example, Meiron Benvenisti calls them "Boy Scouts who demonstrate on Saturday between their naps to cleanse their consciences."[37] Professor Zeev Sternhell (Hebrew University) says that Peace Now cannot provide a political alternative to the government, but can only protest against it.[38]

It is still too early to evaluate the long-term influence of Peace Now's grass-roots work among Israeli youth, in the ethnic neighborhoods, and among Jews abroad. But perhaps the most dramatic testimony to its effectiveness was the manner in which the Likud government and its supporters went to considerble lengths to try to portray the movement as being beyond the bounds of the national consensus. The efforts to delegitimate the movement indicate how much credit the government gave to Peace Now for calling into question the assumption of national consensus on the manner in which it defined Israeli realities.

Mordecai Bar-On suggests: "Imagine what Israel would be like without Peace Now? It makes it easier to be an Israeli!"[39] At least 200,000 Israelis agree and many sympathizers abroad would say that Peace Now makes it easier for them to be a Zionist or a friend of Israel.

Both East for Peace and Netivot Shalom serve purposes similar to Peace Now, but also specific additional ones as well. At a time when the popular perceptions, the media, and even some social-science literature portray Israeli Jews of Middle Eastern background and Jews belonging to the national religious camp as being hawks, anti-Arab, and major obstacles in the path of peace, they refute these stereotypes. Liberal "doves" were minorities in these communities in the period under discussion (and at the time of writing). The peace movements provided forums for like-minded people (disproportionately intellectuals and students) to reaffirm the validity of their views. They also offer more effective points of contact with their communities than do the well-meaning, but suspected, secular Western Peace Now activists. It is their goal to convince their compatriots of the righteousness of their cause.[40] Together with those in the political parties who share their vision, they offer alternative interpretations of Zionism, which they hope, as the domestic, regional, and international conditions become more propitious, will once again become the dominant ones accepted by a majority of their fellow Israelis and its elected representatives. (In the epilogue I shall discuss more recent developments in the peace camp.)

Notes

1. See Rael Jean Isaac (1976: chap. 4) for a good summary analysis of the peace movement in the period following the Six-Day War. For example, a "Peace List" ran unsuccessfully for the Knesset in the 1969 elections and received only half the required number of votes for a seat in the Knesset.
2. Isaac (1981:212), whose political worldview is obviously far from that of Peace Now, concludes her analysis with the following interpretation of the role of *ein breira* in Israeli politics: "Of all the adverse developments that have beset Israel since her 1967 military triumph, the most serious may have been the loss of faith in the traditional slogan, 'There is no choice.' It is a slogan a beleaguered state with an ideological culture can ill afford to relinquish."
3. Peace Now publication in English dated August 1979. Hebrew versions appear in Palgi and in Bar-On. Paraphrasing of Palgi and of Bar-On is based on my own translations of these two important works.
4. Palgi (1979:32) credits a Tel Aviv graphic artist by the name of Arie Tartakover with coining the name "Peace Now" for the original group.
5. This required the pouring of a concrete base in advance and, according to Bar-On (1985:29–30), the Peace Now activists gained the cooperation of the Gush Emunim settlers by saying they were laying the base for a radio antenna. Palgi (1979:45–47) relates how the operation was carried out in secrecy with military precision in planning and execution.
6. Peace Now publication dated August 1979.

7. Peace Now published a brochure in Hebrew entitled "Everything You Didn't Want to Know about Populating the [West] Bank"["Kol Ma Shelo Ratzita Leda'at Al Echluse Hagada"], January 1983.

8. In an interview on May 14, 1983, Bar-On told me that he had told the PLO leader that the PLO would have to remove article 20 of the Palestine National Covenant if it wished to negotiate with Israel. According to Bar-On, Iyad replied that movements do not deny their charters, they make new ones. Baram also discussed this incident in an interview on July 4, 1983. See also Bar-On (1985:41).

9. This is practically identical to a position proposed by Victor Shem-Tov (Mapam) and Aharon Yariv (Labor) to the Labor alignment, but which had not been officially adopted by it at the time it was proposed. This position was articulated by Betzalel "Tzally" Reshef, spokesman for Peace Now, in a meeting with journalists (which I attended) on May 19, 1983, and appears in various publications of the movement.

10. Interview on July 4, 1983.

11. Interview on July 5, 1983.

12. See the Peace Now Hebrew publication "The Unnecessary War: Questions and Answers on the War in Lebanon" ("Hamilchama Hameyuteret"), February 1983.

13. Bar-On (1985:55) and the aforementioned interviews. In fact, in the interview on May 14, 1983, he claimed, "Symbolically, the first victim of the war was a Peace Now activist." Such claims seem to be a reaction against the attempts to delegitimize the Peace Now protestors as traitors.

14. In response to a question by Peretz Kidron at a meeting with journalists on May 19, 1983.

15. Ibid.

16. Interview on May 23, 1983.

17. As a political anthropologist, I have witnessed many public events and ceremonies over the past two decades of professional research in Israel. I can attest that the only public event I have ever participated in that rivaled this demonstration for emotional impact was the first day that the public was allowed to view the Western Wall after the liberation of Jerusalem in 1967 (which I describe in Aronoff, 1981:3). I attended the Peace Now rally with my wife and two teenage daughters. Since I wanted to see the scene from various vantage points we moved around frequently. Although there were masses of people, and Israelis can generally be fairly pushy (as anyone who has ridden Egged buses or tried to buy a movie ticket on Saturday night knows), the crowd politely parted and allowed us to move freely among them without even jostling us!

18. Meeting between Peace Now and members of the press on May 19, 1983. During an interview on July 4, 1983, Reshet elaborated on the point, stating emphatically, "We can't agree to a proclamation that Jews won't kill Jews," but not include Arabs in such a statement.

19. Interview with Tzachi HaNegbi on June 8, 1973.

20. For example, a religious neighbor (a medical student) whom I asked indicated total indifference to the murder of Grunzweig. Yet in a conversation with a friend she expressed grave outrage at the murder of an Israeli woman, Esther Ohana, caused by a rock thrown by an Arab on the West Bank. Similarly, many Peace Now sympathizers seemed much more outraged by the death of Grunzweig than that of Ohana.

21. The Citizens' Rights and Peace movement did actually establish its own youth movement, which stresses principles practically identical to those of Peace Now.
22. Reported by my daughters, who attended the high school.
23. Meeting between Peace Now and representatives of the media on May 19, 1983.
24. Interview on July 11, 1983.
25. East for Peace; "Aims of the Movement" (undated).
26. East for Peace; "Manifesto" (undated).
27. East for Peace; "Guiding Principles" (undated).
28. Daniel Gavron, "Smashing the Stereotype," *Jerusalem Post Magazine*, July 8, 1983, p. 3.
29. Ibid.
30. Ibid.
31. Interview on July 11, 1983.
32. Gavron (1983:4).
33. Interview on January 20, 1983.
34. Ibid.
35. The question of whether there is one or more versions of nationalist Zionism and whether a new political dominance or cultural hegemony has been established is discussed extensively in chap. 6, below.
36. Interview on May 23, 1983.
37. Interview on June 7, 1983.
38. Ibid.
39. Interview on July 4, 1983.
40. Yael Yishai's *Land or Peace* (1987) presents significantly different interpretations of Peace Now and of Gush Emunim.

6

Interpreting Israeli Political Culture

Two basic aspirations underlie all of our work in this country: To be like all nations, and to be different from all nations [David Ben-Gurion, cited in Daniel Shimshoni (1982)].

This chapter addresses the question of whether or not there are symbols and myths with sufficient salience for most Israelis that they provide a common cultural frame of reference strong enough to withstand the strains of the political divisions that threaten to polarize the society. The ideological variations of Zionist visions are examined in order to clarify which cultural idioms unite and which divide different groups in contemporary Israel. The analysis critically evaluates the work and challenges the conclusions of scholars who argue that one particular ideological interpretation of the general Zionist vision has achieved hegemony in contemporary Israeli society. To the present writer it seems possible that an index of national insecurity can be used to gauge degrees of nationalist militancy, which is related to differences in temporal conceptualization of myth and history among types of Zionists. The concluding analysis questions commonly accepted assumptions about the nature of political culture.

Israeli society is presently in a critical transition period. The defeat of the Labor party in 1977, which dominated the political system for nearly fifty years, created both political and ideological vacuums, which the Likud and its partners and allies failed to fill completely. After heading the governing coalitions following the 1977 and 1981 elections, the Likud was forced to share power equally with Labor as a result of the election in 1984. Further, the Likud has failed to achieve the kind of ideological dominance (or hegemony) that is generally thought to have characterized Labor's position at the peak of its power.

There is a scholarly consensus that the consolidation of Mapai as the dominant party in the early formative stages of the development of the political system of the *yishuv* resulted in the emergence of a dominant party system. This dominance expressed itself in both political and ideological realms. Mapai (later Labor) was by far the largest Israeli party. For most of the period of its dominance it had more than twice the number of representatives in the Knesset as its nearest rival. Although it never achieved an absolute majority in the Knesset (as it did in the Histadrut), given the distribution of mandates of the ideologically diverse parties that were elected, and their hostility to one another, no government could be formed without Labor. This enabled Labor to dominate every government through the control of all key ministries, which in turn controlled most of the national budgets.

The second dimension of dominance in a dominant party system is ideological dominance. Most scholars agree that Labor succeeded in identifying itself in the public eye with the pioneering era of early Zionist settlement, the struggle for national independence, the absorption of masses of immigrants, national development, and defense. The general identification of Labor with the epoch of independence and nation building did not mean that a majority of the electorate accepted the socialist interpretation of the general Zionist civil religion. It did mean that Labor's interpretation of Zionist reality enjoyed a significantly superior status because of its association with the formation of the society and the political culture. Even at the peak of its power Labor's specific ideology was probably accepted by a minority, and may have been deeply internalized by a minority of that minority. However, the legitimacy of Labor's leaders was accepted by a very wide public who viewed them as the leaders of the whole nation. Furthermore, most of the politically significant parties and groups could identify with the key symbols, myths, and rituals that constituted the broad outline of the general Zionist civil religion.

The Cases for New Dominance in Israel

Labor acquired ideological dominance before it gained political dominance and lost the former before it actually fell from power. After the Likud came to power it co-opted Gush Emunim, which became a kind of ideological vanguard for the new regime. Ofira Seliktar (1986:74) traces the evolution of revisionism into New Zionism, arguing that it "eclipsed Socialist Zionism." Lilly Weissbrod originally claimed that religious New Zionism (referred to simply as New Zionism), the ideology of Gush Emunim, helped the Likud achieve dominance in the Begin era. She suggested that the Likud moved to the new political center of Israel by New Zionism becoming the dominant ideology (Weissbrod, 1981a:539).

Weissbrod (1981b:798) stated, "New Zionism reformulated the original revolutionary ideology in religious terms, and succeeded in gaining first the support of the young, and subsequently of a large part of the general Israeli public." She argued that the ideology of Gush Emunim did not have to be implemented by a large sector of the population to establish its dominance (Weissbrod, 1983:202). So long as its carriers put into practice its most salient and generally attractive aspects, it was conceded to be the truest expression of the national value system despite serious qualifications by parts of the public (Weissbrod, 1982:273).

Weissbrod (1984:66) has more recently modified her position on the dominance of the Likud and New Zionism by concluding that "no coherent new power center has as yet crystallized that might be granted complete legitimacy." Noting Labor's unique dominance through its association with the heroic period of nation building, she suggests that "possibly, no subsequent power center in Israel will ever attain such a dominant position and enjoy such uncontested legitimacy (Weissbrod, 1984:66–67).

The important pioneering work of Liebman and Don-Yehiya (1983) is the most systematic and thorough treatment of the changing political culture in Israel to date. They trace the role of traditional religion in what they term the civil religions, which have dominated different periods from the early *yishuv* to the present. They define civil religion as "the ceremonials, myths, and creed which legitimate the social order, unite the population, and mobilize the society's members in pursuit of its dominant goals. Civil religion is that which is most holy and sacred in the political culture" (Liebman and Don-Yehiya, 1983:ix). They argue that the *yishuv* and Israel have had more than one civil religion, and they focus their analysis on the extent to which each civil religion appropriated ceremonials, symbols, and myths of religious Jewish tradition. They argue that this is "an important, if not the most important component, of Israeli political culture" (Liebman and Don-Yehiya, 1983:ix).

"In the development of Israeli civil religion we can identify separate periods in which each approach was dominant; although one finds traces of all approaches in every period among different groups" (Liebman and Don-Yehiya, 1984:53). In their periodization they identify Labor Zionism as the dominant of several varieties of civil religion in the *yishuv* period, and statism *(mamlachtiut)* as the dominant civil religion from independence to approximately 1967. "The new civil religion reached a dominant position after 1967. The peak of its influence came with the Likud victory in 1977 (the Likud is more closely identified with the new civil religion than any other party). . . . Its goal was to unite and integrate the society

around its conception of the Jewish tradition and the Jewish people"
(Liebman and Don-Yehiya, 1984:57). This new civil religion is characterized by the importance of Jewish tradition and penetration of religious
symbolism in civic life.

While ostensibly building upon the work of Liebman and Don-Yehiya,
Gary Schiff goes beyond their findings. He argues that "religion is and for
the foreseeable future will continue to be the single most important
political variable, social force, and operative ideology on the Israeli political scene" (Schiff, 1986:43). He contends that "there seems to be no
viable counterideology to religion as a legitimating or motivating force
within the polity today (Schiff, 1986:44).

Critique of the Claim for New Dominance

The evaluation of the claims of these scholars requires the clarification
of their differences. Weissbrod clearly specifies that New Zionism is
synonymous with the ideology of Gush Emunim. Leibman and Don-
Yehiya characterize what they call the new civil religion as a kind of
political folk religiosity, lacking a coherent ideological formulation, centered around certain symbols and myths, and distinctly different from
traditional Judaism. Schiff talks about the political primacy of religion in
general, which in the context of his discussion seems to mean the Orthodox tradition.

The similarities between these positions are more apparent than real.
The differences between the ideologies of Gush Emunim and that of
revisionism, on one hand, and folk or civil religion and traditional religion,
on the other, are more significant than their similarities. The claims of
these scholars that each dominates contemporary Israeli political culture
deceptively appear to be mutually reinforcing. In fact, the claims contradict one another. The national religious messianism of Gush Emunim is
antithetical to the non-Zionist or even anti-Zionist interpretation of traditional Judaism of many of the Orthodox and all of the ultra-Orthodox Jews
in Israel. The amorphous folk religiosity of even traditional nationalist
leaders like Begin are by no means considered by the Orthodox to be
synonymous with, or an acceptable substitute for, their Halachic religious
tradition.[1] If there were a single new ideological form of Zionist civil
religion it could not possibly combine at one and the same time revisionism, national religious messianism, folk religion, and Orthodox tradition.

The rigid conceptual approaches used by these scholars allow for only
static portrayals of political culture. They do not view culture as a dynamic
phenomenon in a constant state of flux and change. They fail to distinguish
between the general symbolic framework of civil religion and the more

specific ideological interpretations of different political movements. Nor do they view dominance as a historically rare phenomenon requiring an exceptional identification between a party, an ideological worldview, and an epoch in the formation or transformation of a political system (except in Weissbrod's most recent formulation).

The scholarly consensus regarding the earlier period of Labor dominance both reflected and helped to reinforce the perception of Labor dominance. Most scholars identified with Labor's version of the Zionist vision and accepted the authority of Labor's national leadership. They rarely questioned the taken-for granted assumption of Labor legitimacy. Their writings helped to produce and to reinforce a historical narrative that contributed to the "consensual" dominance and legitimacy of Labor. Whereas David Ben-Gurion had a few intellectual critics, they were the exceptions, and even they became vocal only in the aftermath of the "Lavon affair."[2] At the peak of Ben-Gurion's (and Labor's) dominance, most of "the intellectuals—some consciously, some not—became legitimizers of a messianic interpretation of social and political reality" (Keren, 1983:153).

The scholarly attention to the reputed dominance of new cultural nationalistic religious forms is differently related to the legitimation of a newly "invented" messianic tradition (Hobsbawm and Ranger, 1983). None of the scholars I here discussed would willingly contribute to the legitimation of the phenomena they analyze. In spite of their very diverse backgrounds, all are critical of various aspects of what they perceive to be a dangerous trend. The fact that not only they, but the majority of Israeli academics, editorialists, and media commentators do not identify with any of the various forms of New Zionism or civil religion reported tends to contradict the assertion that there is a new dominant ideology. The leaders of the Likud, and nationalist politicians in general, have recognized this and have been highly critical of the liberal bias of Israeli opinion leaders whom they derisively call *yefeh nefesh* (literally "beautiful souls," but freely translated as "knee-jerk liberals"). A body named the Media Consumers Protection League crusades against what they call the "leftist mafia" in the media.

Objective indicators, including the "hard" evidence of voting results and survey data on key issues, for example, religious identification and the role of religion in the state, tend to refute the conclusion that either political dominance or ideological dominance of any party or worldview has been established. Rather, the picture that emerges is of a society divided fairly evenly and tending toward polarization. In the 1981 election the two major political blocs achieved near parity (Likud 48 and Labor 47). In 1984 Labor gained a very slight edge (44 to 41). After coalition jockeying and minor party splits from, and alignment with, the major blocs, parity was reestablished, and the new unity government was formed, based on equally shared power and rotation of the premiership. This is hardly the arrangement one would expect in a dominant-party system. As suggested in preceding chapters it bears all the signs of the emergence of a competitive party system that reached an electoral stalemate.

Arian notes the fascinating degree of relative stability over time (1962–81) in the distribution of answers to questions regarding the proper role of religious tradition in public life and personal religious behavior. The respondents are almost evenly divided between those who agree to having public life conducted in accordance with tradition and those who disagree. The proportion of respondents who observe no Jewish religious laws is about the same as those who observe all or most laws (between a quarter and a third). There was actually a decline in religious observance between 1977 and 1981. In response to the question "Do you observe Jewish religious law?" those who responded "To the letter" declined from 14 percent to 9 percent, and those who responded "Not at all" rose from 29 percent to 34 percent. Approximately 40 percent claim to be somewhat observant. "We have before us a picture of a symmetrically divided polity in terms of desired public behavior and in terms of private observance. The issue is a major one and splits the population" (Arian, 1985:217–18). Such evidence contradicts Schiff's notion of a new religious hegemony.

Much of the survey data on public opinion related to a number of other key issues, such as support for settlement in the territories (or willingness to make territorial concessions for peace), is similar to that on religiosity cited above. With variations depending on the actual wording of the questions and the time and contexts in which they are asked, the nation is roughly evenly divided. The major divisions, however, are further subdivided between those who strongly (and even militantly) support their positions and those who are moderate in their views. From this perspective the moderates range between a third and a half of the public (depending on the issue). Again this evidence is more supportive of an emerging competitive party system than the replacement of the old dominant party system with a new one.

Contrary to Liebman and Don-Yehiya's assertion that Israel has had several civil religions identified with specific historical periods, the present writer suggests that Israel has had a single core civil religion from the inception of the Zionist movement to the present. this civil religion is Zionism. Within the general Zionist framework, socialist Zionism, revisionist Zionism, statist Zionism, and religious Zionism (through the different political movements and parties identified with them) have competed with one another for power and the right to claim their version to be the *true* interpretation of *the* Zionist vision.

After Labor's socialist-Zionist version gained preeminence in the *yishuv*, David Ben-gurion transformed the former by inventing a new statist form, which he felt was more appropriate to the postindependence period. Ben-Gurion essentially sacrificed a relatively high level of commitment among a narrower base of supporters for a lower level of commitment among a broader constituency. Whereas he and his followers claimed to be following the same Zionist vision as they had followed previously, others who refused to dilute their socialism (e.g., Min Hayesod)[3] countered that Ben-Gurion had deviated from the true path.

Menachem Begin co-opted Gush Emunim and added a patina of religious symbolism, rhetoric, and rite to the official version of Jabotinsky's secular martial nationalistic version of Zionism, which had become codified in Herut dogma and practice. In so doing Begin invented his own equivalent of Ben-Gurion's *mamlachtiut*. And, like Ben-Gurion, he antagonized some of his most faithful followers when he appeared to compromise the old ideology (e.g., those who left Herut to found Techiya in protest against the Israel-Egypt peace treaty).

Begin's newly formulated reinterpretation of revisionist Zionism was neither a New Zionism nor a new civil religion, but a new ideological variation on an old familiar Zionist tune designed to mobilize a broader electoral constituency. Although selections were borrowed from Gush Emunim's ideology, it is far from synonymous with it. Although appealing to traditional and religious voters, it is clearly distinct from the ideology associated with the national religious camp. It is questionable whether the particular combination of folk religion and nationalism is sufficiently institutionalized (reified) to survive the demise of Begin as leader of the Likud. Clearly his successor as leader of the Likud, Yitzhak Shamir, lacks the ability to act convincingly as its spokesman. Whether this variant will survive or not depends on who succeeds Shamir. If it does it will almost certainly be reinterpreted to fit the style of its articulator and the temper and tempo of the changing socioeconomic and political conditions.

The Constituencies and Components of Israeli Political Culture

In this section we shall consider some of the basic components of Israeli political culture and relate them to different constituencies within Israeli society (and beyond the territorial boundaries of the state). First it must be noted that if Zionism is the main civil religion of Israel, there are significant groups living within Israel who reject or do not identify with its basic myths and values, and there are those not living in Israel who in varying degrees do identify with them.

The core myth of Zionism is based on the biblical concept of exile and redemption. This myth is both a "root metaphor," in that it provides categories for conceptualizing the order of the world, and a "key scenario" in its elaboration of mechanisms for social action (Ortner, 1973). The prophetic promise to the children of Israel of an end to exile in the Diaspora by a return to Zion is the central principle that motivates and legitimates Zionism. It is interpreted as a historic right (or duty) by the secularists and a religious right (or duty) by the religious Zionists. It is rejected by religious and secular non- and anti-Zionists for different reasons. To be an Arab in a Jewish state is a paradox. Consequently the majority of the Arab citizens of Israel (not to mention those living under Israeli military occupation) do not identify with the core myth of Zionism. A small percentage of secular Israelis and a larger proportion of Orthodox Jews in Israel (and abroad) are either indifferent or hostile to Zionism. At the same time there are many Jews living outside Israel who in varying degrees identify with core Zionist beliefs.

Since Zion (Eretz Yisrael, or the biblical land of Israel) is the key symbol identified with Zionism, *aliyah* (literally "ascent," associated with a spiritual ascent to the Temple in Jerusalem or to the *bimah* where the Torah is read in the synagogue), the Zionist term for immigration to Israel, is the primary rite in the civil religion for Zionists born abroad. This is considered to be the right of all Jews and the obligation of every Zionist. The law of return, which guarantees the right of automatic Israeli citizenship to every Jew who immigrates to Israel (passed in 1950) embodies the prophetic vision of the "ingathering of the exiles," a main Zionist key scenario. A litmus test of adherence to belief in Zionism is one's attitude toward the law of return. It is not surprising that most Israeli Arabs are hostile to this law. There are Israeli Jews who are willing to abolish this law as a conciliatory gesture to the Arabs. Such individuals might be called non-Zionists.

Non-Zionist and Anti-Zionist Groups in Israel

I here define as anti-Zionist those groups that reject all aspects of the Zionist civil religion and deny even de-facto recognition of the right of Israel to exist as an independent Jewish state. They do not participate in the electoral parliamentary process, and individuals belonging to these groups (or categories) do not serve in the army. We define as non-Zionist those groups that reject Zionist civil religion (or at least its most central values), but give de-facto recognition to the existence of the state of Israel and pragmatically cooperate with its institutions, including competing in elections. Some individuals belonging to these groups serve in the army but, when they do, are likely to engage in dissident activity (see below).

There are militantly anti-Zionist groups such as those affiliated with the PLO, which, although illegal in Israel, have supporters primarily among the Arabs (both citizens of Israel and Palestinians on the West Bank and Gaza). Some radical members of the Association of Arab University students acknowledge support for the PLO. The militantly anti-Zionist Arab nationalist Sons of the Village reject any form of cooperation with Jews. These individuals and groups operate outside the formal parliamentary political framework in extreme cases through acts of violence and terrorism.

There are other predominantly Arab groups that encourage cooperation between Arabs and Jews. Rakah, the Arab nationalist Communist party, which formed an electoral alliance with noncommunist Arab and Jewish groups to form the Democratic Front for Peace and Equality (with four Knesset members), and the new noncommunist Progressive List for Peace (with two Knesset members) have equal Arab and Jewish representation in the Knesset. Both accept the independent existence of the state of Israel, but in varying degrees reject its Jewish character as expressed in the Zionist civil religion. The views of individual members of these parties range from moderately anti-Zionist to non-Zionist. The parties themselves would most accurately be defined as non-Zionist according to the definitions here adopted. These groups are active in the Knesset, but suffer exclusion from the "club" of what the majority consider "legitimate," namely, Zionist parties. Rabbi Meir Kahane, the single member of Knesset for the most extreme Zionist party, Kach, is treated as a pariah by the vast majority of the members of the Knesset (except by ultranationalists). In this case his antidemocratic and racist views put him beyond the pale of what is considered to be "legitimate Zionist" politics. At different periods there have been other small, predominantly Jewish, non- or anti-Zionist groups.

The other largest groups of non- and anti-Zionist Jews in Israel are made up of Orthodox and ultra-Orthodox Jews. Their opposition is based on their rabbinic interpretations of Zionism as blasphemous because it arrogantly attempts to do what can be done only by divine will (the ingathering of the exiles is to take place with the coming of the Messiah as a prelude to redemption); and because they reject any Jewish state that fails to conform to religious law in its strictest interpretation. Agudat Yisrael is a good example of a Party that was anti-Zionist prior to independence and was sufficiently co-opted to maintain a somewhat ambivalent non-Zionist posture since then. As in the case of the other groups mentioned, views of individual members vary in degrees of militancy as does the position of the group at different periods of time. For example, there are moderate nationalist elements within Agudat Yisrael that come close to the views of the more conservatively Orthodox in the National Religious party and may even serve in the army, and there are militant elements that share anti-Zionist attitudes close to those of Neturei Karta (Guardians of the City). A militant minority of Orthodox Jews maintain an actively hostile stand toward Zionism. Neturei Karta is the best known but by no means the only group of anti-Zionist religious Jews in Israel. Such groups refuse to participate in elections and their activities are consequently of an extraparliamentary (and not infrequently violent) nature.

The official civil religion of Israel, Zionism, had never gained the support of the entire population even at the peak of the dominance of its most powerful ideological interpreters. Those who are either indifferent or actively hostile to it constitute more than a numerically small and politically insignificant minority. They are marginal only in the sense that they do not share allegiance to most central values of Zionist civil religion, yet they constitute groups of significant numbers (increasing faster than the natural rates of most of the mainstream Zionist groups)[4] and have links of sentiment and support from well-organized groups beyond Israel's borders. Given the balance of political power between the two major political blocs, the non-Zionist ultra-Orthodox parties, Agudat Yisrael and Shas, have gained greater power than at any time since Israel became independent. Therefore, they cannot be ignored. It must be determined if and to what extend they meaningfully share a common political culture with those who adhere to Zionism.

Different Zionist Visions and Constituencies

The primary rite of passage that initiates one into full membership in the Zionist civil religion is service in Zahal (the Israel Defense Forces). It is the single most important test, particularly for males, for individual and group acceptance in the mainstream of Israeli society governed by Zionist civil religion. The type of unit in which one (or members of one's group) serves, and even the proportion of casualties suffered by the members of one's group are seen to be proof of the extent of one's commitment and the centrality of the group in the mainstream of society. The fact that kibbutznikim disproportionately served as officers and in elite units that suffered high casualties was always cited as evidence of their vanguard role in the Zionist venture. More recently, in interviews conducted during the war in Lebanon this writer was told by leaders of nationalist religious Jews and of Eastern Jews that the higher rates of casualties suffered by

their respective groups was evidence of their having moved to the forefront
of the national (Zionist) struggle.[5]

Conversely, the increase in protest and dissident activity, particularly
among young kibbutznikim, was repeatedly cited as evidence of the
marginalization of this former elite through their "disloyal" or "treasonous" behavior. It should be noted, in light of efforts to stigmatize critics
of the war, the leading role played by officers of elite combat units in both
the small dissident groups (Soldiers against Silence and There Is a Limit)
and in the much larger protest movement, Peace Now (see Weissbrod,
1984).

The fundamental Zionist premise is the belief in the right of the Jewish
people to an independent Jewish state in the ancient Jewish homeland of
the land of Israel. However, even among those who adhere to this belief as
a primary article of faith, there are deep divisions over what should
constitute the specific "Jewish" character and the territorial boundaries of
the state. The nation is polarized between those who emphasize the duty
of the Jewish people to colonize and incorporate the ancient biblical
heartland of the land of Israel (Judea and Samaria, or the West Bank) at
any cost, and those who argue that to do so would threaten both the
Jewish and the democratic character of the state and would make the
perpetuation of war inevitable. There is an equally deep division between
those who argue that the Jewish character of the state should be based on
conformity with religious tradition and law, and those who strongly reject
this position, arguing for a democratic, liberal, and humanistic adaptation
of Jewish values to contemporary contexts. Although there is considerable
overlap between the two sets of groups that align on both sides of these
two issues, they are not isomorphic.

The complex multiplicity of issues and divisions of Israeli politics cannot
possibly be expressed on a single-dimensional continuum. As Dominguez
(1984) has cogently argued, terms like "left" and "right" are multivocal
and multifunctional. Their shifting referentiality requires contextual interpretation to provide accurate meanings. When this is not done, even
skillful practitioners produce less than completely satisfactory results (see
Arian, 1985: 250–52). On different issues the alignment of parties and
groups would vary on such continua.

The distinction between types of ideological orientation based on the
relation between traditional religion and civil religion, and the division
over the proper role of religion in the state is only one basis for distinguishing between categories of Zionism. By emphasizing a typology based on
intensity of nationalism (each component of which contains religious and
secular versions), a different perspective in understanding Israeli political
culture can be gained. Individuals and groups adhering to Zionism can be

divided into three major categories based on the character and the degree of militancy of nationalism. These categories are not "neat" in the sense that they do not perfectly correlate with the formal divisions between Israeli political parties. The categories tend to overlap parties on their fringes. This is a heuristic analytic typology that deliberately oversimplifies a range of orientations along a continuum, and should never be reified.

Humanist Zionism is the more universalistic orientation, which incorporates basic features of socialist Zionism, statism, and the progressive elements of liberal ideology in Israel. It's ideological utopianism is exemplified by Ben-Gurion's secular interpretation of the messianic prophecy that Israel should be "a light unto the nations."[6] Its programmatic goal is the normalization of the Jewish people in their independent state. I shall discuss the tensions between these goals below. The ideological vanguard of humanist Zionism is represented by the extra parliamentary peace movements, that is, Peace Now, the smaller religious peace movements Oz v'Shalom and Nitivot Shalom, and the peace movement of Eastern Jews called East for Peace. The major parties with Knesset representation in this category are Mapam, the Citizen's Rights movement (Ratz), most (but not all) of Labor, Change (Shinui), Yahad (Ezer Weizman), the most liberal elements within the National Religious party (e.g., the religious kibbutz movement and intellectuals) and the truly liberal Liberals, most of whom have resigned from the Liberal party aligned in the Likud.

Nationalist Zionism in its contemporary form is essentially what Liebman and Don-Yehiya identify as the new civil religion. It is ideologically symbolized by the biblical passage "a people that dwells alone," which to adherents of this version of Zionism stresses the singularity of the Jewish people and the isolation of Israel. The folk religiosity superimposed on the revisionist core and popularized by Menachem Begin remains ideologically distinct from the national religious Zionism of the NRP. This general worldview is attractive to the most activist and nationalistic minority within the Labor movement. The majority of the Likud, and most of the National Religious party, including the Ze'irim leadership (as opposed to the more militant in Gush Emunim), constitute the parliamentary base. Note that this does not necessarily mean that the NRP will not be wooed back into a coalition with Labor or that Shas will not support the Likud even though its main ideological interests are peripheral to the issue. Factors other than ideology operate in the calculus of coalition building.

Ultranationalist Zionism, the most particularistic form of Zionism, also has religious and secular variants. The former is represented by Gush Emunim. The ideological slogan "Esau hates Jacob" vividly expresses the basic assumption of hostility of the non-Jewish world toward the Jews and of the Arab world in particular toward Israel that is universally accepted among adherents of this form of Zionism.[7] The secular version is articulated most cogently in the publications of the ideologue of Techiya, Dr. Yisrael Eldad.[8] This stream of Zionism is represented in the Knesset by a minority of the Likud (led by Ariel Sharon), all of Techiya, Rabbi Drukman, and, in a somewhat more extreme variation, by Rabbi Meir Kahane's Kach. The extraparliamentary expression of this worldview carried to its logical extreme has been expressed in the vigilante and terrorist activities of Jewish settlers on the West Bank, which have been either supported or justified by most of the members of the Knesset factions of the ultranationalist parties (see Weisburd and Vinitzky, 1984; Sprinzak, 1986; and Lustick, forthcoming).

Two Dimensions Differentiating the Opposing Orientations

Nationalism and the Sense of Security

A sense of psychological security has been found to be positively associated with political tolerance in Israel (Shamir and Sullivan, 1983). Clearly, the complex phenomena of variations in ideological worldviews cannot be reduced to a simple psychological explanation. However, underlying social psychological attributes are related to general ideological orientations. The present writer has been repeatedly struck by the association between the extent to which the outsider, or non-Jewish world, is perceived as hostile and the degree of militancy in Israeli nationalism. Liebman and Don-Yehiya recognized the different perceptions of anti-Semitism among the different civil religions, but did not stress this over many other differences in values between them. However, they did stress that the new civil religion was the most ethnocentric of all—stressing both Jewish isolation and Gentile hostility. They also recognized the increasing symbolic importance of the Holocaust, and the key roles of the expressions "Esau hates Jacob" and "a people that dwells alone" in the more nationalistic new civil religion. The former expresses the traditional Jewish sensitivity to anti-Semitism. The biblical prophecy of Balaam, "Lo, it is a people that shall dwell alone and shall not be reckoned among the nations" (Num. 23:9), according to Labor party Knesset member Rabbi Menachem HaCohen was a curse that Gush Emunim has elevated to a blessing.[9]

An index gauging the sense of individual and collective security would, it seems, strongly correlate with the distinctions made herein among the humanist, nationalist, and ultranationalist forms of Zionism. The more secure an individual is about personal and national security, the more likely is he or she to be identified with humanistic Zionism. The more insecure, the more nationalistic the person is likely to be. Caspi and

Seligson (1983:33) found that "those who select anti-Zionists as their target of intolerance are more likely to . . . feel more personally threatened by anti-Zionists than are those who select Zionists as their least-liked group."

For examples of the worldview of the paranoic extreme ultranationalist, consult the writings of Meir Kahane or Amos Oz's interview (1983:87–100 with a self-proclaimed "Judeo-Nazi."[10] Unfortunately (by the use of this word, the present writer deliberately reveals his own political bias), the latter are not just rare idiosyncratic or exceptional cases. Although they may be the most blatant and crude expressions of the ultranationalist orientation, they are by no means the only ones. In field notes from interviews by the present writer with a number of ranking leaders of Gush Emunim and of Techiya, statements are recorded that are somewhat more refined and moderated versions of the aforementioned. However, by no means all of the leaders of these two movements who were interviewed expressed such extreme views. The range of views among Gush Emunim leaders interviewed was even greater than those of Techiya leaders.[11] The leaders of Gush Emunim, while displaying a conspicuous insensitivity to the rights of the Palestinian Arabs, stressed a love of the land of Israel, whereas Kahane relies primarily on the exploitation of the fear and hatred of the Arabs.

For the best example of nationalistic Zionism, one should consult the speeches and writings of its most articulate spokesman, Menachem Begin.[12] Begin's letter of August 2, 1982, to President Reagan, in which he compared Beirut to Berlin and Arafat to Hitler, is a good example of this genre. Begin frequently employed the central theme of "the few against the many" or "them" against "us" to play on the sense of national insecurity (Gertz, 1983). Begin exploited his exceptional rhetorical gifts in the 1981 election to polarize the electorate. He charged that Labor's "Jordanian option" would lead to an "Arafatist state," implying that Labor endangered the very survival of the state (Yavin, 1981:39).[13]

The history of the Jewish people and of the state of Israel provides ample objective evidence to warrant suspiciousness toward outsiders and a sense of both individual and collective insecurity. However, even the most extreme manifestation of anti-Semitism in world history, the Holocaust, produced extremely different reactions on the part of those who survived its unspeakable horror. A ceremony held in honor of the seventieth birthday of Raoul Wallenberg (the Swedish diplomat who saved thousands of Hungarian Jews from extermination), which was held in the Israeli Knesset on May 9, 1983, provided a vivid example of how differently individuals representing the different Zionist orientations interpreted the significance of Wallenberg's heroism.

In his speech Prime Minister Menachem Begin (whose family perished in the Holocaust) stressed how exceptional Wallenberg was and how few Gentiles helped the Jews.[14] Deputy Minister Dov Shilansky (Likud), a survivor of the Holocaust, stressed the impossibility for Jews to live in the Gentile world. Eliezer Avtabi (NRP) and Ronnie Milo (Likud) both drew the lesson that Jews could trust only their own people and must rely on themselves.[15] Professor Shevah Weiss (Labor), on the other hand, stressed that there were other Wallenbergs including the woman who risked her life to hide Weiss and his family even from her own son, who was a Ukrainian collaborator. He stressed the great risks and moral courage that such people displayed. Weiss expressed ambivalence about the intensification of the memorialization of the Holocaust, saying that a balance had to be found so as to draw the positive examples and their implications as well the negative, which he felt were overstressed.

This is but one example illustrative of the type of differences in the orientations toward non-Jews and the sense of trust and security that differentiate humanists, nationalists, and ultranationalists in Israel. Although paranoics can have real enemies, the more extreme form of national paranoia can become a self-fulfilling prophecy by producing the results it most fears. Extreme suspiciousness ends up alienating real and potential allies. This happens when militant nationalists charge non-Jews who disagree with their policies with anti-Semitism. Diaspora Jews who criticize them are accused of being self-hating Jews, and Israeli opponents are condemned as traitors.

If the more Nationalistic versions of Zionism are far less trusting and tolerant of non-Jews, they tend to be more tolerant of Diaspora Jews, on one hand, and of cultural pluralism among Jews within Israel, on the other. As Liebman and Don-Yehiya perceptively show, the socialist Zionists saw a tension in the relationship between the state of Israel and Diaspora Jews; statism negated the Diaspora, and what they call the new civil religion has been more conciliatory to their Jewish brethren residing abroad. Historically, Labor Zionism and its statist variant promoted an Israeli "pressure-cooker" version of the melting-pot approach to "absorbing" immigrants, which demanded cultural conformity. The so-called new civil religion, or what we here are calling the nationalists, who have been preoccupied with realizing the historical boundaries of the Jewish state, have been more tolerant of ethnic diversity (see Lewis, 1984).

Myth as History: The Role of Time in Political Culture

Robert Paine (1983) has suggested that a form of totemism, a nonrational eschatological politics dominated by a mythical rather than a historical notion of time, characterized the political worldview of the Begin era in Israel. He contrasts this with the period of Labor rule, which he characterizes as having been oriented by a more Western, linear, historical worldview. Paine contrasts the semiotics of the sacred under Begin with the "purged" messianism of Ben-Gurion, which he characterizes as lacking eschatological and mystical elements. Clearly there were mystical elements in Ben-Gurion's political messianism, and many rational, pragmatic elements to the policies pursued by Begin during his rule. These types are not mutually exclusive. Recognizing that both properties can be found in every worldview, the distinctions suggested by Paine have heuristic value in determining the influence of each type of orientation to time on particular positions and policies.

Paine's distinction would appear to bear a logical relationship to the index of trust of outsiders proposed above, which posits that the individual or group with the strongest sense of security and trust in the outsider (the non-Jew) is most likely to operate on a more Western, linear concept of time. The most insecure individuals or groups with the greatest distrust of the non-Jew are the most likely to have belief systems characterized by relatively more nonrational, mythical notions of time. The explicit rejection of Western culture (Hellenization) and the messianism of the ultranationalists go hand in hand with their rejection of the possibility, much less the desirability, of national normalization and the explicit goal of preserving isolation rationalized by the notion of chosenness. The relationships between these heuristic categories can be stated as hypotheses, which are capable of being tested. The historically oriented worldview is most likely to be associated with humanist Zionism. The totemic, or mythical, orientation is most likely to be associated with ultranationalist Zionism. Whereas all types of Zionism will contain rational and nonrational elements, nationalist Zionism constitutes an intermediary type, which is even more likely than the others to combine elements of both.

The analysis, in a previous chapter, of the controversy surrounding the state funeral ceremony given to the reputed remains of the fighters and followers of Shimon Bar Kochba can provide a test case for the hypothesized relationships. The heated and controversial debate over the Bar Kochba funeral reveals a number of interesting insights into contemporary Israeli political culture. The fact that the ceremony, in which the prime minister invested considerable personal interest and concern, was so controversial provides additional evidence that his nationalistic ideological interpretation of Zionism had not become accepted as dominant or hegemonic even within his own cabinet, much less among significant sectors of the population. The polarized debate over the contradictory lessons drawn from the same events clearly reveals the continued salience of the conflicting versions of the Zionist vision.

Each of the types of Zionism had a different interpretation of the meaning and appropriateness of the ceremony. The humanist Zionists were the most outspokenly critical. They attacked the ceremony, which they perceived to be a deliberate distortion of history that sought to reinterpret a suicidal policy that brought disaster and dispersal to the Jewish people as a heroic example worthy of emulation. Their protests ranged from the satirical demonstration by the toga-clad youth (clearly Peace Now types), to the publicized boycott of invited archaeologists like Yigal Yadin, to the published work on the *Bar-Kochba Syndrome* of Harkabi. Their concern with the distortion of the historical record was combined with their opposition to the policies that this ceremony aimed to legitimate, namely, settlement of the West Bank. Rabbi Menachem Ha-Cohen, MK (Labor), the scion of an old rabbinic line, explained the importance of reburial in Israel in Jewish tradition dating from Joseph, and condemned the "lack of genuine historical perspective" typified by the ceremony.[16]

The senior cabinet minister from the National Religious party, who did not attend the ceremony, is more difficult to categorize. He had been a member of many Labor-led governments, and was considered sympathetic to most Labor policies. The rise of younger more nationalistic leaders to power in his party led to its alliance with the Likud. The minister, a consummate politician, enjoyed extremely cordial relations with Prime Minister Begin and actively supported his policies during their years of partnership in the government. His sincere and unambiguous criticism of the ceremony was in the context of a confidential personal interview, which took place while Begin was still prime minister. He continued to serve as a minister in the unity government formed after the 1984 election and enjoyed excellent relations with Prime Minister Peres. He could probably best be categorized as a humanist Zionist of the old Poel Ha-Mizrachi type, who is first and foremost a pragmatic politician willing to compromise ideology in order to maintain both his personal and his party's position of power and control over resources—a type common in Israeli politics. Obviously factors other than ideology and orientation toward history play important roles in determining the behavior of politicians in any given context.

Yitzhak Moda'i is a procedural liberal and a strongly nationalist Zionist, but not an ultranationalist. His criticism of the ceremonies was primarily on procedural grounds, namely, the failure "to distinguish between state ceremonials and the personal feelings of leaders. They wanted to emphasize the historic connection with the hills of Judea. In my opinion this was

not the correct instrument." After initially refusing Rabbi Goren's request
to hold an official state ceremony, Moda'i reluctantly deferred when Begin
intervened. This was more an expression of the old adage that discretion
is the better part of valor than out of ideological identification with the
ritual. Although a strong nationalist, Moda'i gave no indication of operat-
ing on totemic time. In fact, his procedural liberalism is as much a part of
the Western tradition as is the humanism of those who were more outspokenly critical of the ceremony. As finance minister in the unity government's cabinet, Moda'i initially developed a close working relationship
with Prime Minister Peres, but later clashed with him repeatedly and was
forced to give up first the finance portfolio and then the justice ministry.
(At the time of writing he is a minister without portfolio.)

Rabbi Goren and Prime Minister Begin both had very practical, rational,
political reasons for promoting the state rites for the Bar Kochba bones.
Yet from personal interviews with Goren and almost all of the key actors
involved in the events, and from examination of the record (including
minutes of the Ministerial Committee on Symbols and Ceremonies), there
seems to have been more to their very strong support than strictly rational
political calculations.[17]

Symbolic of the differences in the orientations between the leaders of
Labor and the Likud was the different dates chosen for the ceremonies.
The committee selected by Ben-Gurion chose a day associated with
mourning the destruction of the second Temple and the later dispersal of
the Jews in the Diaspora, which tended to emphasize the relationship
between the rebellion as a cause of the latter disastrous historical consequence. Whereas Begin and Goren chose a day that emphasized the
heroism of the Zealots while ignoring the direct historical consequences of
their rebellion. This seems to conform to the typological distinction made
by Robert Paine between historical and mythical orientations.

In his proposed typology of the relationship between temporal meanings
and their behavioral consequences, Katzenstein (1987) characterizes Israel
(along with China) as the type of society that operates on a mixed cyclical-
and linear-time framework. Among the characteristics associated with this
type are a preoccupation with the distant past, which is highly salient for
understanding present situations; and a tendency to project the past, which
is recorded as history but treated as myth, into an understanding of the
future. He suggests that factions in China and parties in Israel may be
associated with the different temporal orientations that characterize these
mixed systems.

The humanist Zionists (including the religious variation) would appear
to bridge the causal linear history of the original Jewish tradition and that
of post-Enlightenment modern ideological orientation.[18] The ultranational-

ists (of both religious and secular persuasions) seem to be a more direct link with the postexilic rabbinic tradition dominated by Paine's notion of totemic time or what Mircea Eliade calls archaic time. This perspective is characterized by the interpretation of both the present and the future in terms of the past.[19] The nationalists tend to bridge tenuously, and to oscillate between, the two different orientations. In this particular case, Rabbi Goren and Prime Minister Begin expressed both orientations. In fact, they constitute important personal and ideological links between the nationalist and the ultranationalist Zionists.[20]

Conclusions

Do Israelis share common cultural myths and visions of their destinies? Significant minorities do not identify with or actively reject the most basic symbols of the Zionist civil religion. Among those who do identify with the root cultural paradigms there are fundamental divisions over what should constitute the Jewish character and the physical boundaries of the state. There is a conspicuous lack of consensus on fundamental values and basic public policy among Zionists. These divisions would appear to be linked to profound differences in a relative sense of individual and collective security, trust/distrust and amity/hostility toward outsiders, and temporal worldviews between types of Zionists. Since no hegemonic ideological interpretation of Zionism has gained dominance, what, if anything, constitutes the overarching symbolic framework that provides the commonality in Israeli political culture?

What is shared appears to be very meager given the common assumptions we have about the character of political culture. The fact that secular scholars, religious leaders, and politicians of all persuasions engaged one another in a public debate over the consequences and implications of events that took place 2,000 years ago indicates the existence of a common cultural rubric and rhetoric, which made the debate both possible and meaningful. The contestants shared a common political language (literal as well as figurative), which made their confrontation intelligible to one another. The fact that they engaged in debate rather than physical confrontation indicates that they shared certain assumptions about acceptable rules of the game.

Not all of the actors who accept the rules of the political game in Israel accept the commonly held assumptions of Zionist-defined reality; and not all actors who adhere to the Zionist worldview accept the rules of the democratic game. Finally, there are those who reject both Zionism and the rules of the game, and they tend to be dealt with by the police and the military rather than through the regular political process. Obviously, many factors hold an entity together and provide relative order. Economic interdependence, the threat of violence from without, and the use of physical coercion internally are all factors that reinforce or replace the positive cohesion provided by the shared understandings of a common cultural framework.

Political culture is far more tenuous than it is generally portrayed. It is like a fragile web of symbolic themes that is constantly being stretched in opposite directions by conflicting interpretations. The myths that crown power with legitimacy are constantly threatened by iconoclasts who call into question and undermine them. Old truths are constantly reinterpreted as political realities change, and new cultural traditions are invented by myth-makers who drape emergent groups with the mantle of authority. Political culture, like all culture, is an illusion, but an illusion that is essential for the survival of society and civilization. Like other modern nations, Israel claims "to be the opposite of novel, namely rooted in the remotest antiquity, and the opposite of constructed, namely" a human community "so 'natural' as to require no definition other than self-assertion" (Hobsbawm, 1983:14). Its political culture is particularly vulnerable because so many within and without its borders challenge this claim.

Notes

1. Practically every observant or Orthodox Jew I interviewed stressed this point. In fact, Professor David Flusser, a specialist on religion at the Hebrew University of Jerusalem (in a lengthy interview on January 18, 1983), derided Begin's form of civil religion as "kitch religion" combined with nationalism. The fact that Orthodox Israelis do not mistake Begin's religiosity with their form of observance did not prevent many of them from identifying with him, nor did it detract from his popularity among many of them.
2. The "Lavon Affair" began as a security mishap, but escalated into a complex struggle for power in Mapai which initiated the decline of the party's dominance of the political system. See Medding (1972).
3. Min Hayesod (From the Source) was a group (primarily of intellectuals, kibbutznikim, and officials of the Histadrut) who supported Pinchas Lavon in his struggle with David Ben-Gurion in the Lavon Affair.
4. "According to the Jerusalem Institute for Public Affairs, the average number of children in Haredi families is 8, compared with 3.5 for religious Zionists and 2.2 for secular Zionists. The majority of new immigrants today are deeply Orthodox Jews from North America and Western Europe, while Western liberal Jewish immigrants are a mere trickle" (Thomas Friedman, 1987, p. A12).
5. Sana Hasan (1986:222) reports the following observation of a kibbutznik friend: "I was patriotic once—I was proud of being called to the army after I finished school. But a year later, when I went back to school to attend a friend's graduation ceremony, the headmaster gave a speech and said, 'More graduates

of this school have fallen in the wars than those of any other school.' And he was proud of it!''
6. This expression occurs frequently in political discourse (and not exclusively among humanist Zionists). For example, in a Knesset debate over the possibility of censoring a highly controversial politically satirical play, *The Patriot,* Knesset member Ora Namir (Labor), arguing against censorship, said it threatened the freedom of cultural production. She claimed that if censorship were imposed, "Israel will certainly not be a light unto the nations." It also appears in personal conversations. In an interview with the editor of the NRP affiliated newspaper *Hatzofe,* Moshe Eshon, on January 25, 1983, asked rhetorically, "I ask if we religious are partners in defining what is a light unto the nations?" At a conference on "Israel toward the Twenty-First Century," held at the Van Leer Institute in Jerusalem on March 9, 1983, Professor Gabi Ben-Dor (presently the rector of Haifa University) asked, "Should Israel be a light unto the nations, a Western nation, or a normal Middle Eastern nation?" He answered his question by favoring the Zionist dream to be a light unto the nations (quotation from my notes).
7. See, for example, Harold Fisch (1978); and Ian Lustick's excellent summary of it (Lustick, forthcoming).
8. See, for example, Israel Eldad (1971).
9. Interview with Rabbi Menachem HaCohen, MK (Labor), on December 6, 1982.
10. References to this type of paranoia appeared frequently in interviews. For example, both Gad Yacobi, MK (Labor), and Professor Shevach Weiss, MK (Labor), in separate interviews, on January 4, 1983, argued that the appeal to Jewish paranoia was a basis of the Begin regime. Former Foreign Minister Abba Eban, MK (Labor), suggested in an interview the same day that paranoia was an orientation that became a self-fulfilling prophecy for Begin's government. "Psychologically, Begin wants to be alone, since he knows how to act under siege."
11. In his analysis of the leadership of Techiya, Rosenbaum (1987) suggests that Geula Cohen (whom he calls Techiya's emotional center) presumes that the non-Jewish world is incorrigibly anti-Semitic. Although I have heard her make such statements in public (including a Knesset debate on the Reagan proposal), in private conversation (e.g., an interview on July 12, 1983) she qualifies her statements much more carefully, emphasizing the notion of "a nation that dwells alone." Professor Yuval Ne'eman posits the cultural permanence of Arab hostility and diplomatic duplicity. In an interview on July 4, 1983, he told me that the Jewish terrorists who attacked the Arab mayors "did good work" because it created quiet in Judea and Samaria. The son-in-law of Rabbi Eliezer Waldman was one of the convicted members of the Jewish terrorist underground and he is considered to be one of their spiritual leaders. He considers people like Shulamit Aloni and Yosie Sarid (both of the Citizens' Rights movement) "sick" because they are "oversensitive to what the Goyim [non-Jews] think" (interview on July 11, 1983).
12. See Seliktar (1986), especially chap. 3. Peleg (1987) gives a full analysis of what he calls Begin's neo-revisionism, a fundamental tenet of which is the negation of the outside, non-Jewish world, which he sees as fundamentally anti-Semitic. In an interview on November 1, 1982, Shulamit Aloni, MK (Citizens' Rights movement), suggested that Begin has the minority mentality of the victim, and that "he plays the victim both internationally and locally." She characterized

him as an example of a "slave who became king," who sought to return the people "to its barbaric tribal past."

13. Caspi and Nir (unpublished), Rowland (1985), and Peleg (1987) have analyzed other aspects of Begin's rhetoric.

14. Begin's biographers have all stressed the importance of the Holocaust in his life and in his thinking. See Haber (1978), Golan and Nakdimone (1978), and Perlmuter (1987). Peleg suggests that "Holocaust-fixation" is a major characteristic of Begin's neo-revisionism. In an interview (December 23, 1982) Ehud Olmert, a Likud parliamentarian close to Begin, told me, "For Begin the Holocaust is the single most important event in his life." In an interview on June 7, 1983, Meiron Benvenisti suggested that the fact that Begin left his family in Warsaw, where they perished in the Holocaust, had a profound influence on his vision, for example, in perceiving Arafat as Hitler. Begin is not alone. For example, Dr. Yisrael Eldad (the ideologue of Techiya), speaking at a symposium on "Jerusalem—Personal Perspectives" (at Yad Ben-Zvi on May 11, 1983), emotionally described seeing the apparition of his two brothers who died in the Holocaust during the military parade celebrating the liberation of Jerusalem, which he said was "a response of the Holocaust."

15. In the aforementioned interview, Olmert said, "In the collective memory of this people there is a built-in suspicion of even the pleasant faces of non-Jews in dealing with us. . . . The safeguards a Jew must take differ from those which a non-Jew should take, since we are subject to different treatment."

16. In an interview on June 7, 1983, Rabbi HaCohen explained in detail, citing the Rambam (Maimonides), the importance in Jewish tradition of reburial in Israel. He claimed that "the minute this is made into a state ceremony it becomes a circus, even grotesque. They lack genuine historic perspective. They take things from historical context and place them in the present. When you have an ancient burial in modern uniforms it doesn't work."

17. As Michael Dekel noted (in an interview on November 22, 1982): "Zionism wasn't ever rational."

18. It is significant in this respect that David Ben-Gurion deliberately ignored the period of the Diaspora in Jewish history (and the rabbinic tradition), attempting to build a direct link between the periods of biblical Jewish independence and contemporary Israel.

19. Rosenbaum (1987:12) states: "Tehiya asserts that yielding to the negative aspects of Western culture has weakened Israel: it has produced . . . *a failure to apply the lessons of history*" (italics added).

20. As I was preparing to send this manuscript to press, I received copies of unpublished papers by Handelman and Shamgar-Handelman and by Zeruvabel, and a published essay by Schwartz, Zeruvabel, and Barnett (1986), which treat the role of myth, history, and time in Israeli political culture.

Epilogue

*What was will never be again, and what will be, is
not what was [Amos Oz¹].*

During the better part of the tenure of the national unity government, the leaders of the two major political alignments developed a fairly close working relationship. The fact that their political careers depended upon their successful collaboration undoubtedly induced them to find a common language. Shimon Peres was particularly effective in utilizing the first two years in which he served as prime minister to demonstrate to the nation his leadership ability. It might have been in his and his party's short-term interest to have utilized one of several "crises" that occurred during the government's tenure to break up the coalition so that he would not have had to hand over the premiership to Yitzhak Shamir. Had Peres done so, he would have lost significant credibility.²

Since one of Peres's most important accomplishments had been to overcome the distrust of many who had suspected him of being an unreliable political opportunist, such a move would have been self-defeating in the long run. In addition, the chances for Labor to have built a viable narrow coalition without the Likud were very slim at best, and another election at the time would have in all likelihood reproduced the parliamentary stalemate that initially necessitated the formation of the unity government.

Yitzhak Shamir had a vital personal stake in the continuation of the unity government, since its terms dictated that he personally (and not an unnamed representative of the Likud) was to exchange offices with Peres at the end of two years. Shamir was fighting a rear-guard defense of his leadership against strong challenges from both Arik Sharon and David Levy, so it was imperative for him that the rotation take place without his having to face new elections. Given the complementary nature of their political interests, Peres and Shamir worked together for three years more successfully than anyone had predicted. In fact, the strongest criticism and challenges to their leadership, particularly that of Shamir, came from within their respective parties rather than between them during this period.

Whereas this close cooperation bore tangible positive benefits, especially the withdrawal of most Israeli forces from Lebanon and a significant improvement of the Israeli economy, it also came at a significant cost. The political stalemate that enabled Shamir to block the Peres initiative to hold an international conference that would have provided the umbrella needed by King Hussein of Jordan in order to enter into negotiations was undoubtedly the greatest price. Another significant cost was the lack of a viable parliamentary opposition, which contributed to the erosion of political responsiveness and responsibility. This political *immobilism* in turn has contributed to a crisis in political legitimacy.

This crisis is likely to become conspicuously more manifest after the 1988 election. This would occur if political stalemate results in another so-called unity government that is incapable of acting resolutely on the most critical issue facing the nation, or alternatively, if a narrow coalition government is formed that resolutely follows a policy strongly opposed by approximately half the electorate. Yet another possibility would be that the constraint produced by the knowledge that the government's parliamentary majority is so slim might prevent either a Labor- or a Likud-led narrow government from acting resolutely. Each scenario is likely to threaten the legitimacy of the regime, which could threaten to influence the erosion of legitimacy of the political parties and institutions like the government and the parliament.

The unity government formed in 1984, by far the broadest in forty years of Israeli political independence, failed to undertake electoral reform, which might have significantly strengthened political responsiveness. Nor did it undertake measures that might have strengthened civil liberties, such as the passage of a bill of rights. Political vision and the long-term interests of the nation were sacrificed for political expediency calculated through the perception of short-term interests of the two major parties in the next election. Preoccupation (bordering on obsession) with the interests of the smaller, particularly the religious, parties aborted any attempt at political reform.

Whereas the convergence of the policies of the two major parties and the aforementioned coincidence of political interests of their main leaders enabled the government to function reasonably well, the remaining political divisions prevented the government from communicating even a semblance of a common Zionist vision of sufficient salience to unite or to motivate the nation. On the contrary, the incivility demonstrated within the cabinet among its members toward one another (even within the same party) set the tone for (although did not cause) manifestations of rampant individualism unconstrained by a sense of civic responsibility among the general public.[3]

Obviously many factors contribute to such an absence of civic commitment. Irving Louis Horowitz suggests that it is in part due to "Years of shtetl living which equipped Jews for struggle rather than rule; a middle-east context inhospitable to a civic culture; conflictual (military) solutions to major conflicts rather than consensual (civilian) solutions."[4] The sense of loss of mission characterized by the erosion of political legitimacy and the declining efficacy and salience of Zionism would seem to be an important cause for the felt loss of community and the conspicuous lack of civic commitment and civility.

The advent of the election campaign would have certainly resulted in a heightening of the rhetorical polemics between the coalition partners. However, the widespread civil uprising of the Palestinian inhabitants in the occupied territories (which began in December 1987),[5] and the resultant American diplomatic initiative provided unique conditions in which the "honeymoon" between Peres and Shamir, Labor and the Likud, came to an abrupt end. Clear signs of attempts to delegitimize Peres and Labor, which characterized the 1981 election campaign, are being sounded not only by the ultranationalists, but also by those close to the prime minister, and even by Shamir himself.[6] Peres is being accused of dividing the nation as it confronts the double challenge of the civil "disturbances" of the Palestinians and the anticipated pressure from the Americans. "Shamir's spokesman Yossi Ahimeir told the Reuter news agency that 'it will be very good if Labour decides to leave the government because they are no longer real partners or loyal to the coalition agreement they signed.' "[7] In a meeting in which senior Likud ministers (Sharon and Moda'i) called for the prime minister to fire Peres, Shamir was reported to have "accused Peres of *disloyalty*."[8]

Whereas Shamir's initial response to the American initiative appeared to be conciliatory, an immediate attack from David Levy forced him to beat a fast retreat from his initial manifestation of flexibility. Shamir's balancing act demanded that he not allow Peres to appear to be the only proponent of peace, while at the same time he had to assure his constituents that he had not sold out his commitment to the greater land of Israel.

Similarly Peres attempted to set a course that would, on one hand, differentiate Labor's position clearly from that of the Likud, while, on the other hand, he attempted to attract disenchanted Likud voters and other floating voters to Labor. Since the initial public reaction to the uprising in the territories, and to the demonstrations of support by Israeli Arabs, tended to indicate a shift to the right toward more nationalistic positions, Peres was particularly in a quandary. However, as the uprisings continued and government policies to suppress them aroused greater public revulsion and increased international condemnation, Peres became more outspoken in pushing for a political solution based on the need for territorial compromise. However, he was particularly hampered by the fact that the hardline "bone-breaking" policy being pursued was articulated and implemented by Yitzhak Rabin who, in so doing, became the darling of the nationalist right. Labor also withheld official involvement or collaboration with Peace Now, thereby depriving the largest peace movement of important logistical support.

It is noteworthy that both Gush Emunim and Peace Now, which had been major nonparliamentary actors in earlier periods, had relatively low public profiles during the first few weeks of the uprisings. Whereas individual settlers engaged in acts of vigilante reprisals, they did not appear to be organized.[9] Although both Gush Emunim and Peace Now sponsored demonstrations and issued public statements, particularly from around mid-February, neither was as publicly visible, vocal, or effective as they had been in previous periods.

A number of factors account for these changes. For both, their unofficial co-optation by political parties meant that it was the parliamentary parties rather than the extraparliamentary movements that took the initial political initiative. During this period Techiya, Mapam, and the Citizens' Rights movement (Ratz), among others, sponsored an unprecedented number of votes of nonconfidence in the government.[10] In fact, Ratz and Techiya were particularly active. For example, two Ratz MKs conducted an investigation of conditions in Gaza, documented abuses by Israeli troops, and filed a well-publicized report with the Knesset Security and Foreign Affairs Committee.

Ratz and Techiya were visible outside the parliamentary context as well. For example, Knesset members representing Ratz and Techiya faced each other in a prime-time television interview, which turned into a heated debate. Even more unusually, an Arab Knesset member representing the Rakach-dominated Democratic Front for Peace and Equality participated in this program as well, as did former Chief of Staff Raphael "Raful" Eitan, who had recently split away from Techiya to become a one-man Knesset faction called Tsomet.[11]

Gush Emunim took several weeks to reactivate and mobilize its supporters in response to Shamir's initial responsiveness to the American peace initiative, which implied that he might be willing to make territorial concessions that are completely unacceptable to the settlers. Had Shamir not beat a fast retreat in response to the challenge of David Levy, there would have been a far greater mobilization of the militant Greater Land of Israel supporters to counter such a danger. In fact Techiya initiated such a mobilization (discussed below), which would undoubtedly escalate to violent confrontations with the government among the most militant sectors of the national camp (led by the militant wing of Gush Emunim) if the negotiations would result in Israel agreeing to make territorial concessions on the West Bank.

The peace camp made a very impressive showing during this period. Although it was slow to mobilize, once it did so Peace Now organized four major protest rallies within five weeks, starting in mid-February. However, the largest peace movement lost the initiative to dozens of peace groups that spontaneously sprouted after the uprisings began, like mushrooms after heavy rains. Some established groups like the East for Peace movement made virtually no public impact at all. Others like Yesh Gvul, which had been dormant since the withdrawal from Lebanon, reactivated and began distributing booklets to soldiers outlining their right to refuse illegal orders in the territories and warning them that they were criminally liable for obeying such orders. They also provide counseling to soldiers. Likewise Parents against Silence (the successor to Soldiers against Silence), which was active during the war in Lebanon, resumed its activities.

The two religious peace movements, Oz v'Shalom and Netivot Shalom, joined forces and sponsored a series of well-attended educational lectures on themes pertaining to peace and the territories, which received coverage in the media. Rabbi Aharon Lichtenstein, head of the nation's largest *hesder yeshiva,* has come to play a central spiritual role in the religious peace movement. Whereas "The Chief Rabbinical Council issues a statement calling on the army to 'be strong and courageous in keeping order in all parts of our Holy Land," Rabbi Lichtenstein "spoke of the moral dilemma of soldiers and the need to make 'possibly painful concessions.' "[12] Rabbi David Hartman (director of the Shalom Hartman Institute of Jewish Studies and senior lecturer in philosophy at the Hebrew University) wrote: "If we are seriously concerned over the holiness of Israel and with God's dwelling in the land, then it is imperative that we ask what will happen to the moral character of the nation, what will become of our Judaic heritage if we dispossess or subjugate a vast population?"[13]

In speaking out on the spiritual implications of occupation and the policy of beating demonstrators (which has led to widespread abuses), Rabbis Lichtenstein and Hartman were among a minority of Israel's spiritual leaders. However, they are not unimportant figures. Lichtenstein is a rabbinical authority who is respected even by those who disagree with his views on the need to make territorial concessions in the interest of peace.

Hartman is known to be consulted for advice by Zevulan Hammer, a leader of the National Religious party.[14] Their humanistic Orthodoxy could possibly form the spiritual vanguard of a resurgence of a moderate peace-oriented religious political force. There have been serious discussions among the moderates and doves in the Mafdal about founding their own party. Particularly if they were to team up with Labor Knesset member Rabbi Menachem HaCohen, who is contemplating running on a separate ticket (with Labor's blessing), such a party might find a supportive constituency among the religious public.[15]

Among the approximately two dozen new peace groups that emerged at the end of 1987 and the outset of 1988, one of the more noteworthy is the Red Line. Its twin goals are to press for peace and to bring Jews and Arabs together under the slogan "End the Occupation." It was the first of the peace movements successful to involve Israeli Arabs in its activities. The Red Line sponsored a four-day march, which began on Feburary 28, 1988, in Rosh Hanikra (on the border with Lebanon) with 400 Jewish and Arab participants, passed through Haifa and Tel Aviv where major rallies were held, and ended in a rally in Jerusalem. The organizers claimed the support of some fifty-five groups working for Jewish-Arab cooperation in Israel and twenty-five peace groups (excluding Peace Now, which refrained from giving the march its official support). The Red Line rallies in Tel Aviv and Jerusalem drew the unprecedented support of large numbers of popular entertainers who had never previously taken public stands on controversial political issues. Shortly before the Red Line finale in Jerusalem, twenty-seven students of the Bezalel Academy of Arts and Design were arrested for marching with masks and signs reading "Don't Destroy Our Humanity."

One example of many different types of public gatherings was a convocation of intellectuals in Tel Aviv under the slogan "Talk Peace with the Palestinians." Another meeting organized by the Playwrights Association, held at the Tzavta Club in Tel Aviv, drew 400 intellectuals. The Jerusalem Artists and Sculptors Association was followed by Tel Aviv artists in calling for dialogue with the Palestinians, and various galleries launched special exhibits of artists reacting to the events in the territories.

Ad-hoc coalitions of various groups like Netivot Shalom, Israelis by Choice (composed predominantly of immigrants from English-speaking countries), the Mevakshei Derech synagogue, End the Occupation, and the Association for Civil Rights in Israel set up a hotline of information about events in the territories, legal aid to victims of illegal orders, and a bulletin board of peace camp activities.[16] Others like the Twenty-First Year (of Israeli occupation) called for civil disobedience. In an attempt to overcome the duplication of efforts and the self-defeating consequences of groups with similar goals working at cross purposes (e.g., by scheduling different events at the same time), a grand coalition of twenty-seven peace groups was formed at a conference attended by senior representatives of all of the groups (except Peace Now, which did not send leading figures of the movement) at the Tzavta theater in Tel Aviv on February 25, 1988. Peace Now's fear of alienating its more moderate supporters has cost it the leading role that it had previously played in the peace camp.

Although many factors have influenced these developments, perhaps the most important has been the actions of the Palestinians living under Israeli occupation who are convincing increasingly large numbers of Israelis that the status quo is not a viable solution, and that retention of the territories through the overt suppression of its inhabitants is a price not worth paying.[17]

Until December 1987 the amount of physical coercion required to maintain "order" in the territories was relatively low and was considered to be acceptable to most Israelis. Those who actually used the most violence were restricted to "specialists" in the Shin Bet and the Border Police (the latter especially being composed primarily of Jews from Arabic-speaking countries and Druze). Therefore the bulk of the population, including troops who patrolled the areas, were not generally exposed to the nastier side of the occupation. What people did not see or "know" did not bother their consciences, and they could point to many benefits that the inhabitants enjoyed as a result of the Israeli presence.

However, the mass civil uprising that began in December (which apparently took the authorities completely by surprise) forced the government to use large numbers of troops, regular army as well as reserves, in an attempt to "restore order." Consequently practically everyone in Israel, either directly or through a son, husband, father, or friend, became exposed to things that it had been convenient and comfortable to ignore when it had been possible to do so. The adoption of the policy of beating demonstrators, which led to excesses widely reported throughout the world, brought out the sadist in some, but aroused the consciences of many others. As one reported, "The more I break other people's bones, the more I am broken myself."[18]

In typical Israeli fashion the army dispatched teams of psychologists to help soldiers deal with the psychological problems that resulted from their carrying out duties that were a direct contradiction of the time-honored Israeli military policy of the purity of arms as well as their personal values. Over 500 professional psychiatrists, psychologists, and mental-health workers, most of whom had never been involved in any previous political activities or petitions, published a letter in all Israeli newspapers demanding the government find a political solution to the occupation, which was threatening the mental health of those who enforced the governments policies. They warned of the dangers to Israeli society by the unlikelihood of being able to confine the violence to the occupied territories. They are planning workshops and preparing a study showing the effects of the occupation on Israeli society.

A similar petition, by an ad-hoc group called the Interuniversity Movement for a Political Settlement, and signed by 600 academicians, including leading scholars who had never signed a political petition in their lives, was also well publicized. They also held teach-ins on every campus in the country.

However, if the uprisings have precipitated a reappraisal that is leading many to urge the path of political compromise, they have had precisely the opposite effect on many others. For example, the aforementioned petition of "dovish" professors sparked a petition from a group of 600 "hawkish" academics calling for a firmer stand in the territories, more support for the security forces, and a peace agreement that would not come at the expense of Israel's security. For the militant nationalists and ultranationalists, the violence confirms their belief that compromise is impossible and that the only way to deal with the Arabs is through a show of force. Some even argue for the deportation of hundreds of "trouble-makers," and the most extreme demand the "transfer" of masses of Palestinians across the borders. The extremists were actually pleased when some of the demonstrations of Israeli Arabs on "Peace Day" turned violent, because, they argued, it confirms the unreliability of all Arabs including those with Israeli citizenship. As Techiya leader Geula Cohen put it: "the stones thrown in Judea, Samaria and Gaza had 'opened the heads' of many of those who had thought that a Green Line existed and that the Arabs of Jerusalem, Jaffa, and Wadi Ara wanted anything different from those of Nablus and Hebron."[19]

On February 13 Peace Now held a major rally in Jerusalem to memorialize the anniversary of the murder of Emile Grunzweig. When asked by an interviewer on television, two men who survived serious wounds from the same hand grenade that killed Grunzweig expressed their conviction that what happened to them could happen again. They expressed anxiety that the climate of delegitimization of dovish opinions is beginning again. As if to prove their point, Knesset members of the Likud and Techiya demanded the removal of the parliamentary immunity of Yair Tzaban (Mapam) who (at the aforementioned Peace Now rally) called on Defense Minister Rabin to tell soldiers that "orders to beat in order to break bones are unlawful and should be refused."[20]

Likud faction whip Yehoshua Matza, accusing Tzaban of inciting soldiers to flout orders, said, "That man must be neutralized, and we shall see that he is." Techiya Knesset members set up a tent in front of the prime minister's office in order to collect signatures to a petition calling on the government to "halt the erosion of its policy in the territories." At this Techiya "encampment" Geula Cohen was quoted as saying, "We know those tricks of the left. Mapam, the Citizens Rights Movement, and Foreign Minister Shimon Peres, too, are interested in fomenting and prolonging the riots."[21]

With the doves becoming more dovish and the hawks more hawkish, people who had previously managed to avoid taking a position are being forced to do so. The population is becoming more polarized and the situation is moving in the direction that characterized the 1981 election campaign and the period of protest against the war in Lebanon, which several observers felt, had it continued, might have led to a kind of civil war. Whereas civil war is most unlikely, under certain conditions the situation could rapidly deteriorate into conditions worse than those in the period between 1981 and 1983. A great deal depends on the tone that will be set by those at the helm of government. Since the most likely escalation of polarization would come from intensified and more widespread attempts by the nationalists to delegitimize Peres and Labor by calling into question their loyalty, much will depend on whether Shamir is capable of demonstrating statesmanlike vision and national responsibility to rise above narrow partisan interests and contain the escalation of polarization that has already begun. Thus far he has not shown such statesmanship.

An equally great challenge lies before Peres to display the necessary political courage to lead the nation by persuading its citizens to make sacrifices and to take risks to overcome the present deadlock. Only strong and courageous leadership, and the right circumstances, could persuade a majority of the Israeli public to take the risks and make the sacrifices necessary to achieve peace with the Palestinians and other important Arab neighbors. Much depends on progress being made in the peace process and what kind of settlement (if any) is worked out.

An important factor influencing this process is the structure of the party system. This writer has suggested (Aronoff, 1986b) that as Labor and the Likud compromise to accommodate each other and to compete for the floating vote, they alienate those who remain faithful to their traditional ideological stances. The compromising and movement toward the center of the two major blocs have produced what the present writer has termed the "splinter" parties, which (to a certain extent) have split from them. Labor and the Likud not only compete with each other, they compete with their respective splinter (or satellite) parties—Mapam and the Citizens' Rights movement, for Labor; and Techiya and Tsomet, for the Likud.

These splinter parties compete with their respective "parent" parties, but also compete with what we can term the "marginal" parties, which are on the fringes of the political system. For Mapam and Ratz, the Progressive List and Rakach might be considered competitors, but are less so than is Tsomet and Kach for Techiya. The reason the Progressive List and Rakach are the only qualified competitors of Ratz and Mapam is because they are non-Zionist (and some would say anti-Zionist) parties, whereas Mapam and Ratz are definitely Zionist parties.

The Likud is much more influenced by Techiya, Tsomet, and even Kach than Labor is influenced by Mapam and Ratz. Labor is not in the least bit influenced by the Progressive List or Rakach. There are a number of reasons for this. First of all the Likud is a much less-well-institutionalized and more ideological party than is Labor. Thirty-five-years' dependence upon the authority of Begin makes the competition over succession critical for determining the future character and policy of the Likud. Having spent nearly thirty years in the opposition, Begin and the party he lead could maintain the purity of their ideology. However, once they came to power, pragmatic compromises of ideology were unavoidable.

It is important to keep in mind that whereas Geula Cohen did not lead many of her fellow Herut colleagues away from their parent party when she formed Techiya, the majority of the Likud Knesset faction voted against or abstained on the ratification of the Israel-Egypt peace treaty. Shamir and the successor whom he personally favors, Moshe Arens, abstained. Arik Sharon's ideology is identical to those in Techiya. It is only his desire to become prime minister that keeps him in the Likud. Michael Dekel's call for transfer of the Palestinians places him close to the ideological camp of Meir Kahane, and yet his post as deputy defense minister and his position in the Likud remain secure (as does that of Yosef Shapira in the NRP). The dynamics of the chain reaction of extremism (mentioned in the introduction to this volume) are most operative on the nationalist right.

There are several reasons why the same dynamic is much less operative on the left. First, the most extreme anti-Zionist elements in Israel do not vote, therefore they have less influence on the parliamentary parties, and only a negative influence on the mainstream ones. Second, the votes for which Labor competes with the non-Zionist parties are those of Arabs toward whom Labor has traditionally acted with paternalism. Since Abdel Wahab Darousha split from Labor and established a one-man Knesset faction in protest against Labor's role in the government's policies of brutal suppression of the Palestinian uprising in the territories, Labor will be forced to change fundamentally its attitude toward, and relations with, Israel's Arab citizens if it hopes to stem the loss of their votes, which is anticipated in the forthcoming elections.

Third, since Mapam left the Alignment and Yossi Sarid joined Ratz, the influence of the most outspoken doves in Labor has diminished. The two highest-ranking and most articulate doves, Ezer Weizman and Abba Eban, lack strong constituencies within the party. Weizman is a literal outsider, having come from the Likud, and Eban is a figurative outsider.[22] Although the young doves who constitute an important staff that advises Shimon Peres (such as Dr. Yosi Beilin, political director-general of the Foreign Ministry) are influential, their dependence on his patronage sets clear limits to their influence. On the other hand, many of the militant adherents to the great-land-of-Israel philosophy within Labor abandoned it for Techiya and Tsomet. Consequently, in spite of the fact that Labor is a heterogeneous party that has long been considered to be an ideological supermarket, it is relatively united under Peres in its position on peace negotiations.

What differentiates Labor from the parties to its left, and what it shares with the Likud, is the rejection of the PLO as a possible partner for negotiations. Although Labor favors territorial compromise in return for peace, and the Likud emphatically rejects territorial concessions, neither is willing to consider the possibility of recognizing the PLO as a legitimate representative of the Palestinian people. In the unlikely eventuality that Yasser Arafat would unambiguously recognize the legitimacy of a Jewish state in the pre-1967 borders, renounce terrorism, abrogate the most offensive sections of the PLO charter, and survive assassination attempts long enough actually to engage in negotiations, Labor would agree to sit with him, but it could only do so if it headed a government that was not dependent upon Likud support.

Arafat is unlikely to meet these conditions, and no Israeli government is likely to meet his conditions of complete withdrawal from all occupied territories prior to negotiations. Therefore a peace settlement without the participation of the PLO would depend upon a popularly based Palestinian leadership independent of the PLO. It is highly unlikely that they will achieve complete independence, but, as the recent debate between Palestinian leaders resident in the West Bank and Gaza with the leaders of the PLO over whether the former should meet with United States Secretary of State George Shultz indicates, they are likely to develop greater autonomy and possibly unity than they have ever had previously.[23] The holding of local elections in the territories might possibly offer the means through which Israeli leaders could negotiate with responsible Palestinian leaders who have legitimate claim to representing their constituency. However, the negotiation of some interim arrangement can be successful only if it is agreed that it is temporary and that a permanent one ultimately will offer the prospect of full political sovereignty for the Palestinians.[24]

In a very real sense the challenge of the Palestinians goes much deeper than merely the question of borders. It calls into question the legitimacy of Zionism. The essence of the Palestinian challenge is the rejection of the legitimacy of the claim for a Jewish state. Whereas the mainstream within Zionism has historically made significant pragmatic compromises (ideological and territorial), it cannot compromise the very essence of its worldview, the raison d'être of its existence. That is why even the most dovish Zionists, who recognize the right of the Palestinian people to national self-determination and sovereignty, demand that those who claim to represent the Palestinian people offer tangible evidence that they reciprocally recognize the Jewish right to political sovereignty in Israel. The most tangible evidence that could be offered would be a revision of the PLO charter and the renunciation of terror. Such an act would be the equivalent of Sadat's dramatic visit to Jerusalem, and could have as dramatic an impact on Israeli public opinion as did that historic event. Tragically, moderate Palestinian leaders who have engaged in dialogue with Israel have been systematically assassinated (by Abu Nidal's and other extremist groups). The late Dr. Issam Sartawi is one of many such Palestinian martyrs who paid with his life for engaging in a dialogue with Israel.

In spite of the significant divisions among Zionists, the analysis of which has been the heart of this book, they all share the conviction that the Jewish people have an absolute right to political sovereignty in their ancient homeland. They also share (in greatly varying degrees), along with many Jews who do not consider themselves Zionists, an insecurity and distrust of the intentions of non-Jews toward them, which derives from a historical collective memory of persecution, as well as, for many, bitter personal experiences. The suspicion of outside intentions is particularly strong concerning neighboring Arab states and the leadership of the PLO. The strong conviction of their right to national Jewish sovereignty (although deeply divided over the definition of what should constitute the Jewish character of the nationality and the state) unites Zionists of all ideological persuasions.

What fundamentally divides Israeli Zionists is their evaluation of whether or not the Jewish people and its state are capable of being "normal," and whether or not such a condition (if it is possible) is one that should be sought. Essentially the humanist Zionists, even those who aspire for Israel to be a light unto the nations, aspire to normalcy (even if it may be an unobtainable condition). The nationalists believe that the Jewish people, and consequently its state, are fated to be a nation that dwells alone. The ultranationalists glory in Israel's abnormality, its isolation, and consider this singularity as proof of providential "chosenness." As was indicated in the previous chapter, these orientations are related to varying perceptions of security and different subcultural temporal notions of history. The humanists tend toward greater security, perceive history as a linear process, and aspire to national normalcy. There is an inverse relationship between degrees of nationalism and perceptions of security. There is a positive relationship between degrees of nationalism and perceptions of history as myth, or temporal notions of totemic time.

In a very real sense the present situation is forcing many Israelis to reevaluate and to redefine the essence of Zionism a century after its beginnings and how it relates to the state of Israel in its fortieth year of independence. Such fundamental challenges to perceptions of reality, which have been taken for granted by so many people for so long, are perceived by those thrust into confusion and self-doubt as a great danger. However, with perspective, this situation can also be seen to be a tremendously liberating one, since it allows for considerable freedom in the reinvigoration or re-creation of cultural paradigms, which may also open up new political options.

For example, Meiron Benvenisti has observed, "The whole myth of Jerusalem being different from the West Bank is now out in the open for everyone to see for what it is. For Israelis, it's like spitting in their faces. They're robbed of the illusion that Jerusalem is different."[25] This illusion began with Rabbi Goren blowing the shofar at the newly liberated Western Wall. De'er suggests that this event heralded the birth of Israel's national religious messianism.[26] Whereas all cultural perceptions are illusory by nature, some are more remote from reality than others. The euphoric national religious messianism that engulfed Israel and set the tone for policy during the Begin era was dominated by nonrational perceptions of reality, which blinded policymakers and much of the public to important political realities. These realities have now begun to penetrate the cultural membranes that have filtered them out over the years, and in so doing are calling into question the assumptions upon which they were based.

Ricoeur (1986:16) suggests that utopia's function is to develop new alternative perspectives. He suggests that the imagination itself "has a *constitutive* role in helping us *rethink* the nature of our social life." Such radical rethinking allows the reconsideration of authority and the introduction of "imaginative variations on the topics of society, power, government, family, religion." What Israel most needs at present are courageous leaders, who can combine pragmatic policies that will lead the nation to peace and who can articulate new utopian visions that will give legitimacy to these policies and a meaningful sense of national purpose to all of the people living in Israel. It will require a move away from particularism and tribalism toward universalism and humanism. The old policies have proved bankrupt and the old ideologies have lost their salience. There is no turning back. But the future is rife with as many possibilities and promises as it is with threats and dangers.

Notes

1. Robert Rosenberg, " 'What was will never be again, and what will be, is not what was,' Says Amos Oz," *Jerusalem Post,* February 19, 1988, p. 4.
2. For example, the series of scandals that broke out involving the internal security service (Shin Bet), or the "Pollard affair," were sufficiently serious to have justified a split in the government. There are obviously many factors in addition to the ones I stress that constrained Peres from exploiting these scandals. For example, former security chief Isser Harel claims, "The norms that Peres introduced as director-general of the Defense Ministry and later as deputy defense minister under Ben-Gurion lie at the root of the Pollard affair. . . . As he set up his own foreign affairs network in the Defense Ministry, he set up the forerunner of Lekem"—the scientific liaison unit of the Israeli Defense Ministry, which recruited and ran Jonathan Jay Pollard, the American Jewish naval intelligence analyst serving a life sentence for spying for Israel (quoted from David Richardson's interview with Isser Harel in an article entitled "Spycatcher" in the *Jerusalem Post* February 12, 1988, p. 8). Although the recruitment of Pollard took place when Moshe Arens was the minister of defense, the network continued to operate under Yitzhak Rabin's tenure as defense minister. The head of Lekem (before it was disbanded in the wake of Pollard's arrest), Rafi Eitan, is a very close political associate of Arik Sharon. Therefore both major parties, and most of the top leaders of them, were at least indirectly implicated in the affair, although a government-appointed commission and an investigation by the Knesset Foreign Affairs and Security Commission both reported that Pollard had been run as a "renegade" operation without the knowledge of the responsible ministers.
3. Manifestations of such incivility range from frequent exhibitions of public rudeness, litter, and despoiling of public places and natural areas (in sharp contrast for the care shown for private property) to the shocking neglect of patients in the nation's hospitals during prolonged strikes. I would even suggest that the absence of civility is a contributory factor to the horrendous rate of traffic accidents (the injuries and fatalities of which exceed those suffered in all of Israel's wars).
4. Personal correspondence (12/1/87).
5. Although the government originally labeled them civil "disturbances," as if to play down their significance, before long even they were using the term "uprising" and the Hebrew-speaking public even incorporated the Arabic term *intifada* (uprising) into its vocabulary.
6. This chapter was completed in February 1988.
7. Menachem Shalev, "Shamir, Peres Swap 'Blunt' Statements," *Jerusalem Post,* February 15, 1988, p. 1.
8. Michal Udelman, "Likud Ministers Demand That Peres Be Fired," *Jerusalem Post,* February 16, 1988, p. 2 (italics added).
9. Many were in fact identified with Kahane's Kach movement rather than Gush Emunim.
10. Although other issues prompted such votes as well, e.g., the shocking condi-

tions in government hospitals due to prolonged strikes, the government's handling of the situation in the territories was the primary target of criticism from both the left and the right. There were so many votes of nonconfidence that frequently the responsible members delegated the minister of transportation with replying on their behalf, which on some occasions he did for several ministers at a time, e.g., health, finance, and defense, since he was the only cabinet member present during the Knesset plenum. During the eleventh Knesset up to February 10, 1988, 105 no-confidence motions were submitted, of which 67 were submitted during the last year (Devorah Getzler and Asher Wallfish, "Knesset Unhappy with Its 'Jack of All Trades,' " *Jerusalem Post,* February 11, 1988, p. 2).

11. I note that as long as the two major blocs closed ranks, the criticism by Ratz and Techiya of government policy was ineffective from a parliamentary perspective although it had an effect on the public, which put pressure on the respective parties. I discuss this in more detail below.

12. Haim Shapiro, "Rabbi in the Cause of Peace," *Jerusalem Post,* February 12, 1988, p. 5.

13. David Hartman, "A Religious Perspective on the Conflict," *Jerusalem Post,* February 12, 1988, p. 9.

14. Clearly Hammer does not always follow Hartman's advice. Although Hammer has retreated somewhat from the extreme nationalism of the more militant Gush Emunim positions, he has certainly not returned the Mafdal to the pragmatism and moderation that characterized it under previous leaders.

15. Given the decentralization of procedures for the nominations for Knesset in Labor, HaCohen is unlikely to be renominated, since he lacks the support of an organized branch. Labor would like him to attract the support of alienated moderate Mafdal supporters. A moderate religious party led by HaCohen could be relied upon for support on all issues vital to Labor, and would be an excellent coalition partner.

16. Robert Rosenberg's four-part series of articles on the "Peace Camp" in the *Jerusalem Post* (February 22, 23, 24, 25, 1988, each appearing on p. 4) and Daniel Gavron's essay on "Taking to the Streets," *Jerusalem Post Magazine,* February 26, 1988, pp. 4, 7, provide useful background on the various peace movements and protest activities.

17. Defense Minister Yitzhak Rabin said, "I've learned something in the past two-and-a-half months. Among other things that you can't rule by force over one-and-a-half million Palestinians" (Michael Yudelman, "Rabin: 'Impossible to Rule by Force,' " *Jerusalem Post,* February 22, 1988, p. 1).

18. Israeli army psychologists report that from 10 to 15 percent of the soldiers were "torn apart" by what they were doing, and some have refused to obey orders (reported by Joel Greenberg, "Uncontrolled Epidemic of Police and Army Violence," *Jerusalem Post,* February 12, 1988, p. 1). Most of our friends have sons presently serving in the army, and as tense as they are about the dangers involved in serving in southern Lebanon, many are equally if not more agonized about the moral and ethical problems posed by their sons having to carry out the present policies employed for suppressing the uprisings in Gaza and the West Bank. In a letter to the editor entitled "Licence to Hate," Carol Cook, whose two sons are currently doing their military service, condemns incidents of brutality and maltreatment of Arabs. She says, "And we will not be able to claim, as another people in another time once claimed, that we did

not know. . . . We know these things are happening. We read it in the press and we hear it from our own sons" (*Jerusalem Post,* February 19, 1988, p. 20).

19. Devorah Getzler, "Tehiya Takes Aim at Mapam's Tsaban for 'Incitement' at Peace Now Rally," *Jerusalem Post,* February 15, 1988, p. 2.
20. Ibid.
21. Ibid.
22. In 1977 Eban was asked by a television interviewer if he felt he was "integrated" into Israeli society. I asked my students at Tel Aviv University what they thought about such a question being posed to a man who had served his country for so many years as ambassador to the United Nations and foreign minister. They replied unanimously that they applauded the interviewer and thought he was "right on." Eban's demeanor (arrogant and aloof), appearance (extremely formal in a party and nation where few wear jackets, much less ties), and speech (particularly his rich vocabulary of infrequently used words) make him appear to be a foreigner to most Israelis. He has never been particularly popular in the party, although ironically his image among the public in general appears to have risen since the Labor party lost power. His lack of popularity in Labor and Israel is in strong contrast with his great popularity in the United States, and not just among Jews.
23. Joel Greenberg, "PLO, Palestinians Split over Meeting," *Jerusalem Post,* February 22, 1988, p. 1.
24. Even the most dovish Israelis would insist on demilitarization of a Palestinian state for a prolonged period to guarantee Israeli security.
25. Quoted by Andy Court, "Anata Camp, Angry and Afraid," *Jerusalem Post,* February 19, 1988, p. 7.
26. Benny Morris (1988b:10).

References

Andriolo, Karin R. 1981. "Myth and History: A General Model and Its Application to the Bible." *American Anthropologist* 83:2.

Aran, Gideon. 1985. *Eretz Yisrael Bane Dat V'Politica* (Eretz Israel: Between Politics and Religion). Jerusalem: Jerusalem Institute for Israel Studies, No. 18.

Arian, Asher. 1985. *Politics in Israel: The Second Generation.* Chatham: Chatham House.

———, and Samuel Barnes. 1974. "The Dominant Party System: A Neglected Model of Democratic Stability." *Journal of Politics* 36:3:592–614.

Aronoff, Myron J. 1974. *Frontiertown: The Politics of Community Building in Israel.* Manchester, Eng.: Manchester University Press.

———. 1977. *Power and Ritual in the Israel Labor Party.* Amsterdam/Assen: Van Gorcum.

———. 1979. "The Decline of the Israel Labor Party: Causes and Significance." In *Israel at the Polls: The Knesset Elections—1977.* Ed. Howard R. Penniman; pp. 115–45. Washington, D.C.: American Enterprise Institute.

———. 1980a. "Ideology and Interest: The Dialectics of Politics." In *Ideology and Interest: The Dialectics of Politics, Political Anthropology,* vol. 1. Ed. Myron J. Aronoff; pp. 1–29. News Brunswick: Transaction Publishers.

———. 1980b. "The Creation and Corruption of Civil Religion in Israel." A paper presented at the Burg Wartenstein Symposium No. 84, in Burg Wartenstein Castle, Austria, July 19–27.

———. 1981a. "Dominant Party Democracy: The Israeli Version." A paper presented at the annual meeting of the American Political Science Association in New York City, September 3–6.

———. 1981b. "Civil Religion in Israel." *Royal Anthropological Institute News* 44:2–6.

———. 1983. "Conceptualizing the Role of Culture in Political Change." In *Culture and Political Change, Political Anthropology,* vol. 2. Ed. Myron J. Aronoff; pp. 1–18. New Brunswick: Transaction Publishers.

———. 1984a. "Gush Emunim: The Institutionalization of a Charismatic, Messianic, Religious-Political Revitalization Movement in Israel." In *Religion and Politics, Political Anthropology,* vol. 3. Ed. Myron J. Aronoff; pp. 63–84. New Brunswick: Transaction Publishers.

———. 1984b. "Political Polarization: Contradictory Interpretations of Israeli Reality." In *Cross-Currents in Israeli Culture and Politics, Political Anthorpology,* vol. 4. Ed. Myron J. Aronoff; pp. 1–23. New Brunswick: Transaction Books.

———. 1986a. "Establishing Authority: The Memorialization of Jabotinsky and the Burial of the Bar-Kochba Bones in Israel under the Likud." In *The Frailty of Authority, Political Anthropology,* vol. 5. Ed. Myron J. Aronoff; pp. 105–30. New Brunswick: Transaction Books.

———. 1986b. "Significant Trends in Israeli Politics." In *Israel Faces the Future.* Ed. Bernard Reich and Gershon Kieval; pp. 29–51. New York: Praeger.

———. 1987. " 'Comments' on Ehud Sprinzak, *Fundamentalism, Terrorism, and Democracy.*" Washington, D.C.: Woodrow Wilson Occasional Paper.

———. 1988. "The Failure of Israel's Labor Party and the Emergence of Gush Emunim." In *The New Challenge to Political Parties: Emerging Alternative Organizations.* Ed. Kay Lawson and Peter H. Merkl; pp. 309–37. Princeton: Princeton University Press.

Avineri, Shlomo. 1980. "The Relevance of Ahad Ha'am." *Jerusalem Post,* International Edition, May 4–10.

———. 1981. *The Making of Modern Zionism.* London: Weidenfeld & Nicholson.

Avruch, Kevin A. 1978–79. "Gush Emunim: Politics, Religion, and Ideology." *Middle East Review* 11:26–31.

———. 1979. "Traditionalizing Israeli Nationalism: The Development of Gush Emunim." *Political Psychology* 1:1:47–57.

Bailey, F. G. 1981. "Dimensions of Rhetoric in Conditions of Uncertainty." In *Politically Speaking.* Ed. Robert Paine; pp. 25–38. Philadelphia: Institute for the Study of Human Issues.

Bar-Lev, Mordecai. 1977. "The Graduates of the Yeshiva High School in Eretz-Yisrael: Between Tradition and Innovation" (in Hebrew). Unpublished doctoral dissertation, Bar-Ilan University.

Bar-On, Mordecai. 1985. *Shalom Achshav: Lediukena Shel Tenua* (Peace Now: The Portrait of a Movement). Tel Aviv: Hakibbutz Hameuchad.

Bar-Zohar, Michael. 1978. *Ben-Gurion: A Biography.* Trans. Peretz Kidron. Jerusalem: Steimatzky.

Bauer, Julien. 1985. "A New Approach to Religious-Secular Relationships?" In *The Impact of Gush Emunim.* Ed. David Newman; pp. 91–110. London: Croom Helm.

Beit-Hallahmi, Benjamin. (Forthcoming.) *Despair and Deliverance.*

Bennet, W. Lance. 1982. "Culture, Communication, and Political Control." In *Culture and Political Change, Political Anthropology,* vol. 2. Ed. Myron J. Aronoff; pp. 39–52. New Brunswick: Transaction Publishers.

Benvenisti, Meiron. 1982. "The West Bank and Gaza Data Base Project Interim Report No. 1." Jerusalem: West Bank Data Base Project. Mimeographed.

———. 1984. "The West Bank Data Project: A Survey of Israel's Policies." Washington, D.C.: American Enterprise Institute.

Berger, Peter, and Thomas Luckmann. 1966. *The Social Construction of Reality.* London: George Allen & Unwin.

Blondel, Jean. 1969. *An Introduction to Comparative Government.* New York: Praeger.

Brenner, Uri. 1978. *Altalena* (in Hebrew). Tel Aviv: Hakibbutz Hameuchad.

Brilliant, Joshua. 1988. "Zeevi Encouraged by Response to 'Transfer.' " *Jerusalem Post,* February 23, pp. 1, 4.

Caspi, Dan and Raphael Nir. (Unpublished.) "Electoral Rhetoric—The Televised Debates in Israel." Mimeographed.

Coleman, James S. 1957. *Community Conflict*. New York: Free Press, for the Bureau of Applied Social Research, Columbia University.

Cook, Carol. 1988. "Licence to Hate." Letter to the editor, *Jerusalem Post*, February 19, p. 20.

Court, Andy. 1988. "Anata Camp, Angry and Afraid." *Jerusalem Post*, February 19, p. 7.

Diskin, Avraham. 1983. "Polarization and Volatility among Voters." In *The Roots of Begin's Success: The 1981 Elections*. Ed. Dan Caspi, Avraham Diskin, and Emanuel Gutmann; pp. 113–39. New York: St. Martin's Press.

Dominguez, Virginia. 1984. "The Language of Right and Left in Israeli Politics." In *Cross-Currents in Israeli Culture and Politics, Political Anthropology*, vol. 4. Ed. Myron J. Aronoff; pp. 89–110. New Brunswick: Transaction Books.

Don-Yehiya, Eliezer. 1981. "Origins and Development of the Aguda and Mafdal Parties." *Jerusalem Quarterly* 20:49–64.

Dudman, Helga. 1981. "Collective Resentment." *Jerusalem Post*, International Edition, July 19–25; p. 14.

Duverger, Maurice. 1967. *Political Parties*. Trans. Barbara and Robert North, with a foreword by D. W. Brogan. London: Meuthen. (Originally published in French in 1951 as *Les Partis Politiques*. Paris: Armond Colin.

Eldad, Israel. 1971. *The Jewish Revolution: Jewish Statehood*. New York: Shengold Publishers.

———. 1988. "A Homeland Can't Be Put Up for Sale." *Jerusalem Post*, February 26, p. 11.

Fisch, Harold. 1978. *The Zionist Revolution: A New Perspective*. New York: St. Martin's Press.

Friedman, Jane. 1982. "For Israelis, Bar Kochba Isn't Ancient History." *New York Times*, January 31, p. 22E.

Friedman, Menachem. 1983. "The NRP in Transition—Behind the Party's Electoral Decline." In *The Roots of Begin's Success: The 1981 Elections*." Ed. Dan Caspi, Avraham Diskin, and Emanuel Gutmann; pp. 141–68. London: Croom Helm.

Friedman, Thomas. 1985. "Jewish Settlers Are Put at 42,500." *New York Times*, February 10, p. L17.

———. 1987. "Fight for the Religious Future Builds in Israel." *New York Times*, June 29, pp. A1 and A12.

Furstenberg, Rochelle. 1982. "Ferment in the Yeshiva." *Jerusalem Post*, October 1, p. 9.

Gavron, Daniel. 1983. "Smashing the Stereotype." *Jerusalem Post Magazine*, July 8, pp. 3–4.

———. 1988. "Taking to the Streets." *Jerusalem Post Magazine*, February 26, pp. 4, 7.

Geertz, Clifford. 1973. *The Interpretation of Cultures*. New York: Basic Books.

Gertz, Nurit. 1983. "Miatim Mool Rabim: Retorika V Mivneh B'neumei Ha Bechirote Shel Menachem Begin" [Few against Many: Rhetoric and Structure in the Election Speeches of Menachem Begin]. *Siman Kriah* 16–17 (April):106–14. (Appendix: "Menachem Begin's Speech at Kikar Malkei Yisrael 6.28.1981"; pp. 115–26.)

Getzler, Devorah. 1988. "Tehiya Takes aim at Mapam's Tsaban for 'Incitement' at Peace Now Rally." *Jerusalem Post*, February 15, p. 2.

———, and Asher Wallfish. 1988. "Knesset Unhappy with Its 'Jack of All Trades.' " *Jerusalem Post*, February 12, p. 5.

Gluckman, Max. 1956. *Custom and Conflict in Africa*. Oxford: Basil Blackwell.
———. 1967. *Politics, Law and Ritual in Tribal Society*. Oxford: Basil Blackwell.
Goell, Yosef. 1981. "Gush Country" and "Patriots and Pragmatists." *Jerusalem Post*, International Edition, February 1–7, pp. 9, 22; and February 15–21, pp. 14–15.
Golan, Aviezer, and Shlomo Nakdimon. 1978. *Begin* (in Hebrew). Jerusalem: Edanim Publishers, Yediot Aharonot edition.
Gorni, Yoseph. 1973. *Achdut Ha'avoda 1919–1930: The Ideological Principles and the Political System* (in Hebrew). Tel Avia: Hakibbutz Hameuchad.
Green, Jerrold. 1984. "Religion and Counteremobilization in the Iranian Revolution." In *Religion and Politics, Political Anthropology*, vol. 3. Ed. Myron J. Aronoff; pp. 85–104. New Brunswick: Transaction Publishers.
Greenberg, Joel. 1987a. "Rebels in Gush Emunim Win Share in Leadership." *Jerusalem Post*, International Edition, week ending May 23, p. 4.
———. 1987b. "Split in the Bloc." *Jerusalem Post*, International Edition, week ending May 23, p. 7.
———. 1988a. "Uncontrolled Epidemic of Police and Army Violence." *Jerusalem Post*, February 12, p. 1.
———. 1988b. "PLO, Palestinians Split over Meeting." *Jerusalem Post*, February 22, p. 1.
Haber, Eitan. 1979. *Menachem Begin: The Man and the Legend*. New York: Dell.
Halpern, Ben. 1961. *The Idea of the Jewish State*. Cambridge, Mass.: Harvard University Press.
Handelman, Don, and Leah Shamgar-Handelman. 1986. "Shapes of Time: The Choice of a National Symbol." Paper presented at symposium "Symbolism through Time," No. 100 of the Wenner-Gren Foundation for Anthropological Research, January 12–21, in Fez, Morocco.
Hareven, Shulamit. 1983. "Eyewitness." *New Outlook*, March/April; pp. 13–17.
Harkabi, Yehoshafat. 1982. *The Bar Kochba Syndrome*. New York: Rossel Books.
———. 1983. *Facing Reality: Lessons from Jeremiah, the Destruction of the Second Temple and Bar Kochba's Rebellion* (in Hebrew). Jerusalem: Van Leer Institute.
Hartman, David. 1988. "A Religious Perspective on the Conflict." *Jerusalem Post*, February 12, p. 9.
Hasan, Sana. 1986. *Enemy in the Promised Land: An Egyptian Woman's Journey into Israel*. New York: Pantheon Books.
Hasen, Rick. (Unpublished.) "The Strength of the Gush Emunim Infrastructure," manuscript made available by author.
Hertzog, Hannah. 1985. "Negotiated Society—The Social Boundaries of Israeli Society." A paper presented at the first annual meeting of the Association for Israel Studies, Dartmouth College, June 19–21.
Hobsbawm, Eric, and Terence Ranger, eds. 1983. *The Invention of Tradition*. Cambridge, Eng.: Cambridge University Press.
Honig, Sarah. 1982. "NRP Concerned as Hammer Reveals His Changing Views" and "Gush Emunim Tells Hammer: Don't Visit." *Jerusalem Post*, October 1, p. 1, and October 5, p. 2.
Horowitz, Irving Louis. 1974. *Israeli Ecstasies/Jewish Agonies*. New York: Oxford University Press.
———. 1988. Personal communication, December 1.
Isaac, Rael Jean. 1976. *Israel Divided*. Baltimore: Johns Hopkins University Press.

————. 1981. *Party and Politics in Israel*. New York: Longman.

————. 1988. "Moment of Truth," editorial, March 17, p. 10.

Katzenstein, Lawrence. 1987. "Great Disorder under Heaven: Social Time, Conflict, and the Origins of the Strategic Triangle." Ph.D. dissertation, Rutgers University.

Keren, Michael. 1983. *Ben-Gurion and the Intellectuals*. DeKalb: Northern Illinois University Press.

Kirschen, Jacob. 1983. "Dry Bones." *Jerusalem Post*, February 16.

Landau, Pinhas. 1987. "The Sephardi Revolution." *Jerusalem Post*, International Edition, week ending June 27, p. 11.

Langer, Susanne K. 1942. *Philosophy in a New Key*. Cambridge, Mass.: Harvard University Press.

Lehman-Wilzig, Sam N., and Giora Goldberg. 1983. "Religious Protest and Police Reaction in a Theo-Democracy: Israel, 1950–1979." *Journal of Church and State*, 25, 491–505. Autumn.

Levite, Ariel, and Sidney Tarrow. 1983. "The Legitimation of Excluded Parties in Dominant Party Systems: A Comparison of Israel and Italy." *Comparative Politics* 15:295–397.

Lewis, Arnold. 1979. "The Peace Ritual and Israeli Images of Social Order." *Journal of Conflict Resolution* 23:685–703.

————. 1984. "Ethnic Politics and the Foreign Policy Debate in Israel." In *Cross-Currents in Israeli Culture and Politics, Political Anthropology*, vol. 4. Ed. Myron J. Aronoff; pp. 25–38. New Brunswick: Transaction Publishers.

Liebman, Charles, and Eliezer Don-Yehiya. 1981. "The Symbol System of Socialist-Zionism: An Aspect of Israeli Civil Religion." *Modern Judaism* 1:121–48.

————. 1982. "Israel's Civil Religion." *Jerusalem Quarterly* 23:57–69.

————. 1983. *Civil Religion in Israel: Traditional Judaism and Political Culture in the Jewish State*. Berkeley: University of California Press.

————. 1984. "The Dilemma of Reconciling Traditional Culture and Political Needs: Civil Religion in Israel." In *Cross-Currents in Israeli Culture and Politics, Political Anthropology*, vol. 4. Ed. Myron J. Aronoff; pp. 47–62. New Brunswick: Transaction Publishers.

Lipset, Seymour M., and Stein Rokkan. eds. 1967. *Party Systems and Voter Alignment*. New York: Free Press.

Lustick, Ian S. 1984. "The West Bank and Gaza in Israeli Politics." In *The Begin Era*. Ed. Steven Heydemann; pp. 79–99. Boulder: Westview.

————. 1988. *Jewish Fundamentalism in Israel*. New York: Council on Foreign Relations.

McWilliams, W. Carey. 1984. "The Bible in the American Political Tradition." In *Religion and Politics, Political Anthropology*, vol. 3. Ed. Myron J. Aronoff; pp. 11–47. New Brunswick: Transaction Publishers.

Medding, Peter Y. 1972. *Mapai in Israel*. Cambridge, Eng.: Cambridge University Press.

Meijers, Daniel. 1982. "De Macht van Religie: De Situatie in Israel" (The Power of Religion: The Situation in Israel). *Antropologische Verkenningen* 1:2:194–218.

————. 1984. " 'Civil Religion' or 'Civil War'? Religion in Israel." In *Religion, Power and Protest in Local Communities*. Ed. Eric R. Wolf; pp. 137–61. Amsterdam: Mouton Publishers.

Mendelsohn, Ezra. 1981. *Zionism in Poland: The Formative Years*. 1915–1926. New Haven: Yale University Press.

Miller, Walter. 1961. *A Canticle for Leibowitz*. New York: Bantam Books.

Morris, Benny. 1988a. "Rights and the Man." *Jerusalem Post Magazine,* February 12, pp. 4–6.

―――. 1988b. "Portrayer of the Messianic Wave." *Jerusalem Post Magazine,* February 19, pp. 10–11.

―――, and Menachem Shalev. 1987. Lead story in *Jerusalem Post,* November 1, p. 1.

Nachmias, David. 1973. "A Note on Coalition Payoffs in a Dominant Party System." *Political Studies* 21:301–5.

Nakdimon, Shlomo. 1978. *Altalena* (in Hebrew). Jerusalem: Yediot Aharonot.

Newman, David. ed. 1985. *The Impact of Gush Emunim*. London: Croom Helm.

Niv, David. 1980. *The Irgun Zevai Leumi*. Jerusalem: World Zionist Organization, Department for Education and Culture.

O'Dea, Janet. 1976. "Gush Emunim: Roots and Ambiguities—The Perspective of the Sociology of Religion." *Forum* 2:25:39–50.

Orent, Wendy, 1985. "The Transformation of Hegemony in Israel." A paper presented at the 1985 Annual Meeting of the American Anthropological Association, Washington, D.C., December 4–8.

Ortner, Sherry B. 1973. "On Key Symbols." *American Anthropologist* 75:1338–46.

Oz, Amos. 1983. *In the Land of Israel*. Trans. Maurie Goldenberg-Bartura. New York: Harcourt Brace Jovanovich. (Published originally as *Poh Veshom B'Eretz Yisrael B'Stave 1982*. Tel Aviv: Sifriat Ofakim, Am Oved.)

―――. 1985. *A Perfect Peace*. Trans. Hillel Halkin. New York: Penguin. (Published originally as *Menukah nekhonah*. Tel Aviv: Am Oved, 1982.)

Paine, Robert, ed. 1981. *Politically Speaking: Cross-Cultural Studies of Rhetoric*. Philadelphia: Institute for the Study of Human Issues.

―――. 1983. "Israel and Totemic Time." *Royal Anthropological Institute News,* December.

Palgi, Arye. 1979. *Shalom v'Lo Yotare* [Peace and Nothing More]. Tel Aviv: Ofer Press.

Peri, Yoram. *Between Battles and Ballots: Israeli Military and Politics*. Cambridge, Eng.: Cambridge University Press.

Perlmuter, Amos. 1987. *The Life and Times of Menachem Begin*. Garden City, N.Y.: Doubleday.

Raanan, Tzvi. 1980. *Gush Emunim* (in Hebrew). Tel Aviv: Sifriat Poalim.

Rabin, Yitzhak. 1979. *The Rabin Memoirs*. Boston: Little, Brown & Co.

Rabinovich, Abraham. 1982. "Rate of Settlement to Drop to One Per year, WZO Says." *Jerusalem Post,* September 30, p. 3.

―――. 1987. "Split in the Golden Way." *Jerusalem Post Magazine,* December 4, pp. 4, 6, 13.

Rapoport, David C. "Responses to Questions for I.S.C.S.C. Catastrophe and Political Consciousness Colloquiums," May 28, 1982, Pittsburgh, PA. Unpublished notes.

Remba, Isaac. 1964. "Religion and Tradition in His Life and Thought." *Hauma* 3 (June): 145–66.

Richardson, David. 1982. "De Facto Dual Society." *Jerusalem Post,* September 10, p. 7.

————. 1988. "Spycatcher." *Jersualem Post,* February 12, p. 8.

Ricoeur, Paul. 1986. *Lectures on Ideology and Utopia.* Ed. George H. Taylor. New York: Columbia University Press.

Rosenberg, Robert. 1988a. " 'What Was Will Never Be Again, and What Will Be, Is Not What Was,' says Omos Oz." *Jerusalem Post,* February 19, p. 4.

————. 1988b. Four-part series of articles on the peace camp, in *Jerusalem Post,* February 22, 23, 24, 25, each on p. 4.

Rowland, Robert C. 1985. *The Rhetoric of Menachem Begin: The Myth of Redemption through Return.* Lanham: University Press of America.

Rubenstein, Amnon. 1980. *Mi Herzl od Gush Emunim Ubechazera* (From Herzl to Gush Emunim and Back). Tel Aviv: Schocken.

Rubenstein, Danny. 1982. *Mi L'Adoni Eli: Gush Emunim* (On the Lord's Side: Gush Emunim). Tel Aviv: Sifriat Poalim.

Sartori, Giovanni. 1976. *Parties and Party Systems,* vol. 1. London: Cambridge University Press.

Schechtman, Joseph B., and Yehuda Benari. 1970. *History of the Revisionist Movement.* Tel Aviv: Hadar Publishing House.

Schiff, Gary S. 1977. *Tradition and Politics: The Religious Parties of Israel.* Detroit: Wayne State University Press.

————. 1986. "Post '84 Israeli Politics: The Renewed Centrality of Religion." In *Israel Faces the Future.* Ed. Bernard Reich and Gershon Kieval; pp. 41–51. New York: Praeger.

Schiff, Ze'ev, and Ehud Ya'ari. 1984. *Israel's Lebanon War.* Ed. and trans. Ina Friedman. New York: Simon & Schuster.

Schnall, David J. 1979. *Radical Dissent in Contemporary Israeli Politics.* New York: Praeger.

Schwartz, Barry, Yael Zeruvabel, and Bernice M. Barnett. 1986. "The Recovery of Masada: A Study of Collective Memory." *Sociological Quarterly* 27:2:147–64.

Schweitzer, Avram. 1986. *Israel: The Changing National Agenda.* London: Croom Helm.

Segal, Mark. 1982. "Education Minister Zevulin Hammer Talks to Mark Segal about the Aftermath of the Beirut Massacre." *Jerusalem Post,* October 15, p. 1.

Seliktar, Ofira. 1986. *New Zionism and the Foreign Policy System of Israel.* London: Croom Helm.

Shalev, Menachem. 1988. "Shamir, Peres Swap 'Blunt' Statements." *Jerusalem Post,* February 15, p. 1.

Shapiro, Haim. 1988. "Rabbi in the Cause of Peace," *Jerusalem Post,* Feburary 12, p. 5.

Shapiro, Yonathan. 1976. *The Formative Years of the Israeli Labor party.* Sage Studies in Twentieth-Century History, vol. 4. Beverly Hills: Sage Publications.

Sharkansky, Ira, and Alex Radian. 1982. "Changing Domestic Policy." In *Israel in the Begin Era.* ed. Robert O. Freedman; pp. 56–75. New York: Praeger.

Shipler, David K. 1982. "Israel Buries Bones of Ancient Warriors." *New York Times,* January 31, p. 22E.

Shochat, Orit. Unpublished. "Symbolism and Ritual in the Herut Movement." Unpublished seminar paper submitted at Tel Aviv University.

Shokeid, Moshe. 1984. "A Case of Ethnic Myth Making." In *Cross-Currents in Israeli Culture and Politics, Political, Anthropology,* vol. 4. Ed. Myron J. Aronoff; pp. 39–50. New Brunswick: Transaction Books.

Sprinzak, Ehud. 1981. "Gush Emunim: The Tip of the Iceberg." *Jerusalem Quarterly* 21:28–47.

———. 1986a. "Gush Emunim: The Politics of Zionist Fundamentalism in Israel." New York: American Jewish Committee, Institute of Human Relations.

———. 1986b. *Ish Yashar B'Eino: Illegalism B'Chevra Ha Yisraelit* (Every Man Whosoever Is Right in His Own Eyes: Illegalism in Israeli Society). Tel Aviv: Sifriat Poalim.

Teveth, Shabtai. 1982. *Retzach Alozorov* (The Alozorov Murder). Jerusalem: Shocken.

———. 1986. *Ben-Gurion: The Burning Ground.* Boston: Houghton Mifflin Company.

Torgovnik, Efraim. 1982: "Likud 1977–81: The Consolidation of Power." In *Israel in the Begin Era.* ed. Robert O. Freedman; pp. 7–27. New York: Praeger.

Tzameret, Tzvi. 1983. *Lochame Herut Yisrael (Lehi)* (Israel Freedom Fighters). Jerusalem: World Zionist Organization, Department for Education and Culture.

Wagner, Jane. 1986. *The Search for Signs of Intelligent Life in the Universe.* New York: Harper and Row.

Wagner, Roy. 1981. *The Invention of Culture,* rev. ed. Chicago: University of Chicago Press.

Wallace, Anthony F. C. 1956. "Revitalization Movements." *American Anthropologist* 58:264–81.

Weisburd, David, and Vered Vinitzky. 1984. "Vigilantism as Rational Social Control: The Case of the Gush Emunim Settlers." In *Cross-Currents in Israeli Culture and Politics, Political Anthropology,* vol. 4. Ed. Myron J. Aronoff; pp. 69–88. New Brunswick: Transaction Books.

Weissbrod, Lilly. 1981a. "From Labour Zionism to New Zionism: Ideological Change in Israel." *Theory and Society* 10:777–803.

———. 1981b. "Delegitimation and Legitimation as a Continuous Process: A Case Study of Israel." *Middle East Journal* 35:4:527–43.

———. 1982. "Gush Emunim Ideology—From Religious Doctrine to Political Action." *Middle Eastern Studies* 18:3:265–75.

———. 1984. "Protest and Dissidence in Israel." In *Cross-Currents in Israeli Culture and Politics, Political Anthropology,* vol. 4. Ed. Myron J. Aronoff; pp. 51–68. New Brunswick: Transaction.

Weizman, Ezer. 1987. "Israel and the Peace Process with Egypt." A lecture given at a symposium held in honor of the tenth anniversary of the visit to Jerusalem by President Mohammed Anwar El-Sadat sponsored by the Jewish-Arab Center of the University of Haifa, on November 17, 1987. Quotation taken from the present writer's notes.

Wolfsfeld, Gadi. 1984. "Political Communication and Political Violence: Field Notes from Yamit." *Jerusalem Quarterly* 31:128–44.

Yavin, Haim. 1981. "Al Sidrat Ha 'Nivcharim' B'Televisia: Haya Zeh Mivtza Meshuga" (On the Television Series the "Elected": This was a Crazy Campaign). In *Sefer Shel HaTeoni'im* 1982 (The 1982 Journalists' Yearbook). Ed. Moshe Lehrer; pp. 33–41. Tel Aviv: Association of Journalists.

Yehoshua, A. B. 1981. *Between Right and Right: Israel Problem or Solution?* Trans. Arnold Schwartz. Garden City, N.Y.: Doubleday.

Yishai, Yael. 1987. *Land or Peace: Whither Israel?* Stanford: Hoover Institution Press, Stanford University.

Yudelman, Michal. 1988a. "Likud Ministers Demand That Peres Be Fired." *Jerusalem Post,* February 16, p. 2.

————. 1988b. "Rabin: 'Impossible to Rule by Force.' " *Jersualem Post,* February 22, p. 1.

Zeruvabel, Yael. 1980. "The Last Stand: On the Transformation of Symbols in Modern Israeli Culture." Ann Arbor, Mich.: University Microfilm.

————. 1984. "Israeli Historiography and the Spirit of 'Active Heroism': On the Contemporary Meaning of Masada and Bar-Kochba." New York: Graduate School and University Center, City University of New York. Mimeographed.

————. 1986. "The Holiday Cycle and the Commemoration of the Past: History, Folklore, and Education." New York: Graduate School and University Center, City University of New York. Mimeographed.

Zucker, Norman L. 1973. *The Coming Crisis in Israel: Private Faith and Public Policy.* Cambridge, Mass.: MIT Press.

Name Index

171

Subject Index

Absorption. *See* Immigrants

Altalena affair, 22–23

Amana, 83

American: Jews, 118; peace initiative, 147–48

"Americanization of Israel," 8

Anthropology, xiv

Anti-Semitism, 30, 86, 135; heightened sensitivity to, 62

Arab countries vs. Israel, 8. *See also* Camp David accord

Ashkenazi: dominance, 108; Jews, 112

Authority, xx, 16, 153; abuse of, 98; erosion of, 70; Gush Emunim, 83; holy, 70; Jewish, 113; Labor, 4–5, 27, 70; rabbinical, 149; religious, 69; undermining, 27

Betar, 40–41n1, 61; hymn, 63

Biblical references, 8, 10, 12, 26, 60–61, 62

Block of the Faithful. *See* Gush Emunim

Brit Habiryonim, 61, 62

Brit Shalom, 94

British in Palestine, 21, 22, 61; terrorism against, 21

Bureacracy, 4

Cabinet. *See* Government

Camp David accord, 28, 76, 79, 96–97, 112, 118, 154; Labor support for, 9; and withdrawal from Sinai, 84, 90n13

Citizens' Rights movement (Ratz), 99, 100–101, 148; and high school students, 106; Knesset members of, 100–101; and Shinui, 101

Civic commitment, 147

Civil Religion. *See* New Zionism

Civil uprising, xx, 147–48, 151–52, 158n5

Civil war, 15, 39; potential, 22, 23, 34, 36, 42nn13,15, 89, 153

Change movement. *See* Shinui

Crisis of: confidence, 71, 99; domestic policies, 23–24; identity, 7, 26; legitimacy, xix, xx, 8, 40, 146; increasing population, 5; Zionism, xx

Culture, xiii–xvi; analysis of, xiii; definition of, xi–xii; dominant, xii–xiii; ideology and, xiv; modern secular, 85; rational vs. nonrational aspects of, xv–xvi. *See also* Political culture.

Cultural: change, xiii, 27; dominance, xii–xiii

Debate: over Bar Kochba's funeral, 138–40; national, 11, 32; public, 113–17

Delegitimation: attempts at, 147; Labor's, 153; of Labor's rivals, 3; mutual, 104; of opposition as a means for dominance, 10, 15, 24, 34; Peace Now target for, 103. *See also* Legitimacy

Democracy in Israel, xix, 41n1, 73; ethics of, 36; threat to, 22–24, 32, 35, 73, 104, 115

Diaspora, 116, 130; Jewish communities of, xviii; negation of the, xviii, 61; Samson vs. Jews of, 62

Dominance: Ashkenazi, 108; consequences of, 14–16, 124; cultural, xii–xiii; ideological, 124; Labor, 1–9; lack of, 1–16; Likud's attempts to gain, 9–13, 27, 34; new, 124–29; role of, 1–16; success undermines, 5

Dominant: ideology, 125; party system in Israel, xix; Zionist political culture, xvii

Dovish line, 99, 108, 111, 152, 155; delegitimation of, 152. *See also* Hawkish line

173